P9-APF-972

A CONCISE HISTORY OF BALLET

Frontispiece: Basse-Dance accompanied by viol and lute

A CONCISE HISTORY OF

Ballet

FERDINANDO REYNA

GROSSET & DUNLAP
NEW YORK

TRANSLATED FROM THE FRENCH BY PAT WARDROPER

LIBRARY OF CONGRESS CATALOG CARD NUMBER: 65-18973

PRINTED IN FRANCE BY GEORGES LANG

Contents

Page 9 CHAPTER ONE
The Origins of Ballet

19 CHAPTER TWO
The Cid and the Moresque

27 CHAPTER THREE
The Ballet Comique de la Reine

35 CHAPTER FOUR
The Metamorphoses of Court Ballet

53 CHAPTER FIVE
Louis XIV, the Dancer King

59 CHAPTER SIX
Noverre the Revolutionary

71 CHAPTER SEVEN
The Fortunes of Ballet in Europe

81 CHAPTER EIGHT
Ballet in Italy

95 CHAPTER NINE
The Romantic Ballet

111 CHAPTER TEN
Blasis and Saint-Léon

121 CHAPTER ELEVEN
From Manzotti to Diaghilev

135 CHAPTER TWELVE
Serge de Diaghilev's Ballets Russes

153 CHAPTER THIRTEEN
Les Ballets de Monte Carlo

161 CHAPTER FOURTEEN
Ballet in France

181 CHAPTER FIFTEEN
German Expressionism and the Classical Dance

189 CHAPTER SIXTEEN
Ballet in England

199 CHAPTER SEVENTEEN
Soviet Ballet

209 CHAPTER EIGHTEEN
Ballet in the United States

221 CHAPTER NINETEEN
Ballet around the World

236 List of Illustrations

241 Index of Ballets

250 Index of Names

The Dance, in my opinion, is much more than an exercise, an entertainment, an ornament, a society pastime; it is a serious thing and, in some aspects, even a holy thing. Every age which has understood the human body, or which has, at least, sensed something of the mystery of this structure, of its resources, of its limitations, of the combinations of energy and sensibility which it contains, has cultivated, venerated the Dance.

PAUL VALÉRY

CHAPTER ONE

The Origins of Ballet

The only two forms of dancing known in the Middle Ages were folk dances and court dances with set forms, such as the slow and stately Basse-Dance (*Frontispiece*, *Ill.* 1) in which the gentleman held his partner by her little finger, and moved to music which was invariably out of step with the verses that sometimes accompanied it.

A magnificent wooden chest (intended for a bride's trousseau) now in the Accademia Gallery, Florence, is decorated with painted scenes showing the dances performed in the open air one May day in Florence, under a canopy of shimmering silk, to celebrate the marriage of Boccaccio Adimari and Lisa Ricasoli—members of two of the city's wealthiest families (*Ill.* 4). These dances were orderly and pre-arranged; there was none of the disorder of the medieval rounds. This transformation was the result of the arrival of the Renaissance. After breaking with tradition in every sphere—in religion, painting and philosophy—the Renaissance could not fail to revolutionize dancing, though it was a revolution that was as much a logical development of medieval forms as an imposing of new ones.

Choreography came into being in the Italian courts of the Quattrocento. It was not, however, invented by the nobles, but by men of humble origin whose talents—and here lay the genius of the Italians—won them acceptance, even honour, in society. Among them, which was unusual for the time, were a number of Jews, who even acknowledged their race by adding 'l'Ebreo' (the Jew) after their names. This was because Italy was the only country where the career of dancing-master was open to them, and whereas in Spain they had to practise in secret the medicine they had learned from the Arabs, in Italy they could exercize their talents freely.

Domenico da Piacenza, also known as Domenico da Ferrara, history's first choreographer, was at the height of his fame in the early years of the fifteenth century. His treatise *De arte saltandi et choreas ducendi* (On the Art of Dancing and Conducting Dances), now in the Paris Bibliothèque Nationale, is in two parts. In the first, devoted to the movements of the body, he defines the five elements which constitute the dance, namely Measure, 'Maniera' or Manner, Memory, Division of the Floor, and 'Aiere' or Elevation. Measure is treated seriously; for Domenico, it is the general principle relating the movements, fast or slow, to the rhythm of the music. It is closely linked to the 'maniera corporea,' the dancer's bearing, and is essential if the dance is to be freed from set forms. The approach of a new development is heralded by the importance given to Division of the Floor, recommended for dancer and choreographer alike. Memory, too, now becomes indispensable, since Domenico's are not traditional dances but original compositions. All dancing would be mere physical exercises without the 'Misterio', the mystique, which contained all the inspiration of the dance. According to the master, the movements should be in accord with the music (in itself an innovation for this period). Another innovation is his scale of measures: Basse-Dance, Quadernaria, Saltarello, and finally Piva (Bagpipes), each one-sixth faster than the one before. The following is taken from his treatise:

'I am the Basse-Dance, the Queen of Measures, and worthy to wear the crown. With me but few are successful, and he who dances and plays me well must surely have received a gift from heaven.

'I am the Quadernaria, and if musicians treat me wisely they will find me one-sixth faster than the Queen of Measures. Played rightly, by a good musician, I will be midway between the Basse-Dance and the Saltarello.

'I am the Saltarello, or Pas de Brabant, two-sixths faster than the Basse-Dance, and if musicians treat me as they should they will find I am midway between the Quadernaria and the Piva.

1 Court dance. Treatise by Guglielmo Ebreo

2 Rustic dance with a musician playing the bagpipes

'I am the Piva, and of all Measures I am the humblest, for I am in use among common folk. For my speed, I do so excel that I am twice as fast again as the Basse-Dance.'

The master then sets his pupils tasks of formidable difficulty for dancers trained in the medieval mould.

'By nature: try to give naturally its proper order to each Measure, in distance and tempo; by artifice: learn to separate all the Measures, that is of two beats of Piva make one of Basse-Dance, and of one beat of Basse-Dance make two of Piva... For... all those who meddle with this mystery in the hope of becoming expert in dancing are wasting their time if they cannot perform all these operations.'

A good pupil must have acquired exceptional agility and technical skill after exercises such as these. In the

AD ILLVSTRISSIMVM PRIN
CIPEM ET EXCELLENTIS
SIMVM DOMINVM DOMI
NVM GALEACIVM VICE
COMITEM COMITEM
PAPIAE & CAETERA.

GLORIA SOPRA OGNI GLO
RIA ALTO SIGNORE
CVI STVDIO DI PRVDEN
ZA & DI VIRTVTE
TIRA IN TRIVMPHAL CAR
RO A SOMMO HONORE

Poi che sul piu bel fior di giouentute
va dato il ciel belleza ingegno & gratia
Di quante dote son tra noi uedute
Io come quel che non gia mai si satia
Seruir sforceschi in quanto ho possa & arte
Resarcito ho per uoi quel chaltri stratia
Dico chel danzar sparso in uarie carte
Ho colto in questa opretta e i suoi fragmēti
Chora a uoi mando per faruene parte

3 Illuminated frontispiece from treatise by Guglielmo Ebreo

second part of his treatise, Domenico sets out to enumerate the basic steps, of which nine are 'natural' and three 'artificial'. Natural: the *pas simple*, the *pas double*, the *reprise*, the *contenance* or *pose noble*, the *révérence*, the *tour*, the *demi-tour*, the *saut* and the *mouvement*. Artificial: the *battement de pied*, the *pas couru* and the *changement de pied*. There had now been created, for the first time, a repertory of movements that were independent of their context; choreography was born. Domenico signed his dances, and was at pains to indicate that they were his 'invention', both the music and the choreography. In all there were seventeen Balli and only four Basse-Dances. This indicates that the Basse-Dance, with its rather ponderous evolutions and dignified, gliding steps, was becoming a thing of the past; the Ballo, with its changes of rhythm, spelt freedom.

4 Marriage of Boccaccio Adimari and Lisa Ricasoli

Messer Ambrosio da Pesaro, in his second treatise, defines the dance as 'a demonstrative action, in harmony

with the melody of a few voices'. His work gives fifteen varieties of Saltarelli, Balli, and Basse-Dances, including a French Ballade and one Ballo composed by Lorenzo de' Medici, together with a few dances of foreign origin —German, Turkish, Moorish, and so on.

With Guglielmo Ebreo, or William the Jew, we come to one of the great dancing-masters and choreographers of Quattrocento Italy. After thirty years work, this disciple of Domenico da Piacenza compiled, in 1463, his *Treatise on the Art of Dancing*, richly illuminated and dedicated to Gian Galeazzo Sforza, Duke of Milan (*Ill.* 3). This book gives a fascinating survey of the sumptuous fêtes, the famous names, the great mimed masquerades of Guglielmo's day. His attention to detail extends to instructions for the costume of each dancer, down to the smallest button. He too recommends his pupils to dance 'contra tempo' if they wish to show themselves scientific and intelligent in the art.

The word 'ballet' still did not exist. We meet it for the first time, as 'balleto', in Guglielmo's treatise, where it is a composition entitled *The Ungracious Lady*.

Some years later Antonio Cornazzano, a nobleman and writer who could turn his hand to devotional works or obscene proverbs with equal facility, wrote his code, dated 1465, in which he remarks on the development of dancing in the direction of ballet:

'...In Italy, ballets are now very much the fashion. They are compositions of several measures which may include all the nine movements of the dance, even those which are in appearance contradictory, such as those of the Coquette and those of The Constant Lover, fittingly combined.'

Technique had evolved, and new steps had been added to the repertory introduced by Domenico. Dancing was being stylized, refined and codified, while at the same time there was a growing awareness of the immense possibilities of the human body. Music—which at this period consisted almost entirely of music for dancing—was enriched by a new instrument, the lute. To music and steps were added,

5 Dance with two men, a woman and musicians

as Guglielmo so discerningly puts it, 'certain sweet emotions which, pent up within us contrary to nature, strive to be expressed in movement'.

The creation of ballet is sometimes attributed to Renaissance humanism, sometimes to the invention of a single man. But if ballet seems to be the work of 'inventors', they were drawing on the rich material of past centuries, sometimes deriving from beyond Italy—from as far away as Arabia, land of the Moors.

6 Dance of the Theological Virtues

7 Open-air dancing in Florence. Lorenzo the Magnificent and Poliziano

CHAPTER TWO

The Cid and the Moresque

Without the Cid—so goes the Spanish legend—Europe would have fallen to the Arabs. It did not, but the hero's exploits made such a strong impression on the medieval mind that there emerged the Moresque or Moresca, a chronicle in dance form of the incessant struggles between Christian and infidel. Just as twentieth-century choreographers were to turn for their themes to contemporary problems—to the psychology of the individual, for example—so those of the Middle Ages gave expression to their two greatest concerns, religion and war. These gave us the Mysteries and the Moresque.

On festival days in the villages and ports around the Mediterranean a troupe of players would make their entrance on to the main square. Among them would be the 'Mattacino' (the Moor), with blackened face, wearing a golden turban, a cuirass, bells on his feet, and armed with a wooden sword and shield. To the sound of fife and drum—the only instruments in use at that time—the Moor, Europe's brilliant foe over the centuries, would dance in Oriental style. He was then surrounded by his enemies, likewise armed, and a mock combat followed, which invariably ended with the death of the Moor.

Soon, however, the Moresque lost its warlike character and became mere entertainment. The combatants were reinforced by singers and a female character (played by a man). Drums and fifes still sounded the rhythm for the complicated manœuvres, the gestures of defiance, the thrusts and parries and the traditional leap over the swords. After the battle-dance came the eagerly-awaited 'rosa', the final figure in the pantomime, in which the dancers re-grouped and tossed the Mattacino and his bells high in the air.

Soon the Moresque was even appearing in religious dramas. Carts carrying the scenery, symbolic 'props' and actors of this Italian version of the mysteries would make their way through the streets and halt in front of a church. Here a play such as *The Creation of Adam* or *Adam and Eve Driven from Paradise* would be performed, with more or less music and dancing according to the humour of the town. (Florence preferred beauty; Venice, a hint of sensuality, which was to increase with the approach of the Renaissance.) The carts rumbled off again to the main square of the town, where a danced pantomine, accompanied by music, provided the highlight of the entertainment.

By the fifteenth century, Greek paganism began to mingle with Christian themes. The traditional 'sacre rappresentazioni', derived from fourteenth-century Christian mysteries and legends and from the festivals in honour of Florence's patron saint, were turned by Lorenzo the Magnificent into 'triumphs'—elaborate masked spectacles mounted on chariots, which also inherited something of the medieval masquerades. These 'triumphs' introduced by Lorenzo became, in the Europe of Charles V, the standard ceremony for welcoming important personages, like those put on by Rome for her victorious generals.

8 Fabritio Caroso

Numerous interludes of songs, dances or poetry found their way into the triumphs, often on the slightest of pretexts. In *Saint Cecilia*, a sacred drama, 'they sit down to table, and while they eat there is singing and dancing'. In *Esther*, 'they dance when the messenger arrives'. Interludes were also the custom at princely weddings. When Annibale Bentivoglio married Lucrezia d'Este in 1492, nymphs of Diana advanced to the sound of music, then retreated before the assault of savages, all finally being reconciled at the house of Venus. For the wedding of Guidobaldo di Montefeltro and Elisabetta Gonzaga, one hundred dancers, directed by the famous choreographer Lavagnolo, took part in the festivities, which were organized by the father of Raphael. A festival of international dances was offered by Ludovico il Moro to Gian Galeazzo Sforza and his bride Isabella, Duchess of Milan.

It was not only triumphs and masquerades that were invaded by interludes. Comedies and tragedies in the antique mode, which were very much the fashion at this time, suffered the same fate. Many intellectuals disapproved of these intrusions, which were usually not even justified by the plot. Poliziano's *Orfeo*, for example, was an attempt to revive Greek tragedy, and was intended not as a series of entertainments or digressions but as a coherent work of art. In the end, however, the humanists had the worst of it, and the enthusiastic public kept their interludes—jousts, mock hunts, mime, songs, and above all dancing. The Saltarello, the Gaillarde and the Pavane were all popular, but the great favourite was the Moresque, for it lent itself to every possible kind of dramatic development.

The Moresque, like the sacred drama, was becoming emancipated. It was now extravagant and fantastic, and what with its colour, its cloth of gold and silver, its pantomime and its classical allusions, the original shape was barely recognizable. It could include dances by savages, peasant girls, satyrs and nymphs. Venice became the great specialist in these costly fantasies, and in the fifteenth century created Moresques such as *Jason* and *I Barbieri*. The performers were not called dancers, but 'morescanti'. (It is said to be during this period, too, that the name Moresque—hence Morris—came to be attached to certain ancient country dances in England.) No distinction was drawn between the arts, and all of them—painting, mime, music (already developing the possibilities of the lute), dancing, even horsemanship—were drawn on to make up an entertainment that would please everyone. Great artists such as Leonardo da Vinci and Botticelli designed the costumes of the dancers. It was the period when Italy was unsympathetic to Franco-Flemish music, and when the gaiety and speed of the 'volta' was the rage. Public theatres were about to open, accessible to nobles and petits bourgeois alike.

9 Cesare Negri

The rich disorder of the public squares had to be organized, and reduced to a scale proper for a palace hall. An end had to be brought to the wearisome solemnity of the Basse-Dance. What had until now been a public festivity had to be converted into a private entertainment, of a prescribed length, coloured by individual tastes and ambitions. In short, the semi-improvized had now to be made a work of art.

Domenico da Piacenza was not, then, the 'inventor' of ballet. Born in a rich but unruly century, he merely extracted what was most usable from the abundant material, organized and codified it. After him came men who made use of his ideas, as he himself had made use of those of the Middle Ages.

When Cesare Negri (*Ill.* 9), known as the Trombone, was born in 1530, Milan was the European capital of ballet, and ballet the king of entertainments. In the sixteenth century, as later in the eighteenth, people wrote at length, and with care, on the subject of anything and everything, and Negri was no exception. Like his illustrious predecessors, he waited until his old age before writing his autobiographical treatise, *Le Grazie d'Amore*. From this we learn that he taught dancing very early, and was both star performer and choreographer.

When Don Juan of Austria defied the Turks at Lepanto, Negri was there, dancing before the assembled captains on the deck of the admiral's galley. He danced again for Don Juan of Austria in Milan. On 25 June 1564 he produced a grand masquerade mounted on twenty-five chariots symbolizing every human emotion—Suspicion, Desire, Fear, and so on. In what is now the Piazza della Scala, all the characters in this procession descended from their chariots to dance a gigantic Brando. (The Brando, mentioned by Castiglione in his *Courtier* in 1528, was, like the Moresque, one of the stages in the development of the ballet, and allowed an interesting freedom to the choreographers of the time.)

In the same year, the future Henri III hastily left Poland and began his journey to ascend the throne of France. On 6 August, after attending festivities at Venice, he halted at Cremona long enough to watch Negri and his disciple Farrufino dance. King and dancer once again came face to face at Magenta. From one stopping-place to the next, Negri danced for Henri III as far as the Alps. He had become the dancer of the century.

More than forty of the master's pupils were scattered among the courts of Europe. Agosto Cesare, of Parma, stayed many years with the princes of Flanders. The

Emperor Maximilian engaged Beccaria Carlo. Barbetta Alessandro, of Bologna, went to the court of the Duke of Bavaria, Martinello Stefano to the court of Cologne. Charles V and Philippe II fought over another pupil of Negri, and the Dukes of Poland, too, had their indispensable Italian dancers.

With the arrival of the Italians, the Basse-Dance of the Middle Ages disappeared.

At last, and fortunately for the future of French ballet, the Maréchal de Brissac, Viceroy of Piedmont, had the happy idea of recruiting Diobono of Milan, followed by Tettoni Bernardo, dancer and choreographer. With Bernardo, it is said, came a certain Baldassarino de Belgiojoso, who was to make his name better known later. Once in France, Diobono became tutor to the Duke of Orleans. Henri III—also François II and Charles IX—appreciated the talents of Bernardo. Baldassarino ('little Balthasar'), before making himself famous with the choreographic event of the century, transformed himself into

10 The Battle. *Ballet à quatre* by Cesare Negri

11 *Saut du nœud*

12 *Fioretto*

13 First position for a *double tour en l'air*

14 *Contre-pas* to verses by Ovid

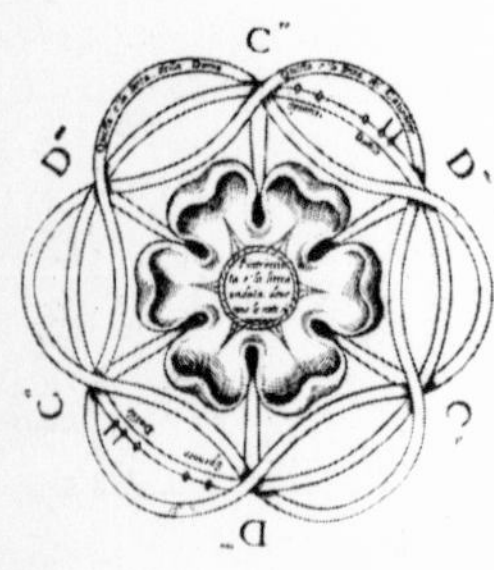

Balthasar de Beaujoyeux, and was described by Brantôme as 'the best violinist in Christendom'. Diobono brought Palvello Ludovico, celebrated performer in sung ballets, to the court of the Valois. Giovan Gallino, the king's dancing-master, became tutor to the young nobles, and developed the strength, grace and skill of his pupils by riding, fencing and dancing. In fact, such were the charms and accomplishments of these inimitable Italians, that they were in constant demand at every royal court.

In 1604 Negri's *Le Grazie d'Amore* was reprinted, under the more accurate title *Nuove Inventioni di Balli*. This work, which lays the foundations of classical dancing, is in three parts: the first is generalities, the second, fifty-five technical rules which are lessons in themselves, the third actual dances—Balli, Brandi, Pavanes—with scoring for lute and details of choreography. Among the variety of steps is the amusing but certainly difficult *saut du nœud* (*Ill.* 11); the dancer had to try to touch the knot of a cord hanging from the ceiling with the tip of his toe.

In the ballets, the *mutanze* represented complete figures, and already corresponded to a fully developed musical theme. It was not, as is sometimes imagined, a time when only slow and majestic pavanes were the rule. Dancers were already moving in very lively style; ten variations for the pirouette alone, six for the *tour sauté*, *cabrioles*... Of course, ladies who took up the art of dancing were very cautious with these elegant acrobatics. 'I piedi in fuora!' Negri would say to his pupils, 'Feet turned out!' Legs and knees were to be well *tendus*, knees bent slightly apart when finishing a jump, the elbow raised a little when turning to give greater grace. The maestro also preferred his pupils to dance on their toes, *à pointe* which was in fact only *demi-pointe*. These standards are, in any event, remarkably advanced for the time.

15 Preparation

Just as advanced, though less organized, Caroso's treatise *Il Ballarino*, published in 1577 and dedicated to the courtesan Bianca Cappello de' Medici, is in some part identical with Negri's work. Fabritio Caroso (*Ill.* 8), born at Sermoneta, near Rome, was not, however, a plagiarist; the similarity between the two treatises simply proves that there was by now a single Italian school of dancing. Of Caroso we know that he traced out his choreography before having it danced. The fifty-four rules in his work indicate the progress in technique since the inspired beginnings sketched out by Cornazzano and Guglielmo Ebreo. And since this is the high Renaissance, Caroso speaks in terms of 'distichs' and 'spondees,' for he made his pupils pattern their steps upon the metres of classical verse (*Ill.* 14). Beyond the Alps a French poet, Antoine du Baïf, was likewise trying to develop the possibilities of using classical metres in French poetry. The music inscribed in *Il Ballarino* merely served the dancing.

The ballet of Caroso and Negri leaves the fifteenth century far behind. In it we can already discern the 'contredanses' of the seventeenth century, just as in the 'balletti' there is already a hint of the sonata.

16 Open-air dancing in Venice

Meanwhile, at the French Court a memorable evening's entertainment was in preparation, organized by the Florentine, Catherine de' Medici.

17 Ballet put on by Catherine de' Medici in honour of the Polish ambassadors, 1573

CHAPTER THREE

The Ballet Comique de la Reine

In France, in the early years of the fifteenth century, interludes in the Italian style with masquerades and 'machines' had begun to appear within the framework of the old medieval entertainments, based until then on the martial exploits used as themes for tournaments. Thus Christine de Pisan relates how in 1401, during a celebration at the palace of the Duke of Orleans, young girls descended, singing, from the roof into the banqueting-hall. It should be remembered that the Duke's wife, Valentina Visconti, was Italian, and that she would certainly not have left her homeland without bringing with her a few Italian artists. The Court continued, nevertheless, to dance to the slow and solemn music of the Basse-Dance.

At the end of the century, Charles VIII and his soldiers returned from Italy enchanted by what they had seen. At Ferrara, they reported, 'He who wants to be transported from this world to the next, let him listen to Pietrobono playing; he who wants the heavens to open, let him experience the liberality of Duke Borso; and he who desires to see Paradise on earth, let him watch madonna Beatrice dancing in a festival'.

In Italy the Renaissance, then in full flower, had come as a delivrance. The French imported from Italy the doctrine of humanism, broader cultural relations, and more brilliant forms of entertainment than before. Thus there were elaborate processions, and Apollo, the Muses and the Nymphs were revived. Du Baïf aspired to a perfect synthesis of music, poetry and dancing, on the Greek pattern. (It should also be said that, years earlier, Caroso had spoken of 'a contre-pas executed with true mathematical exactness to verses of Ovid' (*Ill.* 14).) Du Baïf went so far as to try to undertake a musical and literary reform. But whereas Italy, inspired by the same desire, but guided by her own inventive genius, was moving confidently in the direction of the opera, France failed in her attempt at reform of speech. The Academy authorized by Charles IX in 1540 was dissolved. Nevertheless, the revolutionary ideas of Du Baïf helped to bring about a closer association between music, dancing and poetry, which until then had not achieved any kind of mutual equilibrium.

In the sixteenth century, French ballet consisted of nothing more than interludes in the Italian style—a pleasant medley of songs, miming and dancing, a spectacle more spoken than sung, in the French fashion. Interludes were finding their way into everything—comedies, tragedies, *divertissements*; and, parallel with this, the Italian dances were making their appearance, scandalizing some critics. When Catherine de' Medici became Queen, she was always ready to welcome the latest in entertainment, particularly if it came from beyond the Alps, and furthermore she had a keen sense of publicity. So these Italian-style festivities served her both as enjoyment and as political propaganda. In 1544 she put on, without any ulterior motive, a performance of the Italian Trissino's *Sophonisbe* at Blois; but she also devised another drama, entitled *La Défense du Paradis*, in which Charles IX and his brothers defended the earthly paradise, while Henri de Navarre and his friends attacked it. Naturally Henri and his band, defeated, were to end up in Hell. The meaning could hardly be plainer. And although the sequel to the action showed the Huguenots saved from the eternal flames, these were sinister portents; a few days later, Huguenots were being murdered in the streets. This ballet had been the dress rehearsal for the Massacre of St Bartholomew. Nevertheless, Brantôme says, 'the Queen Mother danced with much grace and majesty, prompt in invention, and in a manner very much her own'.

18 Design for a ballet costume by Bracelli.

Catherine de' Medici also promoted entertainments that were equally political, but more peaceable in nature. One of the tourneys at Bayonne was preceded by a 'triumph' in the Italian fashion. For another festivity, four white mares drew in a large chariot draped in cloth of gold, on which sat a Venus surrounded by little cupids singing verses in praise of the King. Some of these ballets were held inside the palace, some outside. In 1573, when the Poles, dazzled by the successes of the Duke of Anjou, came to France to offer Catherine's son the crown of Poland, the event was magnificently celebrated (*Ill.* 17).

In the hall appeared a gigantic silvery rock, in which were hollowed sixteen niches in the shape of clouds. In each of these was a matron or maiden representing one of the sixteen provinces of France. They emerged from their glittering casket to music by Roland de Lassus, and stepped down on to the floor accompanied by the full orchestra. Thirty violins struck up a lively air, and the sixteen charming ladies began to execute a sequence of patterns and formations, performing 'tours mêlés, contre-tours, détours et arrêts entrelacés' with a precision that left the Polish ambassadors quite astonished.

The author of this 'ballet' was the Italian Baldassarino di Belgiojoso, now known as Balthasar de Beaujoyeux, appointed Intendant of Music and Court Valet by the Queen Mother in 1567 and made organizer of the royal entertainments by Charles IX.

Louis XII had already brought back actors and musicians from Italy, and the fashion had continued; it supplied the creative imagination the courtiers lacked. To succeed at the Court of France in the sixteenth century, however, it was not enough to be Italian. One had also to be a man of intelligence, to preserve something of one's Italian character at the same time as adapting oneself—to do, in fact, what the irascible Lully was to do so well a few years later, for although the Queen Mother, born in Italy, did not forget Florence, the Court judged with French eyes.

Balthasar, then, succeeded where many of his compatriots had failed: he became a courtier at the same time as artistic adviser to the sovereign. At this period the French Court was already extremely logical. Though it found the Italians somewhat comical, with their sing-song speech, it was susceptible to the visual appeal of their ballets, and demanded them in its famous interludes. The display and refinement of the Florentine entertainments were much admired. Henri II brought back a troupe of actors, the Gelosi, in his baggage-train, and France continued to import

19 Design for a ballet costume by Bracelli.

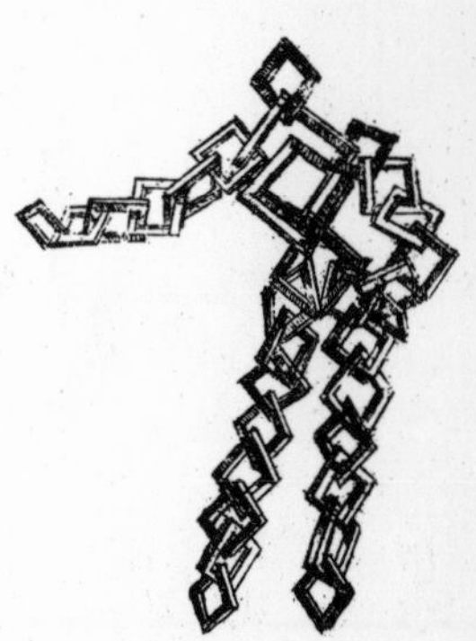

20 Dancing at the court of Henri III

entertainment from Italy—until the day when Balthasar set to work in earnest.

For the marriage of the Duc de Joyeuse, Henri's brother, to Mademoiselle de Vaudemont, sister of the Queen, Catherine de' Medici asked Balthasar to devise a ballet (at this time, any form of entertainment was known as 'ballet'). Balthasar decided to use the scenario of Circe the Enchantress, which had been originally conceived by Agrippa d'Aubigné, but rejected because it seemed too difficult to stage. He retired to the country to work on it. For the lyrics he commissioned Chesnay, for the music de Beaulieu, and for the scenery and costumes Jacques Patin, painter to the King. Around the story of Circe he built up a complete drama, with music, dancing and acting—the first time that anyone had thought of associating the different elements in a dramatic work. The only other theatrical creations to be conceived in this way were the celebrated 'cartels', sets of verses which served as commentaries or 'programme notes' to the action, but which were generally composed by courtiers who did not take part in the performance. Instead of juxtaposing the different elements, Balthasar took the Italian matter and the French manner. This time it could be said that the somewhat mathematical approach favoured by the 'Brigade' (now known as the 'Pléiade') was appropriate, since here for the first time, on the orders of Beaujoyeux, the step was to follow the note, and the note the syllable.

On 15 October 1581, the princes and courtiers assembled around Henri III, were seated on a platform covered by a canopy in the Great Hall of the Petit-Bourbon Palace, to watch the opening of the *Ballet comique de la Reine* (*Ill.* 23). The plot begins with the escape of a prisoner of Circe, come to seek assistance of the King in a long tirade full of political allusions. Circe, vexed at the loss of one of her captives returns haughtily to her castle. At this point comes the first interlude, with the entry of three sirens and a singing triton. A dozen naiads, seated on a chariot, were played by the Queen and ladies of the Court, their faces unmasked. Peleus and Thetis sing a duet, while, from the golden ceiling, an invisible choir responds; twelve pages and twelve naiads dance elegant geometrical figures; suddenly Circe's wand strikes everyone motionless. Mercury then

21 *Ballet comique de la Reine*, 1581. Entry and dance of the satyrs

descends from a cloud and frees the prisoners, and the dance of the nymphs begins again—only to stop once more, for now the goddess has cast her spell over Mercury and lured him into her enchanted garden. There then appear a stag, a dog, an elephant and a lion, Circe's rejected suitors, whom she has bewitched into the shapes of animals.

In the second part come eight satyrs playing the flute (*Ills.* 21, 22), who approach four naiads, bow in hand. The satyrs intone a hymn, followed by a maiden who sings homage to the King. All of them then go to the grotto of Pan, where the nymph Opis entreats the gods to break the spell. In immediate response to this prayer Minerva appears on a triumphal chariot and delivers a speech before the King, followed by a chorus of six voices. There is a thunderclap, and behold Jupiter on a cloud, draped in a golden tunic. Pan, at the head of eight satyrs, leads the attack on Circe's garden; there is a show of resistance; Circe falls, struck down by a thunderbolt from Jupiter. And all the protagonists march round the hall of the Petit-Bourbon Palace paying homage to the King. This was the great moment, the moment of the *Grand Ballet*, described by Beaujoyeux in his memoirs.

'It was then that the violins changed key and began to play the entrée of the *Grand Ballet*, composed of fifteen passages so devised that at the end of each one all turned their heads towards the King. Having arrived before His Majesty, they danced the *Grand Ballet* of forty passages or geometric figures, some diametrically, some in a square, some in a circle, in many and various fashions, and also in a triangle, accompanied by a few other little squares and other figures... These geometric evolutions sometimes took the form of a triangle with the Queen at the top of it; they revolved in a circle, interwove like a chain, tracing various figures with a cohesion and accuracy which astonished those present.'

22 *Ballet comique de la Reine*, 1581. Entry and dance of the satyrs

The evening's entertainment ended at half-past three in the morning. It had gone on for ten and a half hours, but allowing for court ceremonial, refreshments, dances during the intervals, and the still rudimentary 'machines' which had hardly changed since the days of the Mysteries, the show had lasted barely three hours.

This geometrical dancing which so amazed the Court would have been no surprise to the Italians. In Florence they were already in the early stages of the development of opera. In Italy there were theatres, an appreciative public, a tradition of art as part of civic life. In France—the *Ballet comique de la Reine*, the first truly French 'Court ballet', since it had been organized, danced, sung (with the exception of one professional singer) and financed by courtiers and royalty. Its chief importance lay in the way the whole work was co-ordinated. It was, in fact, closer to light opera than ballet. Beaujoyeux, satisfied with his work, wrote: 'I think I may claim to have pleased, with a well-balanced production, the eye, the ear and the understanding.'

23 *Ballet comique de la Reine*, 1581. *Entrée*

24 *Ballet du Noël des Fleurs*, 1618

CHAPTER FOUR

The Metamorphoses of Court Ballet

In spite of the absence of newspapers, Italy quickly learned of the success of Beaujoyeux's production, but Court ballet was to enjoy only a very brief vogue outside France. This kind of entertainment was rather out-of-date in the eyes of the Italians, whose theatres had long been open to the public and were no longer exclusive to the Court.

La Pellegrina, in 1589, marks the beginning of the development of opera. Given in Florence by Count Giovanni di Bardi to celebrate the marriage of Ferdinando de' Medici, Duke of Tuscany and Christine of Lorraine, grand-daughter of Catherine de' Medici, this musical entertainment in seven interludes was an event of great importance; it was the first time, in Italy, that singing and dancing had supported the dramatic action throughout an entire production. The music was composed by Cavalieri, Malvezzi, Marenzio, Caccini and Prete; Rinuccini and Strozzi wrote the verses; and Bronzino and Gian Bologna designed the costumes. In the first interlude, sirens descend from the clouds to pay homage to the noble couple. In the second, the muses sing a hymn followed by a madrigal. In the third interlude there is a battle in which Apollo overthrows the serpent Python. Demons appear in the fourth and nymphs in the fifth. The sixth interlude shows Apollo, Harmony and Rhythm coming down to earth to sing the praises of the bridal pair, and there is a dance in Oriental fashion to the sound of zithers and psalteries. A grand final *ballo* crowns the performance. The operatic flavour of the work was enhanced by a showy and elaborate setting.

For *Il Ballo dell'ingrate*, produced in the ducal palace of Mantua, Rinuccini wrote the scenerio and Monteverdi

25 *Le Nozze dei Dei.* Dance of naiads and tritons, 1603

26 Scene from *Les Dons du Roi des Alpes à Madame Royale*

the music. Isacchino Ebreo was responsible for the choreography. The curtain rose on the gaping mouth of Hell, which belched forth, two by two, the 'ungrateful ladies'. These, after performing some eloquent miming, descended, singing, from either side of the stage into the hall, where they danced the ballet.

In Venice, countless theatres were opening, while in Florence there was also great activity. Here in 1608 Angelo Ricci, ballet-master to the Medici for thirty-seven years, devised the choreography for *La Notte d'Amore*, followed in 1615 by the ballet *I Boemi*. Father Coppola, a priest, composed the verses for a melodrama entitled *Le Nozze dei Dei*, which included a ballet of shepherds in the gardens of Venus, dances by sea divinities (*Ill.* 25), a ballet of the sun surrounded by the signs of the zodiac, and three equestrian ballets on a platform built over the stage.

The Farnese family possessed a magnificent theatre at Parma, where in 1650 the Court danced *La Gloria d'Amore*, a work set in Caledonia, supposed by the poet to be at the other end of the world. This was followed by *Le Vicissitudini del Tempo* and, a few years later, *L'Età d'Oro*.

The Count Filippo San Martino d'Agliè, who lived in Turin, was the devoted lover of Marie-Christine of France, Duchess of Savoy and spent his life—with the exception of a year's deportation to Vincennes on the orders of Richelieu—in loving the queen, defending her when need arose, and composing ballets. Altogether he produced over forty, part verse and song, part dancing, including *La Force de l'Amour* (1626), *Circé* (1627), *Prométhée, voleur du feu céleste* (1630), *Les Montagnards*, given in France a year later, *La Vertu, ennemie des apparences* (1634), a *Ballet comique* (1640), and the famous *Gris de Lin* (*Ill.* 27), staged in Turin before being performed at the Court of France. It was in Piedmont that Court ballet had its longest career, since there French traditions continued. When Marie-Christine died, d'Agliè retired to a monastery.

27 Scene from *Le Gris de Lin*

Court ballet was spreading; at The Hague in 1668 a ballet entitled *Peace*, directed by the Prince of Orange, was put on to celebrate the signing of a treaty between England and Holland. Twenty-two *entrées* told the story of the quarrels between the two countries and their reconciliation, followed by the grand final ballet.

One would not have imagined the methodical Descartes composing a ballet, yet in fact he did. On the occasion of the Peace of Münster in 1646 he wrote, at the request of Queen Christina of Sweden, *La Naissance de la Paix*, which was performed at the royal palace in Stockholm.

28 Ballet on horseback at the court of Turin

29 *Les Dons du Roi des Alpes à Madame Royale.* First tableau

30 Ballet inspired by the Orient

He insisted, however, that his name should not appear on the libretto. Brussels saw the creation of an Italian-composed ballet called *The World*, in which the peoples from the four corners of the globe sang their joy at the marriage of Philippe IV and Maria of Austria. The Court of Hanover did not escape this epidemic of ballets; in 1681 the twenty-three *entrées* of *The Hunt of Diana* showed a hunt on horseback on the stage, with dryads and satyrs in abundance, the entire Court taking part. And the princess, eldest daughter of the Duke of Hanover, danced in *The Charm of Love*, in which a cloud bearing musicians descended from the ceiling. *Le Rendez-vous des plaisirs*, given at Stuttgart in 1688, was sung entirely in French and danced by Courtelle and his wife. In Munich an unusual work was put on, a danced drama without voices entitled *The Conversations of Diana and Apollo*. It is difficult to be certain whether this was the first work of its kind, but it remained, for the time being, without a sequel. England, which had as its form of court entertainment the masque, a sung piece with dramatic episodes, welcomed the *ballet-comique*, and dancing came to have the most prominent part. Once again the balance between the three elements, dancing, singing and poetry, was destroyed, to the advantage of dancing and poetry.

There is one form of ballet that is seldom mentioned but which nevertheless produced some admirable works in the geometric style—the horse ballet, in vogue in the sixteenth and seventeenth centuries. The Middle Ages had been too fond of its tournaments (sometimes fatal to the participants) for later centuries not to have kept a lingering nostalgia for them. And so riders and choreographers endeavoured to combine the ballet and the tournament, and audiences were treated to the sight of dancing horses (*Ills*. 28, 32-4).

This kind of ballet took three months to prepare; the animals learned their steps to the music of a small violin. Not surprisingly, the dancing-master had also to be riding-master and fencing-master. Father Claude Le Menestrier, historian of tournaments and ballets in the seventeenth century, considers 'these equestrian steps [trot, gallop, curvet, cabriole, jump] as true dance figures, in harmony with the sounds and airs which guided the horses in the course of the ballet'. The steeds and their riders illustrated

31 Ballet inspired by the Orient

32 Choreography for ballet on horseback, 1615

a dramatic action in the style of Tasso and Ariosto, the plot of which was outlined before the action began, with sung accompaniment and scenery. Naturally, such spectacles could only be produced in vast squares reminiscent of the jousting arenas of the old days. Duels and chases succeeded one another, interspersed with sung choruses and poems declaimed by actors on foot representing the elements or divinities. The star-turn of the entertainment was the 'abbattimento' (grand battle), the mounted equivalent of the *Grand Ballet*. In 1608 the Court of Tuscany put on *The Tournament of the Winds*, in which one hundred horsemen dressed as Indian nymphs manœuvred to music by Jacopo Peri, while Duke Francesco de' Medici, as Aeolus, guided the winds. For *The War of Beauty* the best artists were brought to Florence, and admirably schooled horses pawed the ground in time to declaimed verses, sung choruses, and the music of an orchestra. Monteverdi put on a mounted ballet to his own music, but of this only the title—*Mercury and Mars*—has come down to us. The entire court of the Medici danced in *Il Mondo Festeggiante*.

France, since the time of Henri II, had not ignored this form of entertainment, but in the German courts ballets on horseback were drilled with the intensity of military reviews. Unfortunately, with the opening of the theatres and the vogue for opera, these vigorous fantasias began to decline. After *The Conqueror of the Centaurs* at Schönbrunn, in which a triple ballet of nymphs, centaurs and satyrs was performed on a stage in the middle of an ornamental lake, the horse ballet disappeared from the courts of Europe.

Henri IV, an economical monarch (Sully watched jealously over the kingdom's finances) put an end to the extravagant spectacles of preceding reigns. The French court returned to Italian masquerades and medieval burlesques, which were less expensive and more in keeping with the gaiety of the '*Vert Galant*' and the broad humour which characterized his reign. The dances of this time —none of which survive today—were similar in style to the mummery of the *Bal des Ardents* (1393), a tragic masquerade in which five noblemen dressed as savages accidentally caught fire and were burnt to death. Strangely, the *Ballet comique de la Reine* had no successors in France. The concept gradually declined into a dry formula, in which spoken declamation predominated. Once again the French temperament had let itself be led astray by logic. But now a new fashion developed which changed the trend again.

33 Choreography for ballet on horseback, 1615

Suddenly ballet, which after the *Ballet comique de la Reine* was tending to become a long series of literary speeches, began to be sung. This sudden change was due to two Italians, Caccini and Rinuccini. Ottavio Rinuccini, a Florentine, was a poet who in the early years of Henri III's reign had been a member of a musical and literary circle, near equivalent of the Pléiade, which met at the home of Count Bardi in Florence. One of the main aims of this group was to revive the sung declamation of the Greeks—recitative. Giulio Caccini, a Roman singer and composer, has been called one of the founders of the musical style of our time. The collaboration between the two men resulted in *Dafne* and *Cefalo* in 1597, and, three years later, *Euridice*, an experiment in opera which was entirely sung but in which each act ended with a ballet.

When Marie de' Medici married Henri IV by proxy, Caccini wrote for her a 'tragedia per musica' which attracted much attention, and the Queen, affected by a tender sentiment towards the composer, lost no time in summoning him to the Court with his colleague Rinuccini. The arrival of these two Italians in France marked a revolution in the ballet. Sung recitative, which the French had always resisted, was now more or less imposed by the sovereign. Dancing still played the most important part, but the carefully-balanced three-part conception of Beaujoyeux was forgotten.

With Marie de' Medici as Regent—Louis XIII was only thirteen—court amusements were no longer restricted by economy. In fact, the year before the murder of Henri IV, an elaborate production had already been staged. It was called *Le Ballet de la Reine représentant la beauté*, and ended with the appearance of Fame singing a poem by Malherbe. Court ballet was back, always extravagant, sometimes disorganized, tending more towards musical comedy than ballet. It was entertainment 'à la mode', the meeting-point of all the arts of the day, and it provided an opportunity for the courtiers who were jealous of the acclaim given to the professional authors of these works. Following the example of the 'cartels', the verses of the ballet were distributed to the spectators, or were added to the spoken 'récits'. These texts, an exalted form of programme notes, proclaimed the literary gifts of their authors, who, however, had often bought the services of less high-ranking but more competent ghost-writers.

34 Choreography for ballet on horseback, 1615

35 *Hercule à Thèbes*, 1661. Finale

36 *La Délivrance de Renaud*, 1617. The Duke of Luynes as Renaud

Confined now to the Court, ballet patterned itself upon the courtier: refinement, splendour, affectation, a romantic dream in which old tales of courtly love were enacted by nymphs and heroes.

So began the period of 'melodramatic' ballet under Louis XIII, a time of direct Italian influence, with spoken tirades largely replaced by 'expressive singing'. *Alcine*, produced in 1610, was a ballet which inclined towards opera, and had some impressive changes of scene against a backdrop of grottoes and fountains. In *Le Triomphe de Minerve* (1615) the spectator followed the thread of the plot through dialogues, verses, choruses and pantomime, with masques and transformation scenes. It should be noted that all the dancers wore wooden or leather masks, partly as a tradition handed down from past centuries, but chiefly as a convenience for the courtiers, whose acting talents were limited. Thus masks, costumes and spoken 'récits' provided what faces were unable to express. The performance ended, traditionally, with the *Grand Ballet*, apotheosis of the aristocracy, which, as it were, set the seal on the work, firmly excluding women and commoners.

A famous melodramatic ballet was *La Délivrance de Renaud* (1617), which told the story of Renaud and Armide (*Ills*. 36, 37, 39, 40). The work opens with Renaud asleep on a bed of flowers, watched over by demons appointed by Armide as his guardians. The demons dance with Renaud, but are interrupted by two knights in search of the hero. Armide casts a spell over the scene, and gardens and fountains rise up from nowhere; but the knights' all-powerful magic wand dries up the water in the fountains, and the water nymph 'dishevelled and naked' is forced to dive back into the fountain-basin. After a struggle between monsters and knights, Renaud, convinced by the crystal shield, at last escapes from his paradise of gardens and grottoes. This display of spells and magic wands gave the opportunity for some beautiful dancing, spectacular changes of scene, and fantastic costumes.

37 *La Délivrance de Renaud*, 1617. The King as a Fire Demon

'Six different monsters... two of whom had the head, wings and feet of an owl, and the body of a judge... Two others had a dog's head, arms and legs, and the body dressed like a peasant... The demons came out of their shells in the guise of old women booted and spurred'...

38 Sixteenth-century masque

Renaud was finally delivered and appeared once more before his king, just in time to dance the *Grand Ballet.*

The great virtue of *La Délivrance de Renaud* was that everything in it was relevant to the action, and the fairytale element was kept under control. *L'Aventure de Tancrède dans la forêt enchantée* (1619) was another masterpiece which possibly surpassed *Renaud* in its scenic effects. Here again there is a battle with demons, for at this period tournaments and metamorphoses were vital to dramatic action. Thus we find a forest, a magician, divinities of the woods, monsters, demons and knights, with those effects of light and shade in which the Italians excelled, and a remarkable setting which ought to have started a new fashion. But neither *Renaud* nor *Tancrède* had imitators. After these two successful productions came *Le Grand Ballet de la Reine*, with strange and fantastic scenery and a dance of the Hyperboreans and Psyche to the music of an invisible orchestra. It was a well-balanced, well-shaped work, but unremarkable. The only other ballet of note was *Apollon*, the object of which was to show Apollo (the Duke of Luynes) killing the serpent (symbolizing the political adventurer, the Maréchal d'Ancre). But Louis XIII was of a melancholy temperament, and the Duke of Nemours, who succeeded Luynes as Intendant des Plaisirs, had to change the nature of court ballet completely.

39 *La Délivrance de Renaud*, 1617. Monsieur de Monpoullan as a Spirit of the Air

Nemours chose the easy way. Melodramatic ballet, after dethroning the *ballet-comique*, was in its turn replaced by the simple *ballet à entrée*. Simple, that is, in its action and setting, which were sketchy in the extreme, but the costumes and machinery were complicated and extravagant. It consisted of a series of tableaux with little link between them and purely visual in character, the theme suggested by almost anything. The 'récits', which in the melodramatic ballets occurred where they were necessary to the action, now had a fixed place.

Nevertheless, these *ballets à entrée* were an opportunity for the dancers Marais and Morel to display their very considerable talents. It is now, in books on the ballet, that we find the names of La Barre, Picot, Delphin, Veyré, Saintot, Le Camus, Paysanne, Prévost. Gradually professionals were beginning to make their way into ballet, and their strict training—originating from Italy—enabled

40 *La Délivrance de Renaud*, 1617

them to display feats of skill of which the courtiers were utterly incapable. Marais had made his very successful début in 1615 in the ballet *Madame;* he then danced *Armide* and Bacchus in *Les Bacchanales.* This dancer was both a fine actor and a remarkable musician. He appeared in *Les Voleurs*, which had a pirate scene, and was brilliant in the role of Guillemine la Quinteuse in the ballet *Fées de la Forêt de Saint-Germain*, the theme of which was devised by Nemours. As the Grand Turk, he danced alongside the King in *La Douairière de Billebahaut.* given in 1626.

1632 marks the first performance of a ballet in a theatre to a paying audience. The man responsible for this startling innovation was the dancer Horace Morel, who has been accorded only a small place in historical works. He was not only a dancer but a fireworks specialist and an organizer of entertainments, and the *Ballet des Effets de la Nature*, put on by him in 1632 in the Salle du Jeu de Paume of the Petit Louvre, had changes of scene showing first a desert, then a volcano in eruption. In the following year Morel staged two other ballets, *Les Cinq Sens de la Nature* and *La Puissance de l'Amour*, but his idea for a theatre open to the public met with no success. Court ballet was determined to remain ballet for courtiers.

Also in 1632, Corneille wrote the scenario for the *Ballet du Château de Bicêtre.* In this, a motley group of people take shelter in a ruined castle, providing a pretext for dances by forgers and other picturesque and disreputable characters. Marais distinguished himself in the role of a magician, and the ballet was danced at the Louvre, the Arsenal and the Hôtel de Ville on the same night. After Corneille, Louis XIII tried his hand as an author, and the ballet *La Merlaison* was entirely his work, including the choreography and all the details of the costumes. The King played the part of a woman, while Marais, dressed as a bird, flew about among the huntsmen.

Richelieu, all-powerful since 1624, made use of the *ballet à entrée* to impress rebellious political opponents. Among these ballets with a political flavour was *Les Triomphes*, which opened with lines composed by that zealous courtier, Ronsard, and in which Louis XIII again took the role of a woman (all women's parts were then played by men). Another was *Les Quatre Monarchies*

Chrétiennes (1635), which had twenty *entrées* depicting the various peoples of the world, each with their appropriate music and costumes. Meantime, the Queen had given birth to a son, the future Louis XIV—a happy surprise, for after twenty-three years of marriage the Court had given up hope. In 1641 Buffequin devised complicated machines for a ballet on the subject of the Franco-Spanish campaigns. In 1642 Mazarin succeeded Richelieu; in 1643 the King died; and in 1644 Jean-Baptiste Lully arrived in Paris.

41 *Hercule à Thèbes*, 1661. Act II

42 *Ballet de la Jeunesse*

CHAPTER FIVE

Louis XIV, the Dancer King

As a sideline to his political activities, Mazarin, a native of the province of Aquila, in Italy, did his best to impose Italian opera on the court of Louis XIV. On 14 December 1645, *La Folle Feinte (La Finta Pazza)*, an opera produced by Torelli, Europe's leading stage designer, with music by Sacrati, achieved a certain success at the Palais Cardinal. The Medicis had 'lent' their choreographer Balbi to Anne of Austria, but this led to difficulties, for though Balbi had a classic style, the dancers were of the school of the Commedia dell'Arte. (The monkeys, bears and Indians of *La Folle Feinte* nevertheless delighted little Louis 'Dieudonné,' the future Louis XIV.) *La Nuova e Curiosa Scuola de ballo*, by Gregorio Lambranzi, published in Germany in 1716, gives a good idea of the style of these dancers. Their movements were grotesque, exaggerated, burlesque, and in complete opposition to the classical dance. La Scala's *corps de ballet* even included dancers known as 'grotteschi' who specialized in the roles of satyrs and buffoons.

The French Court gave a cool reception to Cavalli's *Xerxes* and *Hercule amoureux (Ercole Amante)* and to Cesti's *La Pomme d'Or (Il Pomo d'Oro)*. In vain did the libretti provide a translation of the plot; these spectacles, sometimes lasting nine hours, had no admirers but Mazarin, Anne of Austria and the few Italians living at the Court. Only the ballets found general favour. Though lacking in dramatic action, the graceful costumes and ingenious machines created by Torelli appealed to the spectators. And so it was contrived to introduce ballets into everything, no matter what the form of entertainment might be.

43 Charles-Louis Beauchamp

44 Jean-Baptiste Lully

There was still no question of any French opera until Jean-Baptiste Lully, Italian-born musician, dancer and producer, came to the notice of the King (*Ill.* 44). Lully, drinker and libertine, unpolished in manners yet cunning and even treacherous, seems an unlikely figure for the court of the Roi Soleil. Yet his talents made him Royal Composer of Music before he was twenty, and he played a large part in organizing the royal entertainments. Under him French opera came into being, opera in which ballet rediscovered its former vigour and was linked with the singing. Lully's opera-ballet was immediately adopted.

Though Lully himself directed the burlesque *entrées*, slipping pieces of his beloved Commedia dell'Arte into the classical ballet whenever he was allowed to do so, he did not reign alone. With him were Benserade, poet and librettist, faithful servant of the King, and Beauchamp, choreographer and dancing-master to Louis XIV for twenty years. Beauchamp (*Ill.* 43), born at Versailles in 1636 and descended from a line of artists, became established at Court as a musician and dancer while very young. He was appointed Superintendent of the King's Ballets in 1671, and thereafter composed all the choreography for Court ballets, with Lully supplying the music. By the time he retired in 1687 he had laid the foundations of the 'danse noble'. It can be said that his choreography reflects the style and feeling of Versailles; his *entrées*, gavottes and minuets unfold in majestic curves. For him technique took precedence over figures, and it was through him that the French school of dancing became supreme in Europe, so that French terms are still used today in ballet in Moscow, New York and London. But Beauchamp was not in fact the earliest choreographer in the French tradition. For this the credit belongs to Michel Lecomte, disciple and colleague of the Italian master Francesco Giera who had preceded him at the court of Henri III. Lecomte was royal dancing-master during the reigns of Henri IV and Louis XIII, and it was he who forged the link between the Italian school in France and the French school which was to succeed it.

In the age of Louis XIV dancing at last became the preserve of professionals. Though there were still a few nimble-footed courtiers dancing alongside the King in

Beauchamp's ballets, the King himself inaugurated the reign of the professional by founding, in 1661, the Académie Royale de Danse, whose aim was to 're-establish the art of dancing in its perfection'. Re-establishing the art in its perfection meant, in effect, leaving it to the experts. The Academy's thirteen members were recruited from among the leading dancing-masters of the day. It was too isolated and exclusive a body, however, and ceased to exist in 1780 without having played any appreciable role. Meanwhile the King had created the Académie Royale de Musique, later to become known as the Théâtre National de l'Opéra, whose dancing school (the École de Danse de l'Opéra) declared on its foundation in 1713 that its aim was to 'choose the best pupils and give them teaching free of charge'. The two directors, Fraincine and Dumont, sought out promising boys and girls aged from nine to thirteen in poor families. This school, ancestor of the present École de l'Opéra, has continued without interruption and is the *doyen* of all schools of dancing.

45 Louis Pécourt

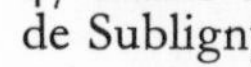

46 Jean Ballon

47 Marie-Thérèse de Subligny

Gravitating around the master, Beauchamp, were other professionals whose names also became famous: Louis-

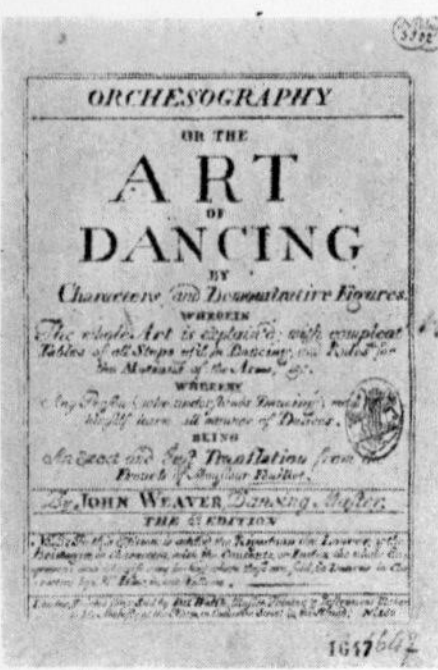
ORCHESOGRAPHY
OR THE
ART
OF
DANCING
BY
Characters and Demonstrative Figures.
WHEREIN
The whole Art is explain'd; with compleat Tables of all Steps us'd in Dancing, and Rules for the Motions of the Arms, &c.
WHEREBY
Any Person (who understands Dancing) may of himself learn all manner of Dances.
BEING
An Exact and Just Translation from the French of Monsieur Feuillet.
By JOHN WEAVER Dancing Master.

48 English version of Feuillet's treatise

49 German version of Feuillet's treatise

50 The three arts of a gentleman, 1742

Guillaume Pécourt (1653-1729) (*Ill.* 45), successor to Beauchamp at the Opéra, who danced with lightness and precision, and Jean Ballon (or Balon) (1676-1739), contemporary of Pécourt, who classed himself in the category of 'danseurs nobles' but was also a remarkable mime (*Ill.* 46). After Pécourt came Blondi (1675-1739), teacher of la Sallé and Mariette, women dancers of the reign of Louis XV. We should also mention Lestang, who exercized his talents as 'danseur noble' until 1702 and then retired to open a school which soon began to produce excellent pupils. With Lestang there was Louis Lasserre, jester of Louis XIV, appointed by the Queen Mother to be Director of fêtes and court ballets, and Deschars, who excelled in comic roles. In the Grand Siècle, Mademoiselle La Fontaine (1665-1738) had a great success in *Le Triomphe de l'Amour*. It was the first time that a woman had danced on the stage of the Académie de Musique, and when public theatres began to open women of the nobility made way for the professionals. After a brilliant career Mademoiselle La Fontaine retired to a convent, where she died. Marie-Thérèse de Subligny (1666-1736), introduced the gigue to France (*Ill.* 47); Desmartins made her début at the age of twelve; and the beautiful Mademoiselle Prévost also began her career at the age of twelve in Lully's *Hesione*. Star dancer of the Académie Royale de Musique, she succeeded de Subligny in 1706, and danced the role of the lovelorn gondolier girl in Campra's *Les Fêtes Vénitiennes*.

It was not until the eighteenth century that a tradition of scandal was to be associated with the figure of the ballerina. The age of Louis XIV kept, at least on the surface, a sense of order and decency that affected dancers, choreographers and musicians alike.

In 1701 Raoul Feuillet, basing himself on the work of Beauchamp, published a *Chorégraphie de l'Art de Décrire la Danse par Caractères, Figures et Signes démonstratifs*, which was immediately translated into English and German and is now considered one of the most important manuals on eighteenth-century ballet technique (*Ills.* 48, 49). It was the first time that French ballet terminology had been stabilized, the five classic positions defined, and the steps codified. Feuillet, who also invented a system of dance notation, did not, however, belong to the Opéra.

The Sun King was also the Dancer King. In 1865, at the age of forty-seven, he took the role of a nymph in *L'Eglogue de Versailles*. We do not know if he was a good dancer, only that he danced often, from a very early age, and frequently played women's parts. Lully would often appear with the King in the ballets he produced, and had no qualms about reproving the sovereign, in a whisper, when the latter stumbled or forgot his steps.

Molière was another dancer who has a place in history (*Ill.* 51). Though far from being a 'danseur noble', or even a classical dancer, he was not without talent, and had a taste for the acrobatic style of the Commedia dell'Arte. His successful *Les Fâcheux* (1661) inaugurated the genre of the *comédie-ballet*, in which acting and dancing were closely linked. In *Le Roi des fêtes de Bacchus* (1651), a ballet whose theme is said to have been devised by him, Molière danced with the professional dancer Robichon and the Count de Saint-Aignan.

51 Molière

In 1653 Benserade provided the scenario for the ballet *La Nuit*, in which the King made a triumphant appearance in the role of the Sun (*Ill.* 52). It was after this performance that Lully was appointed composer of music for the royal ballets. Beauchamp, in his turn, won great success with the creation of the ballet *Alcidiane* in 1658. After this came *La Raillerie* (1659), *L'Impatience* (1661), *Le Ballet des Saisons*, *Le Ballet des Arts*, *Les Amours Déguisées* (1664), *Le Mariage Forcé* after Molière, then the ballet *Le Palais d'Alcine* and *Les Plaisirs de l'Ile Enchantée*. With Moliere's masterpiece *Le Bourgeois Gentilhomme*, in 1670, the triumph of the *comédie-ballet* was assured.

52 *La Nuit*, 1653. Louis XIV as the Sun

Among works with dances arranged by Beauchamp were *Cadmus et Hermione*, a verse tragedy; *Alceste*, *Thésée*, *Atys*, *Isis* and *Psyché*, with Corneille and Fontenelle.

The success achieved by Mademoiselle La Fontaine in the twenty *entrées* of *Le Triomphe de l'Amour*, based on a scenario by Benserade and Quinault, with scenery by the famous Bérain and machines devised by the Italian Vigarani, marks the real starting-point of the history of the *danseuse*.

The right of French ballet to claim supremacy was now undisputed. French dancing-masters and French dancers were in demand all over Europe, laying the foundations of international classical ballet.

53 Jean-Georges Noverre

CHAPTER SIX

Noverre the Revolutionary

'At last we have limbs and an execution such as our predecessors never had,' declared Jean-Georges Noverre proudly in his *Lettres sur la Danse*. And there is no doubt that dancers in the eighteenth century possessed a technique which, although not perfect, was enough to make them into 'stars' whose caprices were numerous and incomes exalted. The men were awarded the title of 'God of the Dance'; the women would ride in carriages presented to them by royalty, and live on allowances provided by titled lovers. That scandalous creature, the ballerina, born in a hovel and queen of Paris at sixteen, enraged the ladies of the nobility, and attracted to the boxes of her 'théâtre érotique' all the great names of salon society. Faced with these celebrities of the dance, novices had to arm themselves either with patience or with powerful support, for they were relegated to the background and, since the sets for the ballets often showed a scene of sea and rocks, they were maliciously described as 'coastguards'.

The performers were much in the limelight; but what had become of the ballet of Louis XV, the choreographers, the Opéra? This is what the caustic Noverre had to say in 1760:

'Dancing and ballet have become, Sir, the craze of our time; the smallest provincial troupe trails after it a swarm of dancers, male and female; why, even fairground quacks rely more on the virtues of their ballets than on those of their medicines.'

As for costume, 'tinsel is everywhere,' used indiscriminately for beggars and for kings. The Curiatii wore gold, the

Horatii silver, and the public was content. Noverre, the reformer, was less so: 'I would have no more of these stiff, cumbersome breeches... I would cut down by three-quarters the ridiculous panniers of our ballerinas.' One advantage of the pannier, however, was that it allowed the ballerina to use the ankle more than the thigh, without the subterfuge being apparent. Men, on the other hand, had to exert themselves considerably to perform the acrobatics that were then in fashion.

In curious contrast to these newly-introduced acrobatics, the music was still that of the age of Louis XIV, ceremonious and slow; 'a ballet-master is hardly allowed even to change the tempo of an old tune.' As can be seen, little mutual harmony existed between the various elements of the ballet. According to Noverre:

'The poet imagines that this art elevates him above the musician; the musician would be afraid to lose dignity by consulting the ballet-master; the latter never communicates with the designer; the scene-painter speaks only to the painters under him, and the stage-setter, often despised by the painter, is in supreme command of the workings of the theatre.'

Moreover, designers, composers and choreographers were all equally at the mercy of the 'stars'.

'...The designer often sacrifices the costume of an ancient people to the prevailing fashion, or to the whim of some well-known dancer or singer. Most composers follow, I repeat, the old formulae of the Opéra; they write passe-pieds because Mademoiselle Prévost performed them elegantly, and musettes because Mademoiselle Sallé and Monsieur Dumoulin danced them attractively and with grace. In fact, Sir, opera is, if I may so express myself, a spectacle for monkeys,' concluded Noverre.

Jean-Georges Noverre—whose times put him in such ill humour, and who was not afraid to confess 'I am sick to death of passe-pieds and minuets'—was born in 1727, of Swiss and French parentage (*Ill.* 53). His father, a former sergeant-major under Charles XII, sent him at an early age to train under Dupré, a great 'danseur noble' of the eighteenth century. The young dancer's début at the court of

Fontainebleau was modest and a little disappointing, but fortunately Noverre was not merely a dancer, but also a man of ideas. These ideas were in line with those of the Encyclopédistes; a synthesis of all branches of human knowledge, each art to follow its own internal logic. Instead of being merely a disjointed medley of entertainment, ballet should be an organized art, conceived as a unified whole. The revival of mime was then a subject very much in the air; in 1678 the philologist Van Meursius had published at Lyons a catalogue of antique dances, Diderot and d'Alembert discussed mime, and Rémond de Saint-Mard wrote: 'I do not say that our dancers should become mimes altogether—it is too late for that—but where would be the harm in their being so to some degree?'

For the Encyclopédistes, mime was only one interesting element among others; for Noverre it became an obsession. He wanted nothing less than the complete reform of a ballet which had become a mere display of technical virtuosity; 'mechanical' dancing was to be replaced by 'dramatic' dancing. First of all, masks had to be discarded, 'those hideous faces which conceal nature, and show us instead a misshapen and grimacing copy.' But Noverre met with opposition, not only from dancers but from the public, who resented anyone spoiling their pleasure. He was more favourably received abroad, however, and was welcomed in Berlin, from where, fortified by success, he returned to Paris by way of Strasburg, Lyons and Marseilles. Here he gave his first *ballets d'action*, in which mime at last made sense out of the plot, the scenery and costumes delighted the eye, and chiaroscuro was used to great effect. *Les Fêtes chinoises* (1749), *La Fontaine de Jouvence* (1754) and *Les Réjouissances flamandes* (1755) won him the post of ballet-master at the Paris Opéra-Comique, a body which was still at war with the troupe of dancers attached to the Comédie-Française. Here he produced his old ballets, and created new ones. Noverre's successes prompted the actor David Garrick to offer him a contract at Drury Lane, and *Les Fêtes chinoises* and *La Fontaine de Jouvence* were chosen for production in London. The moment was an unlucky one, however, for England and France were on the verge of war, and even the presence of the old King George II at the première on 8 November 1755 did not prevent the

54 Marie-Madeleine Guimard

occasion developing into a near-riot. A few days later rioting broke out in earnest, a man was killed, and the show was cancelled. But this brief appearance on the English stage was to strengthen even further Noverre's belief in mime, of which Garrick was a brilliant exponent.

In 1758 the Académie of Lyons offered him the post of ballet-master. Here he presented *Les Métamorphoses chinoises* and his great successes *La Mort d'Ajax*, *Renaud et Armide*, *La Toilette de Vénus*, and *Les Fêtes du Sérail.* In 1760 his *Lettres sur la Danse* appeared, prefaced by a flattering dedication to the Duke of Württemburg which earned him an immediate invitation to Stuttgart. Here he could at last show the full measure of his talent. During his seven years at Stuttgart Noverre produced *Médée et Jason*—one of his favourites—*Antoine et Cléopâtre*, *Renaud et Armide*, *Les Danaïdes*, and many other works, all constructed according to the new theatrical principles preached by the Encyclopédistes. Gaetano Vestris, 'God of the Dance', worked under Noverre at Stuttgart in 1763 and returned to Paris to proclaim the master's genius. An episode in *Lettres sur la Danse* gives us an idea of the kind of effect produced by his tragic ballets. Noverre describes how two Italian poets came to see him after the performance:

'Deeply moved, their eyes still wet with tears, they said to me "Sir, you are today the Shakespeare of your art, but you are too cruel! You should have dried our tears by finishing with a pretty *contredanse*".'

Noverre went on from capital to capital, fêted everywhere, and much sought after in society, for his caustic wit won him friends as well as enemies. At last Marie-Antoinette obtained for him the post of ballet-master at the Académie Royale, an honour which should by rights have gone to Maximilien Gardel. In spite of the animosity which he incurred as an 'outsider', Noverre staged many successful ballets at the Paris Opéra, working both with his friend Gluck and with Mozart, who composed the music for *Les Petits Riens.*

An impressive number of star performers emerged from the chaos of eighteenth-century ballet, and all, or nearly all, had something to learn from Noverre. Only Marie

55 Marie-Anne de Camargo, by Vigée-Lebrun, *c.* 1780

Sallé (*Ill.* 57), born in 1707 while her parents were on tour with a company of strolling players, was not indebted to him for her ideas of mime, for the good reason that she was twenty years older than he. She made her début in her uncle's troupe at the Foire Saint-Laurent in 1718 in an opera by Lesage, later becoming a dancer at the Opéra and being engaged by the impresario John Rich to dance, with her brother, at the theatre at Lincoln's Inn Fields, London. Marie preferred the sober style of English actors to the affectation of the Italians, as Noverre was to do some years later. Mademoiselle Prévost's jealousy—as fierce as that of all ballerinas—caused Sallé to be relegated to the *corps de ballet* with the 'coastguards', but the acclaim of the public soon brought her into the front rank.

In 1729 she caused a scandal by dancing with Laval in town dress, and without a mask. In London she again caused a sensation when, instead of heavy hoops and panniers, she appeared in figure-revealing muslin veils with her hair flowing about her shoulders. *Les Indes galantes*, given in Paris in 1734, marked her greatest triumph—a triumph she needed, for her supremacy was

56 *Pas de deux* from *Sylvie*. Dauberval and Marie Allard

57 Marie Sallé

already being challenged by Camargo. Marie-Anne de Cupis de Camargo—of Spanish origin, and, like Sallé, a pupil of Mademoiselle Prévost—danced in the Italian fashion (*Ill.* 55). Her brilliant technique triumphed over many physical imperfections, but she was limited to a vigorous, acrobatic style, adopting, says Noverre, a 'lively, rousing manner'. Voltaire refused to take sides in the endless battle between the two ballerinas, and wrote:

> 'Ah! Camargo, que vous êtes brillante!
> Mais que Sallé, grands dieux, est ravissante!'

Sallé was indeed entrancing, and with a grace that often served to conceal her lack of technique. When she died, the century of scandals remembered that she had led a completely blameless existence.

In contrast, Marie-Madeleine Guimard (*Ill.* 54) was the incarnation of the scandalous ballerina of the eighteenth century, and everlastingly at war with Noverre, his directors and his musicians. She began as a member of the *corps de ballet* of the Comédie-Française. After the success of *La Mort d'Orphée* and *Vertumne et Pomone* she joined the Opéra, making her début on 9 May 1762 in the role of Terpsichore. Noverre wrote, 'After having long devoted herself to serious dancing, she abandoned it in favour of the mixed *genre* I had created for Monsieur Le Picq.' This mixed *genre* was represented by *Les Caprices de Galatée*, *Jason et Médée*, and others. La Guimard, though she quarrelled with Noverre, followed his advice, for, like the others, she was anxious to expand and develop her art.

58 Ballet headdress. Drawn by Boquet

If Marie-Madeleine Guimard was remarkable for her bird-like thinness ('Her whole body is nothing but salt-cellars', claimed a satirical poet), Marie Allard was unusually stout, which did not prevent her from dancing with surprising vivacity. Her life was a stormy one, and history remembers her chiefly as the mother of Auguste Vestris, third 'God of the Dance', but she won lifelong fame in her own day for her *pas de deux* with Dauberval in *Sylvie* (*Ill.* 56).

Another dancer who owed much to Noverre was Anne Heinel, a German gifted with a grand tragic temperament, who was the wife, for a time, of Gaetano Vestris. 'A proud

59 Dauberval in *La Reine de Jolconde*

60 Auguste Vestris

and elegant figure, with perfect execution, vigour, elevation and brilliance in all her leaps.' Finally there was the gifted Louise-Madeleine Lany, who danced in almost every one of the ballets of Rameau, and whose only fault was her timidity.

The male dancers of the age of Louis XV yielded nothing to the *danseuses*. Dupré was the perfect embodiment of the 'danseur noble' dear to the century of Louis XIV. To be a 'danseur noble' one needed an exceptionally well-proportioned body and harmonious movements. Though this type of performer did not long remain the French ideal, it had a lasting influence abroad, and the tradition has been carried on into the twentieth century by Flemming Flindt and Erik Bruhn. Dupré, after having been himself 'God of the Dance', became the teacher of Gaetano Vestris, who inherited the title and passed it on to his son, the third 'God of the Dance' in a century. The two Vestris, Gaetano and Auguste, took advantage of the lessons of Noverre and of his *ballets d'action* to develop to the full their immense talent, compounded of grace, ease and intelligence. Noverre, who had studied osteology, tells us that Vestris *père* was 'close-hammed... he is the best, in fact the only serious dancer in the theatre.' Vestris *fils* (*Ill.* 60) was the most astonishing dancer in Europe. He once refused to dance before the Queen of France, and relented only when ordered to do so by his father. Jean Lany, brother of Louise-Madeleine, was 'bow-legged, but he is clever enough to turn this defect to advantage; he is the most expert dancer I know'.

Maximilien Gardel made his début when very young at the Académie Royale de Musique, where his ease of execution was admired, though it did not eclipse that of Vestris. In 1781 he took over the post of ballet-master occupied first by Lany, then by Noverre. He made his mark as a choreographer with *La Chercheuse d'Esprit* and *Ninette à la Cour*. His elder brother Pierre was also a creator of ballets, and composed *Le Jugement de Paris*, *La Dansomanie*, *Daphnis et Pandrose ou la Vengeance de l'Amour*, and *Achille à Scyros* to music by Cherubini. His *Psyché* was a very popular work, and the severe Noverre wrote of him: 'He strode with giant steps along the road that I had opened up, the road of the *ballet d'action*.'

Of Dauberval (*Ill.* 59) Noverre says: 'Dauberval, my pupil, though at first modelled by the Graces, became heavy and muscular.' When dancing a *pas de quatre* with Lany, Allard and Pélin, he was indispensable for the perfect ensemble. His best ballet, *La Fille mal gardée*, can be said never to have left the stage since 1789, and is still included in some companies' repertories today. Trained in Noverre's school of mime, Dauberval influenced in his turn Salvatore Vigano.

The near-failure of Noverre and la Sallé—reformers born ahead of their time in this age of great successes—had one fortunate consequence; foreign capitals welcomed them, encouraged them, and developed their ideas. Dancers, too, went abroad to find employment. French ballet could no longer claim supremacy, and the Italian school was regaining a standing it had lost in the age of Louis XIV. But the frontiers of ballet were at the same time becoming less fixed; in St Petersburg, French and Italian dancers would meet, work together, sometimes marry. It was becoming harder to distinguish the different styles, though the Italian school was still notable for its vigour and brilliant acrobatic technique.

While Noverre was writing: 'As for me, Sir, I am now considered as no more than a troublesome old dotard; nevertheless, they still strive to imitate me—but alas! in what a fashion!' two other ballet-masters, elsewhere in Europe, were in their turn trying to introduce much-needed reforms.

61 La Campilli in *Zoraida*

CHAPTER SEVEN

The Fortunes of Ballet in Europe

Franz Hilferding was an Austrian. He was born into one of those families of nomad-actors which seem so common at this period, and after studying dancing in Paris under Blondi returned to Vienna, where he was immediately appointed ballet-master at the Court Theatre. Here he began, as a concession to tradition, by dancing in mask and wig, but resolved to do away with this idiotic custom at the first opportunity. And in fact his first ballet started a new trend by replacing Columbines and Punchinellos with down-to-earth characters such as charcoal-burners, Tyrolean peasants, and Hungarians in national costume, all performing to music the movements appropriate to their various callings, as depicted in the engravings illustrating the *Encyclopédie*. Unlike those of Noverre, his ideas bore immediate fruit in that costumes, scenery, lighting and rhythm were more carefully and skilfully devised. In 1740 he presented at Dresden Racine's *Britannicus*, in the form of a mimed ballet but following the rules of the drama; it was followed by Voltaire's *Alzire* and Crébillon's *Idoménée*. After a period as ballet-master at Stuttgart, Hilferding returned to Vienna as choreographer to the Court Theatre, where he created ballet-pantomimes in the new style, among them *Psyche*, *The Strength of Blood* and *The Rape of Proserpine*. His fame spread so far that the Empress Elisabeth Petrovna of Russia asked Vienna to release him to go to St Petersburg, there to bring about the 'perfecting and renewal' of the ballet.

Hilferding landed in St Petersburg with his entire company, which included the Czech composer Starzer and the stars Santina Aubry, Teresa Colonna and Gaetano

Cesare. Santina Aubry (*née* Zanuzzi, of Padua) had danced in Milan, Venice and Vienna. She was exiled from the Austrian capital by the jealous Empress Maria Theresa, who suspected her husband Francis II of taking an interest in the young dancer that went considerably beyond the bounds of ballet. Casanova, who met her and her husband in the course of his travels through Europe, wrote:

'The first person who came up to me, greeting me with the kisses that are *de rigueur* between old acquaintances, was a young dancer named Aubry, whom I had known in Paris; he had appeared at the Opera and subsequently at Venice, where he won fame by becoming simultaneously the lover of one of the grandest ladies of the city, and the darling of her husband... At the beginning of Lent, the State Inquisitors packed him off to Trieste. He introduced me to his wife, a dancer like himself, who was known as La Santina. He had married her in St Petersburg, from where they had come, and they were on their way to Paris for the winter.'

Teresa Colonna, or La Venezianella, born in Venice in 1734, had begun her career in Italy; she made a triumphant début at St Petersburg, where she was to stay until 1778. Gaetano Cesare, or Cesari, whose feet 'never touched the ground', joined the Russian Imperial Ballet, and later created *Poor Yourka*, to music by Starzer, on the occasion of the coronation of Catherine the Great.

As for Hilferding, he left Russia in the summer of 1764, never to return. His theatrical ventures had completely ruined him, and he died in poverty in Vienna four years later.

Next to be summoned to St Petersburg was Gasparo Angiolini. Born in Florence in 1721, he had begun his career as a dancer, and composed his first ballets (for which he also wrote the musical scores) at the Teatro Reggio, Turin. From there he went to the Court Theatre, Vienna, where he met Hilferding, and took his place as ballet-master when the latter left for Russia. In 1761 he wrote the scenario and composed the choreography for *Don Juan or the Stone Feast*, to music by Gluck. This work aimed to enhance the prestige of the ballet-pantomime at the expense of classical dancing. Next came *The Siege of Cythera*, an *opéra-comique* by Favart, and in 1762 *Orpheus*, again to Gluck's music—the first opera fully to embody the new principles of dance drama. Between 1763 and 1764 he staged a series of heroic ballets, *Cleopatra*, *Peleus and Thetis*, *Iphigenia*, and *Semiramis*, after Voltaire. The unusual subject-matter and conception of these works aroused fierce controversy, but Angiolini persisted in his theories, practising them in St Petersburg, where his *Dido*—to his own music and choreography—was much admired. After this came *The Chinese in Europe*, this time with his own scenario as well as music, and a ballet with theme and music derived entirely from Russian folklore which was an enormous success.

Other works produced by Angiolini in Russia were *The Defeat of Prejudice* (1768), *Rinaldo and Armida* (1769), *The Refuge of Cupid* (1770), *Pygmalion*, given in 1772 at the home of Prince Viazemsky, *Theseus and Ariadne*, and the *Orphan of China*, as well as the danced *divertissements* for operas by Manfredini. His *Eagle of Virtue*—a ballet that combined poetry, drama and dance, and for which he devised the scenario—marked the appearance of the first notable Russian dancer, Boublikof Timofay Semenovich, a pupil of the St Petersburg Academy of Dancing. This was an important event, for until now only French or Italians had won promotion to the rank of star dancers.

62 Michele Fabiani

While on a visit to Milan Angiolini met Noverre, who was then staging his own great ballet-pantomimes at the Teatro Ducale, and the famous quarrel between them developed. Noverre, who had a justifiable pride in his *ballet d'action*, claimed to be its sole originator, whereas Angiolini maintained that the idea was the outcome of the collaboration between himself and Hilferding. There was a heated exchange of letters and pamphlets, and feelings ran high. In reality, all three had taken part in the birth of this ballet, and no single one could claim to be its creator.

In 1788 Angiolini left Russia, laden with honours and provided with a royal pension, and settled in Milan. After witnessing Bonaparte's triumphal passage through the city he had the unfortunate notion of planting a tree of Liberty in his garden; the Austrians, who were not far away, returned to Milan and promptly deported him.

Through the good offices of General Moncey, Angiolini regained his liberty but he did not live long enough to enjoy it.

As we have seen, Russia had become the more or less temporary refuge of many French and Italian dancers, thanks to the efforts of three successive Tsarinas, Anna Ivanovna (reigned 1730-1740), Elisabeth Petrovna (1740-1762) and above all Catherine of Russia (1762-1796). Catherine had no special passion for the arts, but she was perceptive enough to see that they afforded pleasure to others, and so did her best to encourage opera and ballet. That ever-curious eighteenth-century journalist, Casanova—travelling round Europe now in the comfort of a 'dormeuse', now in a 'berline', hastening to give the slip to some unfriendly Government—noted what she had to say on the subject:

'One evening, as we were coming out of the opera-house after a performance of Metastasio's *Olympiad*, I overheard her remark: "Everyone enjoyed the music of this opera, and on that account I am delighted, but I found it tedious. Music is a fine thing, but I cannot conceive how one can love it passionately unless one has nothing else important to do or to think about. I am at present bringing Buranello here, and I shall be curious to see whether he succeeds in making the music interesting to me, though I doubt it, for I fear I am constitutionally unfitted to appreciate it".'

St Petersburg, at the time of Casanova's visit, swarmed with Italians. Cosimo Damiano Tesi, dancer and choreographer, had arrived with his wife in 1735; when he went back to Europe he was replaced by Antonio Rinaldi, who had come from Venice, via London. Rinaldi produced several works in the Russian capital, among them *The Force of Love and Hate* (1736), *False Nino* (1737), and *Ataxerxes* (1738) with a scenario by Metastasio. Unfortunately, though promotions were swift, falls from favour were no less rapid, and as the result of an intrigue Rinaldi had to flee from Russia and take refuge in France. Here he danced with Barbarina Campanini (1721-1779) whose artistic talents, combined with a remarkable temperament, were to make her a favourite in all the capitals of Europe (*Ill.* 65).

At the same time, St Petersburg engaged the French ballet-master Jean-Baptiste Landet, or Landé, to teach dancing at the newly-founded Imperial Theatre School. The composer Araya had Rinaldi recalled to Russia to create, and dance, the ballets for the operas *Seleuco* (1744) and *Cupid and Psyche*. Russian dancers appeared on the stage for the first time; there were about twenty of them all told, among them Axinia Baskakova in *Scipio* and Caterina Azarevich Lobiankova.

Next to arrive in Russia was Locatelli, a composer and producer, with an excellent company of singers and musicians and a seasoned troupe of dancers, including Antonio Sacco, his two sisters Andreina and Libera, and his wife Anna Conti de Sales. The company gave successful performances of *Cleopatra's Feast*, *The Ladies of the Seraglio*, *The Sailors' Return*, *The Fair of London*, and many others. A few years before Angiolini's departure from Russia, the Petrovsky Theatre engaged the Italian choreographer Giuseppe Salomoni, who had worked in Venice, Naples,

63 Décor for *Les Cannibales vaincus*

64 Pierre Gardel

65 La Barbarina in a *ballet champêtre*

Lisbon, Turin and Milan, and he produced for them more than fifty ballets. In 1790 he became ballet-master to Prince Cheremetief, in Kousov.

It should not be thought, however, that success in St Petersburg was easy. The Russian public was exacting, and the Empress, in spite of her lack of appreciation of the theatre, showed no mercy to small talents, though she was more indulgent towards those with greater gifts. As an example, here is the disillusioned account of Valville, a young actress and amateur singer welcomed to the Russian capital, as recorded by Casanova:

'I know that in Paris one sings, dances and acts without ever having learnt how to... But here, alas, things are very different!'

The Tsarina, however, could be merciful, as the story of the seduction of Mlle Chitroff, a beautiful dancer at the Imperial

Theatre, shows. The Tsarina had taken the greatest exception to this, but she eventually forgave the dancer, recalled her seducer, and the affair ended with a marriage.

Frontiers counted for little at this period for the artistic, the well-connected, or the wealthy, or even for the merchant, on his way to reinstate some aristocrat's fallen fortunes. Artists moved freely through Europe; an Italian ballerina would be arriving in one place, the choir-master Galuppi and his friends in another, and this exchange between capitals fortified and enriched the ballet.

66 Peter Crux

In Berlin, Court ballet, which was already flourishing, was given fresh impetus by the arrival of Barbarina (*Ill*.65). On her advice, Frederick the Great established, in 1742, the Königliche Opera (Royal Opera House). Barbarina, however, did not like to stay long in one place; she went to Paris to dance with Rinaldi, and from there to England, promising to return after that to her royal admirer in Berlin. In London, however, she fell in love with a lord, and the couple ran off to Venice, in the hope that there one more scandalous *liaison* would not attract attention. But Frederick the Great reacted violently and threatened the Venetian Republic with dire reprisals if the culprits were not handed over. The city thought it wiser to comply; but, Barbarina being a star, everything was settled amicably, and the ballerina became a kind of Madame La Pompadour of Frederick the Great, while still continuing to dance.

After Barbarina's day the Berlin public's interest in ballet waned, until the arrival of the French dancer and choreographer François-Michel Hoguet (1773-1871). Hoguet was immediately appointed ballet-master, and stayed in Berlin for fifty years, composing ballets such as *Robert and Bertram* (1841) and *Aladdin or the Wonderful Lamp* (1854).

In Vienna the tradition of court ballet, which went back to the Italian masters of the sixteenth century, was continued in the first half of the eighteenth century with Anna Scio, wife of the French ballet-master Alexandre Philibois. Another name of importance is Peter Crux (*Ill.* 66), an Austrian, the pupil of Gardel, who made his entire career on the Viennese stage and bore comparison with the best artists from Paris. Then came Hilferding, Angiolini, and, in 1767, Noverre, with his *Apothéose d'Hercule*. They were followed by Antoine Pitrot, who produced many successes.

67 Antoine Bournonville

Warsaw made the fortunes of a husband-and-wife team, La Binetti and her husband Le Picq:

'The King declared that he would pay a thousand ducats to have them come to Warsaw for eight days... In three days, Le Picq had arranged a ballet: costumes, scenery, orchestra, performers, everything was ready... The couple were such a success that their engagement was extended to a year, and they were given *carte blanche*. This greatly displeased Catai, not only because Binetti outshone her as dancer, but because she enticed away her admirers.

'In ten days or so Binetti was installed in an elegantly furnished house: two dinner services, one plain, one in silver gilt, a cellar with exquisite wines, an excellent cook, numerous admirers... The two ballerinas shared out the theatre between them, for although Catai's talent was as nothing compared to Binetti's, she was determined not to abandon the field to her rival. One star danced in the first ballet, the other in the second; those who had applauded the former were silent when the latter appeared, and vice versa.'

In Riga Casanova found Campioni, 'a dancer at the very top of his profession,' who told him with satisfaction: 'I left St Petersburg two years ago, and I live well here, for I have pupils who are a credit to me.'

Through the efforts of Henri Malter, mime-ballet had a successful career in Stuttgart, encouraged by the founding of a *corps de ballet* of about thirty pupils by Michel de Agata and François Sauveterre in 1758. Two years later came Noverre with Vestris, Dauberval, Gardel, Heinel and Luisa Toscani. Their success was considerable, but after Noverre's departure Stuttgart's interest in the ballet declined until the arrival of Taglioni and Romanticism.

John Weaver may be considered as the creator of pantomime and of the English school of ballet. Born in 1673, he was dancer, ballet-master and choreographer from 1700 to 1736 at the theatres of Drury Lane and Lincoln's Inn Fields. He also published an adaptation of Feuillet's work under the title *Orchesography*, and many other works on dancing. Nor should we forget Robert Aldridge (1738-1793), an Irish dancer and teacher, who composed a number of ballets in Dublin and London, finally opening a dancing school in Edinburgh. His pupil Simon Slingsby, who appeared at the King's Theatre, London, with Baccelli and Vestris, was probably the first Englishman to win a high reputation as a dancer, at a time when it was customary in England to import dancers from the Continent. Italian singers, clowns, ballerinas and castrati were popular on the English stage, and Andrea Giovanni Gallini directed the Royal Opera House, also writing books on the ballet.

68 Vincenzo Galeotti

Among the dancers of the Royal Opera of Copenhagen were the two Saccos, husband and wife. Sacco, notably in *L'Amour plus fort que la Mort* and *Le Cosaque Jaloux*, succeeded in giving his ballets the dramatic content sought by Noverre, Angiolini and Hilferding. His place was taken in 1775 by Vincenzo Galeotti (*Ill.* 68), who produced *Le Berger et la Fée*, *la Foire d'Amsterdam* and *Les Caprices de l'Amour et du Maître de Danse*—the latter destined to be revived in the twentieth century at the Paris Opéra by the Dane Harald Lander under the title *Les Amours de Cupidon*. Galeotti had a long career at Copenhagen where he died in 1816. One of his pupils was Antoine Bournonville, whose son Auguste (1805-1879) was to establish the great Danish dancing tradition, continued in our own day by Flemming Flindt and Erik Bruhn.

At the time of the foundation of its Opera House Stockholm already possessed a *corps de ballet*, under the direction of the French ballet-master Gallodier (1773-1803) who had trained at the Paris Opéra. The Swedish public gave an enthusiastic welcome to foreign dancers such as Mademoiselle du Tillet, Giovanna Bassi, Louis Gallodier and Louis Frossard. It continued to take an interest in the work of Antoine Bournonville (*Ill.* 67), Gallodier's successor, but in spite of the efforts of Filippo Taglioni (who had married the daughter of the Swedish actor Karsten), ballet gradually entered a decline. Anders Selinder's early attempts to introduce folk dances to the stage met with failure.

69 Costume design of the eighteenth century

CHAPTER EIGHT

Ballet in Italy

In the late eighteenth century Italian ballet, strongly coloured by ideas of mime and dance drama, had turned in the direction of tragedy. Performances of heroic dance, given in such diverse settings as the Padua Fair and the amphitheatre of Verona, were as popular as the cinemas of today. Schools of dancing were springing up everywhere: the Regio Theatre School, Turin, in 1754, the San Carlo Theatre School, Naples (founded by Salvatore Taglioni at the instigation of King Murat) in 1812, and the La Scala School in 1813.

Turin, capital of Piedmont, attracted a stream of Italian ballet celebrities, as well as French stars. Gaetano Grossatesta, the Venetian choreographer, visited it in 1743, and in the same year came the French dancers Lany, Vestris *père* and the latter's mistress, Marie Allard. Later, Gasparo Angiolini and his wife Teresa Fogliazzi gave a programme which included *Antigone*, *The Discovery of America*, and *Flemish Peasant Dance in an Inn*. In 1759 Dauberval produced a number of his ballets at the Regio Theatre. He partnered Anna Campioni in *Isaeus* (1761), in which Carlo Taglioni—ancestor of the famous dancing family—appeared as a member of the *corps de ballet*. In 1790 Andrea and Antonia Vulcani (dancers), Muzzarelli (choreographer) (*Ill.* 73) and later Pietro Angiolini, son of Gasparo, all came to the Regio Theatre. When Piedmont temporarily became a republic, the ballets given in Turin had republican themes.

Naples was no less devoted to the ballet. In 1735, under the reign of Charles III, the Viceroy, giving orders to impresarios to organize the theatrical season of San Bartolomeo, insisted on the inclusion of two ballets performed by

70-1 Maria de Caro

artists of the first rank, with choreography by Grossatesta and Aquilanti. On 4 November 1737 the San Carlo Theatre opened, with a performance of Metastasio's *Achilles in Scyros*. To the great misfortune of Johann Christian Bach, Filippo Beccari and his sister Colombe, a brilliant and graceful dancer, arrived in Naples in 1761. The younger Bach's opera *Cato* won great acclaim, but the unhappy composer, a victim to the charms of Colombe, pursued his courtship even in the theatre. The usher called him to order, but to no avail. The same scene was repeated the following day, and Bach was expelled from the theatre forever.

On 30 May 1737 Le Picq and Binetti presented in Naples a programme of French dances which were entirely without acrobatics or excessive pirouettes 'à la Vestris'. They feared that these relatively new dances would not be popular, and were surprised when their sober style, in complete contrast to the Italian manner, was a complete success. Anna Ramoni Binetti, who provoked a duel between Casanova and an officer in Warsaw, danced successively in Venice, Stuttgart, London, Innsbruck (Hilferding's *Aeneas in Italy*), Milan, Monaco and Naples, ending her career in Venice. Noverre found in Le Picq all the indispensable qualities :

'A finely-proportioned figure, a noble face, magical harmony of movement, and, to crown all, a brilliance of execution that is all the more astonishing in that it is completely unforced, and physical effort is always concealed by grace.'

Maria de Caro, a pupil of Vestris and Noverre, was not beautiful, but her dancing earned her a positive triumph at the San Carlo Theatre (*Ills.* 70, 71).

The presence of the Pope in Rome did not prevent ballet from being equally popular there. Women were still not allowed on the stage, and women's parts were taken by men *en travesti*. Noverre wrote in his *Lettres:*

'The new Rome seems, in this respect, to have modelled itself upon the old. Women's roles are sung by adolescent boys, and young men fulfil the functions of *danseuses*.' Although this custom was inspired by a laudable concern for morality, the remedy was worse than the disease; men

72 Rehearsal of a pastoral ballet by Pietro Longhi

would be given the title of 'première danseuse', and though they were perfect in adagios and allegros, their frenzied spins would reveal a pair of black under-shorts—strictly obligatory for ballet dancers—which made a comical contrast to their decolleté and short skirts.

In Padua *The Destruction of Carthage*, a heroic ballet with mime composed by Dominique Ballon, opened in 1792, with the author and Thérèse Ballon in the leading roles.

Acrobatic ballet was the rage in the theatres of Venice. The adventuress Sarah Goudar, explaining in one of her books on music and ballet the difference between a French and an Italian dancer, censures the Italians for their exaggerated turns, and recalls the exploit of a dancer who landed *d'aplomb* on his right foot and remained balanced on it for eight minutes. In 1764 Giuseppe Salomoni produced *Circe's Enchanted Island* and *The Magician*. Even more spectacular were Metastasio's *Olympiad*, in three acts, with music by Bartoli, in 1765, and at the San Cassiano Theatre *The Loves of Zephyr* and *The Enchanted Garland* by Fabiani, 'dancer to the Empress of All the Russias'. Galeotti (*Ill.* 68) produced a few works in Venice before going on to found the Copenhagen ballet, and Gasparo Angiolini, with Antonio Campioni and Catherine Kurtz, appeared at the San Benedetto Theatre in 1773 in *The Departure of Aeneas* and *Art Conquered by Nature*. Other famous names of the period were Caterina Ramaccini, La Brugnoli, Anna Conti, La Burgioni, La Mantovanina, Margherita Fusi and the two Campionis. Antonio Campioni and his wife Ancilla had already won a considerable reputation abroad. He was the son of the actor Giuseppe Campioni, of Parma, and made successful appearances with his wife in London, Vienna, Warsaw and St Petersburg. She, if we are to believe 'le Président de Brosses' (author of *Lettres sur l'Italie*), 'was considered the most beautiful woman in Italy.' The Taglioni family also came to Venice: Carlo produced his *The Abducted Wife* at the San Moise Theatre, and also *The Dutch Fair*, with Filippo and Giuseppe Taglioni as 'premiers danseurs', Domenico Turchi as 'premier grotesque', and Luigia Taglioni as 'première danseuse'.

Milan's Teatro Ducale—later to take the name of La Scala—opened in the mid-seventeenth century. The

73 Antonio Muzzarelli

74 Gaetano Gioja

performers at first remained anonymous, but gradually their names and those of the choreographers, with titles and grades, began to appear on the bills. In 1758 the first detailed libretto was produced, for a ballet entitled *The Fable of Bacchus and Ariadne*. The *ballet d'action* began its reign at the Teatro Ducale, and in 1773 Noverre arrived to put on a season of his own works. The Milanese, though acknowledging his genius, found his style somewhat violent, and less moving than Noverre would have wished. He was not discouraged, however, and returned some time later to produce *Médée et Jason*, *Renaud et Armide*, *Adèle de Ponthieu*, and *Les Horaces et les Curiaces*, which were similarly received.

On 2 February 1776, the Teatro Ducale burned down, and two years later La Scala Theatre was inaugurated with the opera *L'Europa Riconosciuta*, with music by Salieri and a grand ballet called *Pafio e Mirra* by the choreographer Claude Legrand. This had no fewer than sixty dancers, with grandiose scenery painted by the Galliari brothers, and included such 'attractions' as a circus, wild animals, and armed rebellions—in a style not very far, in fact, from 'revue.' The choreographer Canziani did even better with *Apollo Placato*, in which a band of corybantes, satyrs and fauns gambolled to the sound of drums, cymbals and castanets. The sung parts alternated with danced ensembles, *pas de deux* and *pas de quatre*.

General Colli in Rome, or the Pope's Ballet. This startling title brought the Milanese to La Scala in crowds on the eve of the Napoleonic occupation, which for the Italians seemed very like a liberation. According to the librettist, the idea for this ballet came from none other than Napoleon (whose troops were then about to march on Rome). The scenario was by Salfi, music by Pontelibero, and choreography by Paolino Franchi. Pope Pius VII, danced by Dominique Lefèvre, is hesitating between the counsels of the Father Superior of the Dominicans, who preaches peace, and those of the Cardinals, who are clamouring for war. As a result of sentimental intrigues by his two nieces, the princesses Braschi and Santacroce, the Pope entrusts the defence of the Eternal City to General Colli. In the fourth act the Pope watches a ballet in the Vatican, showing, says the libretto 'all the passion he feels for the prettiest, the most agile pair of legs...' In the fifth act General Colli is reviewing his troops in St Peter's Square when a messenger brings news of the French victory at Mantua. The Pope falls in a faint; the Father Superior of the Dominicans offers him a Phrygian cap; General Colli indignantly rushes forward to snatch it from him, but the people intervene, and the Pope puts the red cap of liberty on his own head.

In spite of the somewhat scandalous character of this work, all Milan was in the theatre on the night of the première. There was an uproar at the end of the fifth act when a group of French officers noisily demanded that the Pope and General Colli should dance a 'Périgourdine'; both dancers at once obliged. *The Pope's Ballet* ran for nine performances, but upon the signing of the Peace of Tolentino between Pius VII and Bonaparte it promptly disappeared from the bills.

Next at La Scala came *Porzia*, a tragic ballet by the choreographer Filippo Beretti; *Romeo and Juliet*, which had the second act set in the amphitheatre of Verona, with dances and tournaments; and *Fair Zoraida*, by Giuseppe de Rossi, which was set in Peru. Antonio Muzzarelli (*Ill.* 73) composed for the Cannobiana Theatre *The Loves of Igor*, *Captain Cook in the Indies*, etc. Francesco Clerico specialized in tragic mime-ballet : his *Death of Hercules* was followed by *The Fall of Troy* and *Lodovico il Moro*.

Gaetano Gioja (Naples 1768-1826) had once, as a very young man, seen Vestris dance, and had sworn that he would one day become a dancer himself (*Ill.* 74). After studying under Traffieri he made his début at the age of nineteen, and in 1789 produced in Vicenza his first ballet, *Sophonisbe*, which opened all doors to him. Whereas Noverre had been criticized for having too much walking and too little dancing in his ballets, Gioja's works put dancing before mime, and when Salvatore Vigano saw *Caesar in Egypt* (also by Gioja) he did not hesitate to declare it greatly superior to his own ballets. Gioja's habit was to work late at night, composing choreography and music simultaneously. After creating more than two hundred and fifty ballets, he died as a result of a fall on the stage.

Next to enter the limelight was Salvatore Vigano (*Ills.* 77, 79). He came of a family composed exclusively of

75 The Viganos. Drawings by Shadow

dancers, and so when he was born in 1769 his career was decided in advance. He made his début in Rome in a *travesti* role, going on to dance in Venice, then in Spain. It was in Madrid that he met the French dancer Dauberval, who was to have a decisive influence on his career. Another important encounter was with his future wife, the beautiful Austrian dancer Mayer, known as Maria Medina (*Ills.* 78-80). Vigano produced *Raoul* (1791) and Dauberval's *La Fille mal gardée* (1792) in Venice, and in Vienna *Richard Cœur-de-Lion*, after Sedaine and Grétry, in 1793. The appearance of himself and his wife in Vienna aroused fanatical enthusiasm. Carolina Pichler gives an account of it in her book *Events of My Life:*

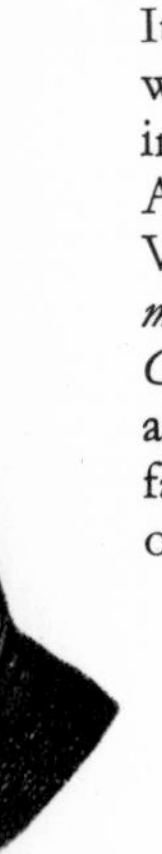

76 The elder Vigano, 1835

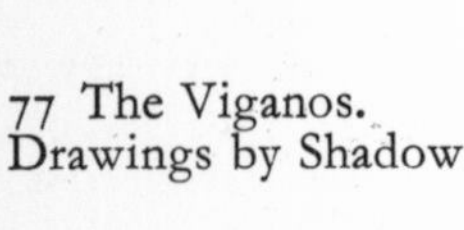

77 The Viganos. Drawings by Shadow

'In the so-called *pas de deux roses*, Maria Medina wore nothing over her flesh-coloured tights but two or three crêpe skirts, one shorter than the other, and gathered in at the waist by a dark-coloured belt. This belt was really all she wore, for the crêpe concealed nothing. As she danced her skirts rose and floated out, revealing her body, which in the natural-coloured tights appeared completely naked. The effect produced by this woman and the ballets her husband created for her was sensational; it was the triumphant culmination of an old art and a new manner.'

After touring Europe the Viganos returned to Vienna, where they stayed until 1803, when Maria Medina disappeared from Vigano's life.

78 Salvatore Vigano

79 The Viganos. Drawings by Shadow

On 28 March 1801 the première of *The Creatures of Prometheus*, to music by Beethoven, took place at the Court Theatre, Vienna, with Maria Cosentini and Salvatore Vigano in leading roles, and the mime Cesari as Prometheus. This ballet won, in the end, only a *succès d'estime*. In 1812 came the première of *The Walnut of Benevento*, a half-fairytale, half-allegorical piece, and in 1813 Vigano produced in Milan a second *Prometheus*, with music from Haydn's *Creation* as well as Beethoven's score. Also given at La Scala were *Coriolanus*, *Sammete and Tamiri*, and *The Strelitz*, danced by Jean and Teresa Coralli, which recounted the bloody suppression by Peter the Great of a military revolt. The ballet *Othello* (1813) opened with a festival scene whose boldness of conception was praised by Stendhal

80 Maria Medina Vigano

and in which Antonia Pallerini and the mime Nicola Molinari, both specially coached by Vigano, succeeded in making their roles particularly terrifying. After *Mirra* came *Daedalus*, a somewhat obscure work, and *The Vestal Virgin*, undoubtedly Vigano's most moving and poignant ballet, which caused Stendhal to describe him as 'the Shakespeare of the dance' (*Ill.* 81). *The Titans* was Vigano's last great work. He had begun on another, entitled *Dido*, when he died as the result of a chill brought on by overwork.

81 *The Vestal Virgin.* Ballet by Salvatore Vigano, 1818

Vigano's style disappeared with him. His achievement consisted in having realized, with acuteness, that one could not produce French-style choreography and Italian-style pantomime at one and the same time, and that ballet was not tragedy. Mime there must be, but it must be supported to a very large extent by dancing and above all by the character of the music. Vigano preferred the manœuvring of large ensembles, interspersed with solos and *pas de deux*, to a series of individual dances. At last the *corps de ballet* assumed its full importance. Noverre would have been satisfied.

'The patient, slow Vigano,' wrote Stendhal, 'took the time to ensure that the very last member of the cast who had not been sure of his role could perform it perfectly.' The newspapers, on the other hand, wondered why his works had so little dancing in them. 'Why does he not have a few good classical dancers in his company?'

82 Samengo
and Amalia Brugnoli
in *The Magic Ring*

CHAPTER NINE

The Romantic Ballet

In 1760 Noverre had complained:

'Unfortunately the pirouette has not remained exclusive to Vestris, but has become the standard routine of thirty other dancers... The dancing of the Opéra seems to have unknowingly adopted the system of Descartes; it is losing itself in whirlings.'

And the great choreographer pleaded for the return to ballet of 'those graces which have disappeared from the theatre through an excess of awkward spins and technical difficulties.'

From 1799 to 1815 the Paris Opéra had been under the sway of Pierre Gardel and Milon, both of them rigidly opposed to the slightest innovation. While in Paris ballets in a fast declining genre such as *Persée et Andromède*, *La Fête de Mars*, and *L'Enlèvement des Sabines* followed one another in quick succession, French dancers and choreographers were roaming the world and absorbing fresh influences.

The works of Henry (Henri Bonnachon) were, according to his contemporaries, fired with the true poetic spirit. *Le Bal masqué* ran at La Scala, Milan, for a full season, to be followed by *Le Château des esprits* and *Hamlet*, which fully justified their author's reputation. After these triumphs Henry settled permanently in Italy. François-Albert Decombe (known as Albert), on the other hand, made his début in Paris at the Théâtre de la Gaîté. He was initiated into the pure Romantic technique by Coulon, and in 1813 joined the Opéra, becoming first 'premier danseur', then choreographer. He appeared successively in London,

Vienna, Naples and Paris, where he produced *Le Séducteur au village* in 1818, and *Cendrillon* in 1823. Some years later he returned to London to stage *Daphnis et Céphyse*, but this was in 1830, and in another year was to come the first assault of the Romantic ballet. Jean Aumer (*Ill.* 84) made his début at the Opéra in Dauberval's *Le Déserteur;* as choreographer he produced *Jenny ou le Mariage secret* and *Les Deux Créoles* at the Théâtre Porte-Saint-Martin, *Antoine et Cléopâtre* at Lyons, and *La Somnambule ou l'Arrivée d'un nouveau Seigneur* (1829) at the Paris Opéra. A fourth distinguished French choreographer of this period was Jean-Baptiste Blache, born in Berlin of a family of French dancers, who joined the Opéra but left it again to replace Dauberval in the Grand Théâtre of Bordeaux. His *Mars et Vénus, ou les Filets de Vulcain* (1806) ran for over two hundred performances and won him a gold medal from the King of Prussia.

At the Paris Opéra at this time many brilliant ballerinas were emerging: Fanny Bias, who is shown in a lithograph of 1821 standing on her points; Emilia Bigottini, a fine dancer in spite of having only a tolerable ear for music (*Ill.* 85); Geneviève Gosselin, who triumphed in *L'Enfant prodigue*, but crossed swords with the all-powerful Gardel, who saw in her a dangerous rival to Miller, his wife; and Clotilde Chameroy, who was establishing a reputation second only to Vestris when her brief career was cut short by death. The curé of Saint-Roch refused her Christian burial, but earned himself a reprimand from the Archbishop of Paris for a harshness unworthy even of the age of Molière.

83 Maximilien Gardel

While the Romantic climate (derived from Germany) was developing, Jean-François Coulon and his son Antoine were working on the Romantic technique. Noisy pirouettes and jumps 'à la Vestris' were succeeded by silence and an atmosphere of ethereal purity; the loudly-tapping heels of the eighteenth-century ballerina were replaced by the dainty, noiseless satin slipper of the Directoire era, with its logical consequence—the point.

On 21 November 1831, the Parisian public, which in spirit was still with Vestris and the Muses, woke up with a start at the third act of *Robert le Diable*. Gautier had said 'Enough of dryads, now let us have witches.' The dance of the lapsed nuns, rising up with Marie Taglioni from their tombs in the cloister in eerie moonlight, had an electrifying effect on the spectators. Coralli (*Ill.* 96) had created this macabre choreography to music by Meyerbeer, Ciceri's set was faithfully modelled on the cloisters of St Trophime, and gas lamps swathed in yellow veils cast an appropriately lugubrious light.

84 Jean-Pierre Aumer

A few years before Marie Taglioni had been surprised to see La Brugnoli dancing on her points, and had commented that her arms were faulty. It was Taglioni herself, however, who inaugurated the reign of the point on 12 March 1832, with *La Sylphide* (*Ill.* 91). This fairytale ballet-pantomime, created by her father, Filippo Taglioni, was set amid the romantic mists of Scotland, through which glimmered the white skirts of the Sylphide, or spirit of the air, gliding silently on impeccable points. The third great landmark of the Romantic period—which was to last only ten years—was *Giselle*, with scenario by Théophile Gautier. *Giselle ou les Wilis* (1841) was the very apotheosis of Romantic ballet (*Ill.* 87). All the characteristics were there: the aerial points, the swaying, bell-like white *tutus*, the Germanic romance of the first act, the other-worldly realism of the second, the drama supported and intensified by a perfect technique, and—Woman, absolute mistress of the Romantic ballet.

These legendary ten years of *ballet blanc* were shared by three ballerinas, Marie Taglioni (*Ills.* 86, 91, 97, 100), Carlotta Grisi and Fanny Elssler. Marie Taglioni's family had been dancers for two generations. Her father had been 'premier danseur' in Italy, then at the Royal Theatre, Stockholm, before going to Warsaw to produce his works and reorganize the *corps de ballet*. He himself trained his daughter, imposing on her an iron discipline, and launched her in 1822 at the Court Theatre, Vienna, in a ballet of his own composition, *La réception d'une jeune nymphe à la cour de Terpsichore*. The Viennese public and critics were enthusiastic, but the reaction of the Théâtre de la Porte-Saint-Martin was only mediocre. It was not until 1827, when she made her début at the Opéra, that Paris 'discovered' Taglioni. It discovered not only a perfect technique (her father is said to have declared 'If I heard my daughter dance, I would kill her'), but a lyrical grace and a tempera-

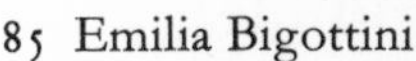

85 Emilia Bigottini

ment which transfigured physical prowess into 'modesty and naivety'. Besides her father she had Coulon, creator of the Romantic style, as her teacher. After creating the role of *La Sylphide* in 1832, she remained as Sylphide for audiences all over Europe; she started fashions, such as the Sylphide turbans, and hairstyles 'à la sylphide'; and Victor Hugo wrote verses in her honour.

Carlotta Grisi (*Ills.* 88, 92, 98), daughter of an Italian Land Registration official, studied at La Scala, Milan, then with Carlo Blasis. At the San Carlo Theatre, Naples, she met the French dancer Perrot, who fell in love with her violet eyes and vowed to make her a star. In this he succeeded, for Grisi was acclaimed in Milan, London, Munich, Naples and finally Paris. She became the great love of Théophile Gautier, who wrote for her the scenario of *Giselle* (music by Adolphe Adam, scenery by Ciceri) in which she starred in 1841, partnered by Lucien Petipa. *Giselle* was an unprecedented success. After this Grisi danced *La Jolie Fille de Gand*, *La Péri*, *La Esmeralda*, *Le Diable à Quatre*, *Paquita*, and finally *Giselle* once more at the Maryinsky Theatre, St Petersburg in 1850.

The triumph of Fanny Elssler (*Ill.* 93) does not, strictly speaking, belong to the Romantic ballet, though she is generally considered as a Romantic dancer. She made her debut in *La Tempête* in 1834, and danced the cachucha in *Le Diable boiteux*, in which she seemed the very incarnation of fiery, passionate Spain. But she failed when she tried to take her rival's role in *La Sylphide*. Contemporaries called her 'a man's dancer', and Taglioni 'a woman's dancer'. 'I love Fanny to the point of lying for her,' declared Barbey d'Aurevilly. Critics never tired of contrasting the 'taqueté' of Elssler with the 'ballonné' of Taglioni, and in fact the difference between them was more than professional rivalry, it was a clash of opposing styles. Taglioni was always 'the sylph' and Elssler 'the lovely girl whose dancing makes so much noise...'

86 Marie Taglioni

Taglioni had nothing to fear from the success of Lucile Grahn. Born in Copenhagen in 1819, she trained in the *corps de ballet* of the Danish Royal Theatre, following the Romantic idiom of the day. After a quarrel with Bournonville she left Denmark to become an international star, dancing *La Sylphide* in Paris and St Petersburg, and inter-

87 *Pas de deux* from *Giselle*

88 Carlotta Grisi in *La Péri*, 1843

89 Lucile Grahn in *La Esmeralda*

preting many works of Perrot, for she had both technique and poetry.

Fanny Cerrito (*Ill.* 95), however, was a more serious rival. Neapolitan by birth, she had made her début at the age of fourteen in Salvatore Taglioni's *L'Horoscope;* she had beauty, vivacity, and a sure technique, and was young, whereas Taglioni's charms were already beginning to fade. In 1845 Cerrito married Saint-Léon, dancer, choreographer and talented violinist. She appeared at the Paris Opéra with her husband in ballets he had composed, becoming finally the 'prima ballerina assoluta' whose technique was praised by Gautier. But to admire Cerrito was already to be unfaithful to the true Romantic ballet.

When Taglioni was on the point of retiring from the stage, Lumley, manager of Her Majesty's Theatre, London, had the brilliant idea of bringing together in a *pas de quatre* the four greatest dancers of the century. It was difficult to include one without offending another, and after a number of incidents, and diplomatic manœuvring by Lumley to spare the ladies' pride, the ballet finally took place on 26 June 1845. Taglioni, still on top of her form, shared the stage with the young, graceful Cerrito, the vigorous yet romantic Grahn, and Grisi. This famous work was successfully revived in our own day by Anton Dolin, after the original score had been discovered in London.

The creator of the memorable *Pas de Quatre* (*Ill.* 100), was Jules Perrot the only great male dancer of the Romantic ballet. Brought up in the theatre, Perrot was taught by the younger Vestris, and his ease and lightness of movement made him well-suited to appear in a ballet in which women played the major parts. He visited London, Vienna and Milan, producing *Alma ou la Fille de Feu* in 1842, *Ondine* in 1843, *Éoline ou la Dryade* and *Pas de Quatre* in 1845, and *Faust* in 1848. He was given an enthusiastic reception in Italy, and finally went as ballet-master to St Petersburg in 1848, there to be succeeded by Arthur Saint-Léon.

Taglionis, it was said, were ten a penny at the Opéra; in fact there were four of them, including Marie, whose names figure in ballet history. Filippo Taglioni, Marie's father, after his great triumph *La Sylphide*, produced *La*

Révolte dans le sérail, *Brésilia*, and *La Fille du Danube;* in Russia, *La Gitane*, with Fanny Elssler dancing in Spanish style; and in London, *L'Ombre*, and *Aglaé ou l'élève de l'amour*. But, try as he would, he could not create a second 'Sylphide'. He retired from the theatre in 1852, and died, afflicted by blindness, in his villa on the shores of Lake Como. His son Paolo, Marie's brother, known as 'Paul the Great', made his début at Stuttgart in *Zémir et Azor* on 4 November 1825. After appearing in Vienna, Munich and Paris he visited Berlin, where he met and married the ballerina Amalia Galster; of their three children, only Marie, born two years before *La Sylphide*, became a

90 Poster for *Giselle*, 1841

bureaux seront ouverts à 7 h. | ACADEMIE ROYALE DE MUSIQUE. | On commencera à 8 h. très-précises.

AUJOURD'HUI LUNDI 28 JUIN 1841,

LA PREMIÈRE REPRÉSENTATION DE

GISELLE

OU

LES WILIS

Ballet-Pantomime en 2 actes.

Précédé du 3e ACTE DE

MOÏSE

Opéra, paroles de M. JOUY et ***, musique de M. ROSSINI, décorations de M. *Cicéri.*

HANT: Mrs LEVASSEUR, F.-PREVOT, WARTEL, MOLINIER, SAINT-DENIS, OCTAVE Mmes WIDEMANN, ELIAN, Lagier.

ANSE dans le Ballet: Mrs SIMON, MABILLE, PETIPA, Quériau, Coralli, Desplaces 2e, Mmes ROLAND, NATHALIE FITZJAMES, CARREZ, FORSTER, SOPHIE DUMILATRE, ADÈLE DUMILATRE, CARLOTTA GRISI, Breistreff, Dimier, Wiéthoff, Caroline.

Les Entrées de faveur sont généralement suspendues.

Employés chargés de la distribution des billets aux Bureaux, étant dans l'impossibilité de savoir au juste, à chaque instant, combien il reste de places disponibles dans la Salle, l'Administration a l'honneur de prévenir les porteurs de billets pris aux Bureaux que, dans le cas où ils ne trouveraient pas à se placer, elle s'empresserait de leur rendre leur argent.

adresser, pour la Location, au Bureau de l'Académie royale de Musique, rue Grange-Batelière, Hôtel Choiseul, tous les jours, de 11 h. à 4 h.

dancer. His works included *Théa ou la fée des fleurs*, *Electre ou la Pléiade perdue*, with Carlotta Grisi, *Flik et Flok*, a fantasy-ballet danced by Amina Boschetti, and a number of ballets of a grandiose, spectacular character such as *L'Incendie de Ninive*, the last act of which featured the burning of the funeral pyre of King Sardanapalus and required a cast of three hundred. Paolo Taglioni was already conceiving ballets on the grand scale of the spectacles of the future Eden Theatre. He died in Berlin, during a rehearsal, in 1888. Another member of the Taglioni tribe, Salvatore (the ballerina's uncle) studied dancing under Coulon, distinguished himself in the ballets of Gardel, married the dancer Adelaide Perraud, and appeared with her and Marie at the San Carlo Theatre, Naples, in *Pas de Trois*. His *Barbier de Séville* so much delighted Murat, then King of Naples, that he founded a school of dancing in the city with Salvatore at its head. After *Ines de Castro* the King appointed him permanent choreographer at the San Carlo Theatre. In 1838 he staged Goethe's *Faust*, and composed in all more than two hundred and fifty ballets derived from all kinds of historical and literary sources including *La Flûte enchantée*, *La Conquête de Malacca*, *Roumanoff*, *Christine de Suède*, and *Les Fiancés* (from Alessandro Manzoni's famous novel *I Promessi Sposi*). Salvatore died in 1869.

Jean Coralli Peracini *(Ill.* 96), born in Paris in 1779, must also be awarded his due place in the story of Romantic ballet. According to Saint-Léon, Coralli's was an 'essentially French' style, all delicacy and poetic refinement. *Giselle*—at least in part—was his work, and also *La Folie de la Danse*, *Armide*, *L'Amour et l'hymen au village*, *L'Union de Flore et de Zéphyr* (which, with *La Statue de Vénus*, a ballet dedicated to the ballerina Heberlé, triumphed at La Scala, Milan) and a number of works produced at the Théâtre de la Porte-Saint-Martin. When he was finally appointed choreographer at the Opéra, then under the direction of Doctor Véron, he composed *Le Diable boiteux*, *La Tarentule* and *La Péri*, all classics of the Romantic era.

Whereas Vigano had had real musicians to write his scores, the Romantic ballet neglected the music. All that was demanded of Adam and Schneitzhoeffer, the composers of *Giselle* and *La Sylphide*, was music that fitted the

92 Carlotta Grisi and Jules Perrot dancing a Polka

91 Marie Taglioni in *La Sylphide*

93 Fanny Elssler in *La Esmeralda* at the Theatre of St Petersburg

94 Set for *La Fille du Danube*

choreography and the atmosphere. The scores for both ballets are equally immemorable. Not until the Diaghilev era do we find music which actively enhances the ballet.

Marie Taglioni made her final farewells in London in 1847, after twenty-five triumphant years; but after *Giselle*, there remained nothing new to say. Romantic ballet was dead, its possibilities exhausted. A new technique, the point, had been discovered and exploited to its very limits;

95 Carlotta Grisi, Marie Taglioni, Fanny Cerrito and Lucile Grahn in Jules Perrot's *Pas de Quatre*, 1845

now it was destined for new uses. On 27 April 1884 Taglioni, the brilliant star of the Paris Opéra, died in Marseilles, completely forgotten. Emma Livry, her pupil, whom she had hoped to make her successor and heir to the Romantic tradition, had died twenty years before, from burns received when her dress caught fire during a rehearsal of *La Muette de Portici*.

Outside France the Romantic ballet existed only in the form of plagiarisms and adaptations. To the Court Theatre, Vienna, came *Les Pages du Duc de Vendôme*, *Paul et Virginie*, *Le Déserteur*, and *La Sylphide*. Mary Ann Lee was the first to dance *Giselle* in America; a month after she had appeared in it in Boston, Caroline Fuchs took the same role in New York. Mary Ann Lee had learned the Cachucha, the Cracovienne and the Bolero from Fanny Elssler when the latter toured America in 1842, and had gone to Paris to study under Coralli, returning to star in *La Fille du Danube*, *La Jolie Fille de Gand* and *Giselle* with her partner George Washington Smith. Smith, also a great admirer of Fanny Elssler, had studied under Silvain in the United States, and after a number of successful tours opened a school of dancing in Philadelphia. Spaniards, too, came to Paris; in 1807 a School of Classical and Theatrical Dancing had opened in Madrid, whose teachers had visited the schools of Milan and Paris and returned full of enthusiasm for the new style. The bolero was then at its height, and the period was at last over when the Marquis d'Aranda could, as the fancy took him (and the Inquisitors), grant or refuse permission to dance the fandango 'which contains the whole history of love, from beginning to end'—the fandango which made such an impression on Casanova. A number of famous Spanish dancers crossed the frontier, among them Pepita de Oliva, Camprubi, and Lola de Valence, who was painted by Manet and immortalised in verse by Baudelaire. *La Sylphide* found its way to La Scala, Milan, in a version by Antonio Cortesi, who had already composed *Les Mystères de Paris* (after Eugène Sue) for the Teatro Communale of Bologna, and *Le Dernier Jour de Missolonghi ou la mort de Byron* for the Regio Theatre, Turin. *Giselle* was also given in Turin, a year after the Paris première, with Nathalie Fitzjames (*Ill.* 99) as Giselle, Arthur Saint-Léon as Prince Albrecht, Amalia Ferraris

96 Jean Coralli

(aged fifteen) as Myrtha, and the mime Belloni as Hilarion. Fanny Elssler's *Giselle* at Milan had three acts instead of two, the choreographer Bajetti having spun out the work with character dances. Copenhagen, where *La Sylphide* was danced by Lucile Grahn and Bournonville, went one better and discarded the original music altogether, substituting a score by Lovenskyold. But it was in Russia that the Romantic ballet was to arouse the greatest enthusiasm; French choreography, imbued with the Russian spirit, was to be the inspiration of Marius Petipa.

In the final analysis, the Romantic ballet would seem to have rested on the fragile, prettily rounded shoulders of one young woman, inaugurating the silent ballet-shoe of her master Coulon, and dressed in white gauze by the chaste Restoration. Once she was dead, there remained a virtuosity that was now classical, a ballet without men, and new generations of over-vigorous Italian dancers, who were soon to be the inspiration of the Russians.

97 Marie Taglioni in *Joko, le Singe brésilien*

98 Carlotta Grisi and Lucien Petipa in *Giselle*

99 Nathalie Fitzjames

100 Jules Perrot's *Pas de Quatre*. Marie Taglioni taking her curtain call

101 Carlo Blasis

CHAPTER TEN

Blasis and Saint-Léon

Once the Romantic ballet had disappeared, Italy—which had never taken very happily to the Romantic style—returned to prominence, and competition between France and Italy began once more. The competition was entirely friendly, however; Carlo Blasis would train dancers on one side of the frontier, while on the other Saint-Léon would bring out their talents in the ballets he created.

Until now the ballet-masters of the school of La Scala had been content to give their pupils a conscientious, but somewhat narrow, training, leaving the essential part of the work to the French. This arrangement came to an end in 1837, when Carlo Blasis and Virginia, his wife, took over the school.

Blasis (*Ill.* 101) was born in Naples in 1797, and studied first under Dutarque, who had spent long periods in Russia, then with Pierre Gardel, under whose guidance he made his début at the Paris Opera. He began as a dancer, but became in the course of his career ballet-master, choreographer, composer and finally historian. In 1820, in Milan, he published an elementary treatise on classical dancing, followed in 1830 by *The Code of Terpsichore*, which still forms the basis of classical training today. A lesson with Blasis would be divided as follows: arabesques, point work, *temps terre-à-terre* and *temps de rigueur*, *enchaînements* and *grands ronds de jambe*, exercises at the bar and in the centre, *pliés* in all positions, *grands et petits battements sur le cou-de-pied*, *aplomb*, and *grands fouettés sur place* and *en tournant*—already, in its essentials, the lesson as we know it today. Blasis also demanded daily practice, but, unlike some, he was opposed to 'forced labour', and rejected tours de force as being 'fit only for charlatans', stressing instead elevation and *ballon*, and never tiring of repeating to his pupils 'the height of art is to conceal art'. The point was the great novelty of the day, and Blasis gave it a leading place in his teaching fifteen years before Taglioni set her seal on it in *La Sylphide*. As well as dancing, Blasis also included mime in his curriculum; but without the inspiration he succeeded in passing on to all his pupils, his teaching would have been reduced to those frenzied gymnastics that were later to become characteristic of the Italian school. By 1840 his fame as a teacher had spread far and wide, and by 1847 he had pupils starring in forty-four theatres in Europe and America, including Fanny Cerrito, Amalia Ferraris (*Ill.* 106), Giovanni Casati, Sofia Fuoco (*Ill.* 102), Hippolyte Monplaisir, Claudine Cucchi, Pasquale

102 Sofia Fuoco in *La Rosière*

Borri, Vittorio Rota, the American Augusta Maywood, the Russian Elena Andreianova (*Ill.* 104), Amina Boschetti and Carolina Rosati (*Ill.* 105).

In 1851, as a result of an elaborate network of intrigues, Blasis found himself refused admittance to the Imperial Dancing Academy of La Scala. He continued his teaching in a private school, however, and from there went to London, Paris, Moscow and St Petersburg, where he taught, wrote, and republished his manual of dancing. When he finally returned to Italy to spend the last years of his life, in the tradition of dancers of the day, on the shores of Lake Como, he was succeeded by his pupil Giovanni Lepri.

A succession of Blasis's remarkable pupils appeared at the Paris Opéra. *Vert-Vert*, in 1851, marked the début

103 Olimpia Priora

of Olimpia Priora (*Ill.* 103), a fifteen-year old dancer from Venice who won praise from Théophile Gautier:

'... her dancing is vigorous, precise, correct, her points very strong, her balance firm; one of the finest evenings we have had since Grisi and Taglioni.'

Nadejda Bogdanova, a dancer with a perfect figure and superb legs, came from her distant Russia to dance with Cerrito and Lucien Petipa in *Gemma* in 1854. Contemporary accounts describe her as gay, refined and intelligent, in temperament far removed from the gloom of Romanticism, and more at home in the allegro than the adagio. The Crimean War obliged her to return to Russia, and she paid only one more visit to Paris before finally retiring to her native country, where she died in 1896. Carolina Rosati

104 Elena Andreianova

105 Carolina Rosati

made her first appearance at the Opéra in 1853 in *Jovita ou les Boucaniers*. As in her previous triumphs in Verona and London, she danced in Paris in grandiose productions requiring an elaborate *mise en scène* and a large cast, and which easily occupied a whole evening. (The scenery, which was mass-produced, was signed with such names as Cambon, Thierry and Deplechin; there was no thought of employing the services of real artists.) Rosati also appeared in St Petersburg, where she was given an enthusiastic welcome. In 1856 the Opéra engaged the Italian star Amalia Ferraris, who caused a sensation in *Les Elfes* by dancing a formidably difficult solo with effortless ease, accompanied only by a harp. Her vigorous, rapid point work, executed with suppleness and unusual elegance, astounded her audiences. But when in an attempt to revive

106 Amalia Ferraris

the competition of the Romantic era, the Opéra set Ferraris and Rosati side by side in *Marco-Spada ou la Fille du Bandit*, neither critics nor public could decide between them. And in fact, from the profusion of dancers in Italy, it would have been difficult, if not impossible, to award a first prize.

107 Set for *Coppélia* at the Paris Opéra, 1870

After the Italian stars came Italian choreographers. Pasquale Borri produced *L'Étoile de Messine* in 1861, a spectacular ballet in which crowd movements alternated with *pas de deux*. He was not fortunate in his collaborator, the composer Gabrielli, who borrowed rather too freely from the works of his colleagues. *La Maschera ou les Nuits de Venise*, for which Paris had commissioned Vittorio Rota, was a success, but it was the ballerina, Amina Boschetti (another pupil of Blasis) who attracted attention. She inspired Baudelaire to write the sonnet beginning:

'Amina bondit, fuit, puis voltige et sourit;
Du bout de son pied fin et de son œil qui rit,
Amina verse à flots le délire et l'esprit.'

Martha Muravieva, another Russian ballerina, after a brilliant *Giselle*, appeared at the Opéra in 1864 in *Diavolina* and *Néméa ou l'Amour vengé*, with choreography by Saint-Léon. *La Source*, also by Saint-Léon and starring the Italian dancer Guglielmina Salvioni, introduced the enchanting music of Léo Delibes. It was followed in 1870 by *Coppélia* (*Ill.* 107), a ballet-pantomine also with music by Delibes, danced by Giuseppina Bozzachi, and based on the story from the *Tales of Hoffmann* of the doll Coppelia, 'the girl with the enamel eyes,' with whom a young man falls in love. Since we are no longer in 1842, the ballet has a happy ending. Saint-Léon's choreography was so perfectly composed—this was his last, and greatest, work—that *Coppélia* was added to the repertories of theatres all over the world. A few weeks after this encouraging success came the Franco-Prussian War and the Siege of Paris; the hardships it brought were beyond the endurance of the young star Bozzachi, who died during the Siege at the age of seventeen.

Saint-Léon (*Ill.* 108), whose name recurs so frequently in the second half of the nineteenth century, was the only choreographer in France capable of using the dancers trained by Blasis. Born in Paris in 1821, he was a dancer and violinist before becoming a choreographer, and, while he did not revolutionize ballet, he devised a new system of dance notation, published in 1852 under the title *Sténo-chorégraphie*. In 1845 he married Fanny Cerrito, but eventually separated from her. Like all the great French ballet-masters he worked in St Petersburg, where he was appointed successor to Didelot and Jules Perrot, and where he met Marius Petipa.

Saint-Léon was the last choreographer of talent France could offer to match the Italians. Soon Italy was to dominate the Paris theatrical scene with a series of triumphs at the Eden Theatre (*Ill.* 110).

108 Arthur de Saint-Léon

109 Fanny Cerrito and Antonio Guerra in *Le Lac des Fées*, 1839

110 The Eden Theatre

CHAPTER ELEVEN

From Manzotti to Diaghilev

Paris and Milan had hitherto been the twin poles of ballet. But now, whereas in Italy ballet flourished in richness and profusion, in France it was slowly disappearing from the bills. Between 1850 and 1881, however, a few notable Italian masters tried to breathe new life into a declining art.

Giovanni Casati's output was prolific. He was choreographer at La Scala, Milan, where he created *Isolde of Normandy*, *Manon*, *Sardanapalus*, *The Star of the North*, *The Daughters of War*, *A Midsummer Night's Dream*, and others. In 1866 he obtained the post of Director of the La Scala school of dancing, but he was not an inspiring teacher and students preferred Giovanni Lepri, who taught in Florence. Giuseppe Rota, a man of wild, romantic temperament, produced a number of strange works. 'With the public in the state it is,' he once remarked bitterly, 'one must employ the most extreme resources of art.' His *Vampire* seemed derived from Edgar Allan Poe or Ann Radcliffe, and his *Daughter of Satan* had the same cruel demoniac strain. After *The Loves of Rinaldo and Armida*, came *Blacks and Whites*, which recounted a tragic episode of racial segregation in the United States, and *The Gambler*, which showed a man torn between his passion for gambling and the love of a woman. *The Count of Monte Cristo* and *The Countess of Egmont*, given in Vienna, won him a much-prized tribute from a declared enemy of ballet, Richard Wagner. Wagner's praise was well-deserved, for Rota's ballets, though romantic in conception, contained modern dances and some original ensemble work.

Pasquale Borri, 'an energetic and intelligent dancer, always elegant, vigorous and vital,' who had left Italy as a young man to try his chance in Austria with *Rübezahl*, soon became famous. He married the ballerina Carolina Pochini (*Ill.* 111), who, after making her début in Milan at the age of thirteen, had danced in Perrot's *La Esmeralda* in Trieste, and had rivalled Fanny Elssler in *La Jongleuse*. Among the ballets created by Borri were *The Prodigal Son* (starring the French ballerina Victorine Legrain), *Rodolphe* (after Eugène Sue), and *The Goddess of Valhalla*, with a complicated plot based on ancient Norse legends.

Luigi Manzotti, born in 1835 into a modest merchant family, dreamed, as a boy, of nothing but the theatre. He soon left his parents and joined a company as choreographer, producing *The Moor of the Antilles*, *Michelangelo* and *Rolla*, all of which involved a very large cast. *Pietro Micca*, the story of a Piedmontese soldier who sacrifices his life to save Turin, was given in an arena at Milan, with soldiers and cannons. After *Sieba* came the spectacular *Excelsior* at La Scala (*Ill.* 112). This ballet—typical of the 'Belle Époque'—was a resounding success in several countries. A cast of over five hundred, their arms and legs synchronised with amazing precision, celebrated successively the invention of the telegraph, the building of the Suez Canal, the piercing of the Simplon Tunnel, and Volta's electric pile. It was, in fact, not really a ballet, but a new style of choreographic revue. In Paris it was decided to build a new theatre worthy of such a lavish production, and so the Hôtel Hortense Schneider in the rue Boudreau was knocked down to provide a site for the Eden Theatre. This vast Pagoda, encumbered with 'neo-Indian' statuary, boasted two winter gardens, one Russian and one Chinese; its incongruous mixture of styles, characteristic of the period, was set off by long corridors lined with innumerable mirrors. It seated twelve hundred, and had a stage almost as large as that of the Opéra. On 11 January 1881 it opened with *Excelsior*, brought by Manzotti from Milan. The ballet was rapturously received by the Parisians, who greeted it as something approaching a miracle. Male dancers, such as Saracco, Bonesi and Cecchetti, really danced, and performed feats such as carrying the ballerina on the upraised palm of the hand. At last the man was taking his place alongside the 'danseuse étoile'. The venture was a triumph for Manzotti; his ballet ran at the Eden Theatre for an

111 Carolina Pochini

112 *Excelsior*. Ballet by Manzotti

113 *Amor.* Ballet by Manzotti, 1886

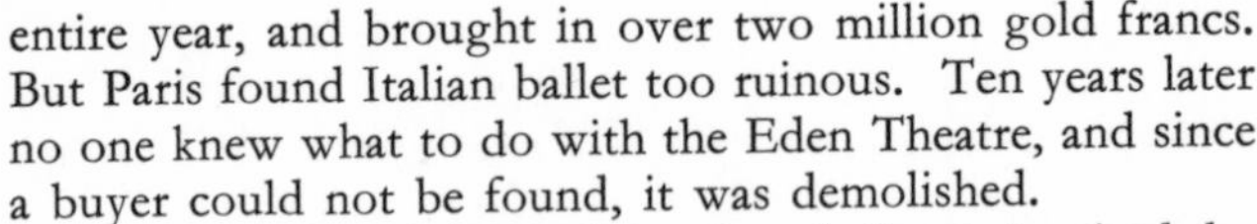

entire year, and brought in over two million gold francs. But Paris found Italian ballet too ruinous. Ten years later no one knew what to do with the Eden Theatre, and since a buyer could not be found, it was demolished.

114 Caterina Beretta

After *Excelsior* Manzotti produced *Sport*, inspired by such themes as the Venice Regatta and the ascent of Mont Blanc, and again nearer to music-hall than ballet. But these fabulous productions exhausted his inspiration, and until his death in 1905 he created only mediocre works.

The Italian genius was in fact slowly dying in these tedious ballets, which had nothing more to offer than light, nudity and emptiness. Legs and arms moved amid grandiose settings, but no longer expressed anything, and the public, bored and indifferent, soon lost interest. The critics declared in chorus that the ballet was not worth serious attention. The soul of the dance had abandoned its chosen country.

In Paris, ballet was restricted to providing *divertissements* for operas, and of these only eleven new works appeared over a period of thirty years. The Opéra ballet school still remained intact, however, and continued to produce excellent ballerinas, but no male dancers. Louis Mérante (*Ill.* 115), ballet-master, staged a number of his own works, including *Sylvia, the Nymph of Diana* (1876) with music by Léo Delibes and with Rita Sangalli and the mime Magri in the leading roles, followed by *Le Fandango*, *Yedda*, *La Korrigane*, and Messager's *Les Deux Pigeons*. Altogether these creations contained much technique, but little art, though they had a certain musical interest. Mérante was succeeded in 1889 by the Dane Hansen, who staged *La Tempête*, *Le Rêve*, *La Maladetta*, and *L'Étoile*, starring the buxom Rosita Mauri. In 1905 he created *La Ronde des Saisons* for the slender, exquisite Carlotta Zambelli, a dancer from Milan who quickly won promotion to the rank of 'première danseuse étoile' and was later ballet-mistress at the Opéra for many years.

Meanwhile, Italians had invaded the last stronghold of the ballet—St Petersburg. Virginia Zucchi, whose dancing had captivated Europe, set off to conquer Russia, where she made her début in 1885 at a *café-concert* (*Ill.* 118). She

115 Louis Mérante

116 Zina Richard

117 *Korrigane* at the Paris Opéra

completely enchanted both critics and public, and Plestcheev, historian of Russian ballet, wrote enthusiastically: 'A waltz on points to music by Chilovski became—do you remember?—a real poem through her execution.' She would take her curtain-calls with bold, almost aggressive charm, wearing not the chaste Romantic *tutu*, but short, gossamer-thin skirts which revealed her well-shaped legs. This wheel-shaped *tutu* was at once baptised the 'tutu à l'italienne'. Was it her daring costume or her seductive dancing that bewitched the young Alexandre Benois, future designer of the Ballets Russes? Whatever the cause, there is no doubt that his lasting admiration for 'the divine Virginia' had a considerable influence on his art. After Zucchi had been engaged by the Imperial Theatres to dance in *La Fille du Pharaon*, the Maryinsky Theatre drew full houses.

Antonietta Dell'Era, who made her Russian début in cabaret in 1883, also triumphed at the Maryinsky Theatre, but with a chaste, distinguished style reminiscent of Taglioni's. In 1892 she starred in Tchaikovsky's *The Nutcracker*. Carlotta Brianza, Emma Bessonne and Elena Cornalba still shared the favours of the Russian public. In 1889 Giovanna Limido and Enrico Cecchetti (*Ill.* 122) were engaged, again for a *café-concert*. Giovanna was described as 'the quintessence of the classical spirit', while her partner impressed audiences with his rapid pirouettes. Cecchetti became a teacher at the Imperial School, and was later to take over the teaching of Diaghilev's company.

Next to dazzle St Petersburg was the amazing Pierina Legnani (*Ill.* 120), a pupil of Caterina Beretta, who had already triumphed in Milan, Paris, London and Madrid, and who made her début at the Maryinsky Theatre in 1893 in *Cinderella*. *Le Journal des Spectacles*, which was published in French in St Petersburg, caught some echoes of this memorable event:

'The great attraction of the evening, however, was the début of Mlle Pierina Legnani, the prima ballerina who is a true Italian despite her fair hair. She has a very fine sense of mime, great lightness of movement, superbly modelled poses, strong legs and unfailingly perfect balance (so that she rarely needs the support of a partner), and finally, powers of endurance and a technique so staggering that in this respect she can be compared only to Maître Cecchetti. In the second act she performed considerable feats, without refusing to encore even the most difficult; but in the last act she drew positive cries of admiration from the audience by turning herself around an infinity of times (thirty-six, they say), repeating this tour de force a moment later with even greater energy and precision.'

Legnani next starred in *Swan Lake* (choreography by Petipa, music by Tchaikovsky), and stayed in St Petersburg —where her very personal charm won her a host of admirers—until 1901.

118 Virginia Zucchi, by Clairin

The impetus had been given, and Russian dancers now began to compete with these brilliant Italians. New blood and new inspiration were soon to bring back life and soul to the ballet. Among the earliest stars of the Russian school, products of a rigorous, intensive training, were Oblakov, Olga Preobrajenska and Mathilde Kschessinska. The two last, true representatives of the Imperial School of St Petersburg, won fame in Paris and other European capitals. Marius Petipa, their teacher, however, was not a Russian but a Frenchman.

Petipa (*Ill.* 124), born in Marseilles in 1822, studied under his father, Jean Petipa, and Vestris. After dancing in Brussels, Nantes and in the United States he came to Paris, partnering Carlotta Grisi at the Comédie-Française and

119 Carlotta Brianza in *La Esmeralda*

120 Pierina Legnani in *Le Corsaire*

Fanny Elssler at the Opéra. In 1847, on receiving the following concisely-worded letter, he went at once to St Petersburg:

'Monsieur Petipa: His Excellency M. Guedeonoff, Director of the Imperial Theatres, offers you the post of 'premier danseur'. Your salary will be 10,000 francs per year, plus one semi-benefit performance.'

There he again met Jules Perrot, then ballet-master, who was not to return to France till 1859. Petipa was soon appointed professor at the Imperial School, and finally succeeded Perrot as Inspector of Dancing. He was now able to launch pupils of his own (among them Sourovchikova, who later became his wife), but his ambition was

121 *The Sleeping Beauty*. Olga Preobrajenska in the role of the White Cat

122 Enrico Cecchetti

not limited to teaching; he wanted to create, and his talents at last found full expression in a series of marvellous ballets. His first work, *La Fille du Pharaon* (1862), was created for the last appearance of Carolina Rosati, an established star who enjoyed Imperial protection. The work was universally applauded, but once Rosati had gone, Petipa determined to try to supplant foreign stars by the Russian dancers he had trained himself. Muravieva and Marie Petipa (his daughter) (*Ill.* 125) made successful appearances at St Petersburg, Berlin and Paris, while Vazem (Petipa's

123 *The Sleeping Beauty* at the Bolshoi, Moscow, 1899

favourite pupil) danced in *Les Deux Étoiles*, *Le Papillon*, *Les Brigands*, and *La Fille des Neiges*. Nevertheless, in spite of a perfectly-trained *corps de ballet*, the public was cool towards the Maryinsky Theatre's productions, and it took the arrival of the Italian ballerinas to revive interest in ballet—an event welcomed by Petipa, for it meant that his career was no longer in danger.

Petipa's was a graceful, elegant style, marked by a strong personality. He lacked the abundant imagination of Perrot and Saint-Léon's faculty for adaptation, but he was extrem-

124 Marius Petipa

125 Marie Petipa in *Le Marché des Innocents*, 1861

ely methodical. After studying minutely the scenarios that were to provide the basis for his works, Petipa would give all his attention to the passages for the soloists, tailoring each step to suit their capabilities. He chose his music with care and scrupulously respected composers' scores, though he liked to specify which instruments he wanted. Three world-famous works are associated with his name, all to music by Tchaikovsky: *The Sleeping Beauty* (1890) based on the fairytale by Perrault; *Swan Lake* (1891) a romantic fantasy; and *The Nutcracker* (1902), on a theme borrowed from the *Tales of Hoffman* —ballets with all the majestic grace of the age of the Roi Soleil.

At the end of the nineteenth century major changes were taking place on the artistic scene. Avant-garde painters were increasingly appreciated, and modern composers such as Strauss and Debussy were winning applause for their works. Petipa's own pupils, Gorsky and Fokine, considered their master's ballets old-fashioned, and were successfully putting on (outside the Imperial Theatres) works in a new style, which combined splendour of décor with the astonishing technique of male dancers who jumped with a vigour forgotten since the days of Vestris and his pirouettes. The public, its curiosity aroused, followed these performances first with interest, then with passion.

Petipa continued, regardless, to follow the path he had set himself; but time had caught up with him. Soon he was obliged to give up the title he had held under four Tsars, and after enduring a number of vexations was unceremoniously retired in 1904. In 1906 he published his Memoirs, and died in his adopted country in 1910. His ballets, which were forgotten at the time of his death, were soon to be brought to life again.

In 1909 Paris was already preparing for the arrival of Serge de Diaghilev's Ballets Russes at the Théâtre du Châtelet. This year marks the birth of modern ballet.

126 *The Nutcracker* at the Maryinsky Theatre, St Petersburg

127 *Swan Lake* at the Maryinsky Theatre, St Petersburg

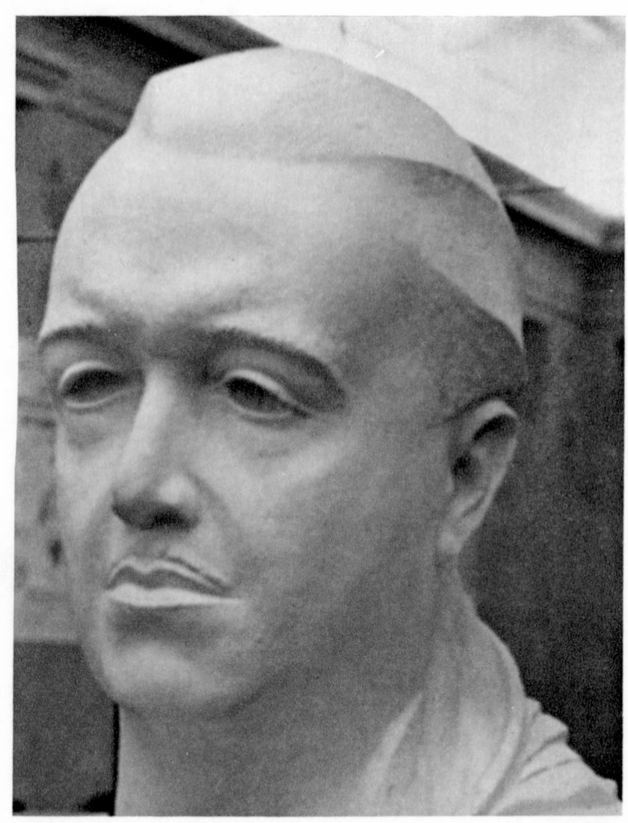

128 Serge de Diaghilev, by Gurdjan

CHAPTER TWELVE

Serge de Diaghilev's Ballets Russes

At this time an American dancer, Isadora Duncan, arrived on the continent, bringing with her a new form of expression. Draped in a Greek peplum, she would improvise in front of a curtain to Bach, Chopin or Schubert, expressing the emotions and states of mind aroused in her by the music. 'I did not invent the dance,' she was to say later, 'it existed before me, but it was sleeping, and I woke it up.' In 1905, when she appeared in St Petersburg, Michel Fokine saw her and was fascinated; and it was under the influence of her style that he created (in the same year) *The Dying Swan*, to music by Saint-Saëns. Isadora Duncan battled tirelessly against the canons of classical dancing to impose her own free, expressive style, but she left no school behind her, only a legend. She was to die tragically in Nice, accidentally strangled by her own scarf.

In Russia the revolution in ballet was inexorably advancing. Serge de Diaghilev *(Ill.* 128), a pupil of Rimsky-Korsakov and a true aesthete, came to ballet through his interest in music and art. At the turn of the century he had founded the magazine *Mir Iskoustva (The World of Art)* with his friend Walter Nouvel and the painters Léon Bakst, Golovine, Korovine, Roerich and Alexandre Benois. Between 1904 and 1909 Diaghilev organized exhibitions of Russian art and a series of Russian concerts in Paris, and presented *Boris Godunov*, an opera by Mussorgsky sung by Chaliapin, in 1908. In 1909 he decided to return to Paris with a troupe of dancers from the Maryinsky Theatre: Mathilde Kschessinska, Anna Pavlova, Tamara Karsavina, Ida Rubinstein, Michel Fokine (*Ill.* 135), Vaslav Nijinsky and his sister Bronislava, Adolphe Bolm,

Michel Mordkin, and others. Kschessinska quarrelled with Diaghilev after the company's arrival in Paris, but she was a powerful figure in the ballet world and before long was dancing *Coppélia* at the Opéra.

On 18 May 1909 the Châtelet Theatre was packed. Ministers and ambassadors jostled with stage celebrities, there was a dazzling array of jewels and magnificent evening gowns, and 'le Tout-Paris' waited in a fever of anticipation. At 8.30 p.m. precisely the curtain rose on the fairytale setting of *Le Pavillon d'Armide*. Fokine's choreography, Benois's scenery and costumes, and the virtuosity of Nijinsky and Karsavina roused the distinguished audience to wild enthusiasm. The first ballet was followed by *Prince Igor*, danced by Elena Smirnova and Adolphe Bolm to music by Borodin, and the unforgettable evening ended with *Le Festin*. Serge de Diaghilev had indeed conquered Paris. Years later a critic was to write: 'There were two epochs in my life, before and after the Ballets Russes.'

The second production included *Les Sylphides*, in which Fokine, recapturing the spirit of the Romantic ballet, expressed the indefinable charm and tender melancholy of youth. The scenery was by Benois, the dancers Pavlova, Karsavina and Nijinsky, and the music a score of Chopin orchestrated by Stravinsky. A greater impact was made by *Cléopâtre* (*Ill.* 137), an exotic work starring Karsavina and Nijinsky, in which Ida Rubinstein won a well-deserved triumph.

Of these wonderful dancers, who put so much grace, virtuosity and intelligence into the service of their art, the most remarkable was undoubtedly Vaslav Nijinsky (*Ills.* 136, 138). He was born in Kiev in 1890, became a pupil of Nicolas Legat and Oboukhov, and by the age of eighteen he was taking leading roles at the Maryinsky Theatre. A year later he met Diaghilev, a meeting which was to decide his whole future career. Cocteau has left us a somewhat unsympathetic portrait of him:

'Nijinsky was below average height. In soul and body he was all professional deformity. His Mongol-type face was joined to his body by a very long, broad neck. The muscles of his thighs and calves stretched the stuff of his trousers

129 *Petrouchka*. Costume by Benois

Joueur d'Orgue de barbarie.

Mlle Bourgeois

Alexandre Benois 1947

and made him look as if his legs were bent backwards. His fingers were short, as if cut off at the joints.'

But this ugly little man, as soon as he began to dance, seemed to grow taller, to quiver and vibrate with energy, and his talent—a very cerebral one—gave him the power to idealize the least gesture. Nijinsky was to suffer the loss of his reason, and he danced his last role at the age of twenty-seven. He died in an asylum in London in 1950.

Anna Pavlova was winged grace itself (*Ill.* 130). Trained by Cecchetti, she evolved a style which was shown to perfection in the solo. *The Dying Swan* will always be associated with her name; the title at once evokes the harmonious curve of her arms, her unreal points, the drooping line of her fragile white neck. In 1910 she left Diaghilev and began touring the world with the small company she had recruited. She remained faithful to her own essentially poetic style, and had the same triumphant success all over the world. She died in The Hague in 1931 after contracting pneumonia.

Tamara Karsavina, however, remained prima ballerina of the Ballets Russes until 1914 (*Ills.* 133, 134, 136). She was the daughter of a dancer of the Maryinsky Theatre, and possessed great expressiveness and charm as well as a perfect technique.

In 1910 Diaghilev took on a number of new dancers, including Lydia Lopokova and Catherine Geltzer (*Ill.* 132). Five great choreographers were to bring their art to the service of the master and his company: Fokine, Massine, Balanchine, Nijinska, and later Lifar. For its second season the Ballets Russes appeared at the Paris Opéra with *Giselle*, starring Karsavina and Nijinsky (*Ill.* 138). In spite of the personal triumph of the two dancers, the ballet was not a great success, its style being thought academic and out-of-date. It was after a performance of *Giselle* at the Maryinsky Theatre that Nijinsky (in 1911) felt compelled to hand in his resignation; the audience, though thrilled by his technique, thought the costume designed for him by Benois indecent, all the more so since Nijinsky refused to wear the regulation breeches over his tights.

The Firebird was to make Igor Stravinsky famous. Karsavina personified the brilliant bird with its fluttering wings, and the ballet had an enthusiastic reception (*Ill.* 133). An even greater sensation was caused by *Scheherazade*, which evoked an atmosphere of exotic sensuality with the warm, bold colours of its setting. Parisian women at once adopted the semi-oriental fashion inspired by this work, abandoning pastel shades and button boots for the dresses in rich fabrics and bright colours designed for them by Poiret, the great couturier of the day.

In 1909 Diaghilev had formed his own company, the Ballets Russes de Serge de Diaghilev. After opening at the

130 Anna Pavlova in *The Dying Swan*

Théâtre du Châtelet with *Le Pavillon d'Armide*, *Le Festin* and *Polovtsian Dances*, he produced, on 13 June 1911, *Petrouchka*, with choreography by Fokine to a score by Stravinsky. This great ballet is set in a fairground where three puppets endowed with human feelings—the pretty Ballerina, the unhappy Petrouchka, and the foolish Moor—act out their tragedy, while around them whirls the frantic bustle of the fair.

French composers, too, inspired the Russian choreographers. In 1912 came Debussy's *Après-midi d'un Faune* and Ravel's *Daphnis and Chloë*. The former, based on a poem by Mallarmé and danced by Nijinsky, was an attempt

131 Vera Trefilova

132 Catherine Geltzer in *La Bayadère*

133 Tamara Karsavina in *The Firebird*

134 Tamara Karsavina, by Jacques-Émile Blanche

135 Michel Fokine

to evoke the archaic style of dancing shown in Greek bas-reliefs, and in it Nijinsky, the little Mongol faun, caused another scandal by his scanty costume and erotic poses. The solid Parisian bourgeoisie were shocked and offended, for the crowd always revels in scandal, and accepts or rejects, applauds or boos with equal facility. *Daphnis and Chloë* suffered from this failure, which prevented the public from judging the work on its true merits. Fokine's choreography, based on the pastorale by Longus, was suffused with religious feeling and enchantment.

In 1913 the Diaghilev company produced *Jeux* at the Théâtre des Champs-Elysées (*Ill.* 136). This *divertissement*

136 Nijinsky, Tamara Karsavina and Ludmilla Schollar in *Jeux*

on the theme of Sport, despite a fine performance by Nijinsky, was not successful. It was followed by *Rite of Spring*, in which Stravinsky let loose a barrage of disturbing, haunting, syncopated rhythms. The work showed a primitive people, dominated by a merciless Nature, convulsed and intoxicated by the return of Spring, and the first night caused an uproar which will long be remembered in ballet history. Nijinsky, influenced by new theories of eurhythmics, had conceived a daring choreography in an emphatic, jerky style, in which the dancers leapt up or crouched down as if chained to the strident, powerful music.

137 *Cléopâtre.* Costume by Bakst

138 Vaslav Nijinsky in *Giselle*

During a tour of South America that same year Nijinsky married a Hungarian dancer, and Diaghilev, greatly vexed, dismissed him from his company. In 1914 came the Great War, which found the indefatigable Diaghilev still seeking his way amid the tortuous bypaths of Western art, though many of his dancers had returned to Russia. His next venture was opera-ballet, and in the first year of the war he staged *Coq d'Or* in Paris, with choreography by Fokine, music by Rimsky-Korsakov and scenery by Goncharova, and *Le Rossignol*, an opera in three scenes by Stravinsky in which Olga Spessivtzeva made her first appearance with the Ballets Russes.

The Legend of Joseph, by Richard Strauss, marked the début of Léonide Massine, a young man of eighteen

139 Léonide Massine in *Soleil de Nuit*

with a powerful gift for mime who was later to emerge as one of the greatest choreographers of modern ballet. He created *Soleil de Nuit* (*Ill.* 139), *Les Femmes de bonne humeur*, *Parade*, and *Les Contes russes*. *Parade*, with scenario by Jean Cocteau and music by Erik Satie, was given at the Châtelet in 1917, and had sets designed by Pablo Picasso (*Ills.* 142, 143). It was produced at one of the most critical periods of the war, and the ironical, mocking tone of the ballet angered and shocked the audience, preoccupied as they were with political events. The performance ended in a riot, and Cocteau and Picasso had great difficulty in leaving the theatre.

Massine, after one of his many visits to Spain, created *The Three-Cornered Hat* to music by Falla, which evoked

140 Tamara Toumanova and Léonide Massine in *The Three-Cornered Hat*

the rich, colourful atmosphere of Spain at the end of the eighteenth century (*Ill.* 140). In *La Boutique fantasque*, scenery and costumes by Derain (*Ill.* 141), Rossini's music, orchestrated by Respighi, seemed to sweep Karsavina and Massine off their feet with its frenzied rhythms, and the choregraphy is among the most perfectly successful ever devised. Massine produced two more works, *Astuzie Femminili* and *Pulcinella*, before leaving the Ballets Russes in 1921.

Diaghilev now adopted as his choreographer Bronislava Nijinska, sister of the famous dancer. The ballets she

141 *La Boutique Fantasque*. Backcloth by André Derain

142 Chinese costume designed by Picasso for *Parade*, 1917

created were to move away from Cubism towards Futurism, Surrealism and pure acrobatics. The master had just suffered a serious setback with *The Sleeping Beauty*, which he had staged in London in a splendid and elaborate setting, with Carlotta Brianza (who had danced the role of the Princess under the Tsar) as the Fairy Carabosse. The public's reception of the ballet was so lukewarm that it had to be withdrawn. Diaghilev, bitterly disappointed, could not bring himself to abandon *The Sleeping Beauty* altogether, and he re-grouped some of the dances from it and presented them the following year in Paris under the charming title *Aurora's Wedding*. It was now that Boris Kochno, a young Russian poet, joined the company and became the valued collaborator of Diaghilev, who entrusted to him the writing of the scenarios for many of his ballets.

In 1922 the company put on *Mavra*, a comic opera, and *Renard*, with music by Stravinsky and choreography by Nijinska. In 1923 came *Les Noces*, a cantata on the theme of village wedding rites, with Felia Doubrovska in the leading role. Nijinska's choreography, supported by the haunting music of Stravinsky, was a triumph. Among new members of the company at this time were Alice Nikitina and Anton Dolin. The latter, Irish by birth and a pupil of Nijinska, was an athletic dancer who excelled in acrobatic roles, though he was also suited to the classical style. Another creation of Nijinska's was *Les Biches* (1924), a ballet in eight scenes, music by Francis Poulenc and scenery and costumes by Marie Laurencin which parodied high society of the 'twenties (*Ill.* 145). Next came *Les Fâcheux*, *La Tentation de la Bergère* and *Le Train bleu*. In this last work, which was more like a danced operetta, Anton Dolin's perilous acrobatics to music by Darius Milhaud roused great enthusiasm, and *Les Matelots* was equally successful. Massine, who had in the meantime returned to the company, created *Zéphire et Flore* in 1925, starring Dolin, Nikitina and Lifar.

Serge Lifar, a newcomer to the company, who had joined it only two years earlier, had come from Kiev with four other pupils of Nijinska. He came to the notice of Diaghilev, who entrusted him with increasingly important roles, until by 1925 he 'was premier danseur' and appearing in all the ballets. Another notable addition to the Ballets Russes was George Balanchine, a former pupil of the Imperial School of Ballet, who had recruited a small company with which he toured England and Germany. He was appointed choreographer by Diaghilev in 1925, and his first work was *Barabau*, a comic ballet. Diaghilev also recruited a young girl of fourteen, Alicia Markova, soon to become a very great star, a 'new Taglioni'.

Surrealism now made its appearance in *Romeo and Juliet*, for which Max Ernst and Miró painted the scenery, and Serge Lifar and Karsavina danced the leading roles. On the first night there was indescribable pandemonium both in the auditorium and on the stage, and the police had to be called. Then came *Jack-in-the-Box* (dances by Erik Satie orchestrated by Darius Milhaud, scenery by Derain), which featured Negro art, and *The Triumph of Neptune*, which evoked the popular colour prints of the Victorian era, danced by Lifar, Danilova, Sokolova, Idzikowsky and Balanchine. Both ballets were enthusiastically received.

Olga Spessivtzeva now returned to the Ballets Russes. While Balanchine worked on *La Chatte*, to music by Sauguet and with a Futurist décor of mica and celluloid, Massine was preparing his *Pas d'Acier* to music by Prokofiev, an evocation of a factory where robot-men work to an infernal, mechanical rhythm, producing considerable dramatic effect. After this came *Oedipus Rex*, with scenario by Cocteau, and in 1928 a masterpiece, *Apollo Musagetes*, the work of Stravinsky, Balanchine and Lifar. *The Gods Go a-Begging*, music by Handel orchestrated by Sir Thomas Beecham, scenery by Bakst, starred Danilova and Woizikowsky; Massine's *Ode*, danced by Lifar, had a complicated but ingenious *mise en scène* in which dances alternated with cinema projections. In 1929 Lifar re-staged the delightfully comical *Renard*, with a setting by Larionov (*Ill.* 144) and music by Stravinsky, and Balanchine devised *Le Bal* to music by V. Rieti, with scenery and costumes by Chirico. The Parisian season ended with *The Prodigal Son*, scenario by Boris Kochno, music by Prokofiev, in which Balanchine's choreography, revealing its affinities with the modern school, was given added richness by the scenery of Georges Rouault, and Serge Lifar gave a magnificent performance. The company now left Paris for England, Germany and Venice.

143 Curtain for *Parade*, designed by Picasso, 1917

In Venice Diaghilev, who had been ill for some time, died on 19 August 1929. He was buried in the cemetery of the Island of San Michele. After his death no one ventured to succeed him, and the company dispersed to the four corners of the earth to found new schools.

144 *Renard*, 1922.
Costumes by Larionov

145 *Les Biches*, 1924.
Design by Marie Laurencin

146 The Ballets Suédois in *Les Mariés de la Tour Eiffel*, 1921

CHAPTER THIRTEEN

Les Ballets de Monte Carlo

Diaghilev's work was not carried on after his death. But one lasting achievement of this dilettante of genius was to have furthered interchange between the two cultures of East and West. Thanks to him, Russian dancers and choreographers, French composers and painters, Italian and Spanish musicians, had been brought together and had combined their ideas in a common cause. At this period Paris was undoubtedly the most important artistic centre in the world.

In 1919 some members of the Ballets Russes had joined the Paris or Monte Carlo Opera companies. Other companies had been formed under the aegis of wealthy patrons, in the vain hope of rivalling Diaghilev's successes.

The Ballets Suédois, founded by Rolf de Maré and directed by the dancer-choreographer Jean Borlin, produced between 1920 and 1924 a number of interesting avant-garde works. Among them was *Les Mariés de la Tour Eiffel*, in which Cocteau, using music by Tailleferre, Auric, Honegger, Milhaud and Poulenc, recounted a series of burlesque adventures, full of extravagant ideas caricaturing the bourgeois spirit of the Belle Époque (*Ills.* 146, 147). *L'Homme et son désir*, with scenario by Paul Claudel and music by Darius Milhaud, *La Création du Monde*, devised by Cendrars, and *Jarre*, inspired by Sicilian folklore, were followed by *Relâche*, a farcical ballet by Picabia to music by Erik Satie with a film interlude by René Clair, which aroused the most conflicting reactions. In spite of these praiseworthy efforts, the Ballets Suédois did not have enough internal unity to survive long, and it was disbanded in 1925.

147 Curtain by Irène Lagut for *Les Mariés de la Tour Eiffel*

In 1924 Count Étienne de Beaumont, a talented amateur of music, founded the Soirées de Paris. He produced his entertainments at the Théâtre de la Cigale, a famous Montmartre *café-concert*, and the reportory included ballets by Massine, Offenbach's *Beau Danube*, Milhaud's *Salade*, Satie's *Mercure*, and *Romeo and Juliet*, in which Cocteau used Shakespeare's text as the basis for a mime-ballet. But this company had a very brief existence (17 May to 30 June 1924).

After the First World War, Ida Rubinstein founded a ballet company, which gave performances at the Paris Opéra and subsequently all over the world. She was more of a mime than a ballerina, and her productions were composite in style. They included Ravel's *Bolero*, Stravinsky's *Le Baiser de la Fée*, and works with scores by Ibert, Auric and Sauguet. André Gide gave her the text of his mime-drama *Persephone*, and Paul Valéry those of *Amphion* and *Semiramis*, the latter based on the life story of the Queen of Babylon. Although Ida Rubinstein took care to surround herself with artists of established reputation (Nijinska, Massine and Jooss as choreographers, Vilzak, Lichine, Schollar, Dolin and Ashton as dancers), she eventually had to renounce her ambitions and dissolve her company in 1935.

Meanwhile Bronislava Nijinska had been producing a number of ballets in Paris. In 1931 she staged a Bach *Étude*, an 'abstract' ballet with variations in a dry, austere, geometric style; *Les Comédiens jaloux*, with characters taken from the Commedia dell'Arte; and *Variations*, to music by Beethoven, another abstract ballet with very stylized décor. This company included Alexandra Danilova, Anatole Vilzak, Thadeo Slavinsky, Vera Nemchinova, Nina Tikanova, and Tatiana Uskova. For Nijinska ballet was less a form of expression than an art in which movement was used for its own sake. She sought to develop new forms of choreography, and contributed, both by her teaching and by the work she created, to the enlargement of the vocabulary of ballet.

148 René Blum

In 1932, in association with the Théâtre de Monte Carlo, the first company of the Ballets Russes de Monte Carlo was founded, under the direction of René Blum (*Ill.* 148) (who was attached to the Theatre of Monaco) and Wassili de Basil, better known as Colonel de Basil, an ex-officer of the Imperial Russian Army (*Ill.* 149). The troupe attempted to carry on the Diaghilev tradition by gathering together some distinguished members of the old company, among them Léonide Massine and George Balanchine. To these were added Tamara Toumanova (*Ill.* 153), Irina Baronova, and Tatiana Riabouchinska, three fifteen-year-old ballerinas whose technical virtuosity and youthful freshness amazed and charmed the public. The two undisputed stars of the company, however, were David Lichine and Alexandra Danilova (*Ill.* 152). First to be produced were two ballets by Balanchine: *Concurrence*, a pantomime with extravagant costumes created by Derain (*Ill.* 150) and music by Georges Auric; and *Cotillon*, with music by Chabrier, in which Christian Bérard evoked alternating moods of light humour and melancholy. Next Massine staged *Jeux d'enfants* with music by Bizet and scenery by Miró, followed in 1933 by *Le Beau Danube* and *Beach*, which saw a return to the classical style, with music by Françaix and scenery by Dufy. But *Les Présages*, with Surrealist décor by André

149 Colonel de Basil

Masson, marked a new development; it was a choreographic symphony in four parts to Tchaikovsky's Fifth Symphony, symbolizing man's struggle with destiny, and was the first of several great symphonic ballets created by Massine which were to culminate in *Symphonie Fantastique*. In 1934 Massine produced *Union Pacific*, a ballet in the American idiom which showed his mastery of the handling of groups and ensembles, and Lichine created *Les Imaginaires* to music by Georges Auric. It was now that Colonel de Basil left the Ballets Russes de Monte Carlo to form his own company.

150 *Concurrence.* Costume by André Derain

The second company of this name was founded by René Blum in 1936. He secured as his choreographer Michel Fokine, who had returned to Russia after leaving Diaghilev, but soon left it again and sailed for America. Finding conditions there uncongenial for the development of his art, he returned to Europe, where he produced *Diane de Poitiers*, *Semiramis* and Ravel's *La Valse*. The Ballets Russes de Monte Carlo put at Fokine's disposal enough technical and financial resources and enough talented painters and musicians to enable him to give full rein to his genius. In 1936 he produced for them *L'Épreuve d'amour*, which was set in China, with music by Mozart

151 Costumes by Christian Bérard

and scenery by Derain. After *Les Elfes*, in which the dancers were costumed in iridescent tights with delicate wings, in 1937 Fokine composed the choreography for *Don Juan*. This majestic work was danced to the same score that Gluck had composed for Angiolini's original production in Vienna, and had costumes designed by Mariano Andreu.

A few years later Michel Fokine returned to America and worked for Ballet Theatre, for which he created *Bluebeard*, danced by Dolin, and *Lieutenant Kije* in 1941. After a tour in Mexico he fell suddenly ill, and died in New York on 22 August 1942. His intelligence, allied to a profound musical sense, made him not only a great dancer but a choreographer of the very highest order. He believed strongly in dancing as a means of dramatic expression, and sought consistently to weld the three elements of ballet, music, painting and dancing into a unified artistic whole.

The Ballets de Monte Carlo now had in its company some very distinguished stars. Alexandra Danilova, the company's 'prima ballerina assoluta', had left Russia to join first Diaghilev, then René Blum; she interpreted the most varied roles with equal ease. Alicia Markova's style recalled that of Taglioni: the same poetry, the same

152 Alexandra Danilova

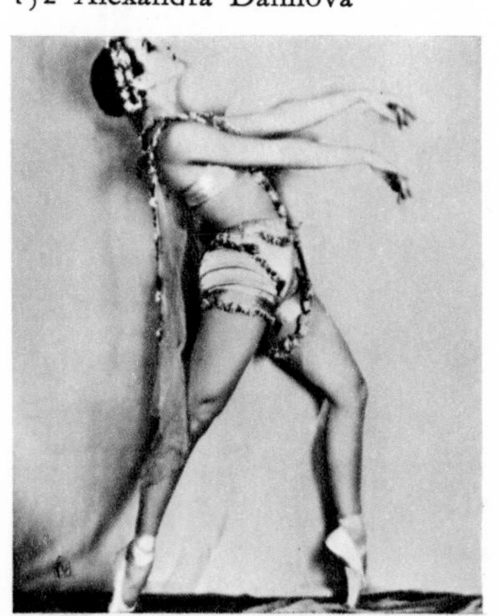

153 Tamara Toumanova

lightness, the same mysterious grace. With Massine, the ballet-master, appeared Youskevich, Franklin, Doukoudovsky and George Skibine. The company had been welcomed in all the great capitals. Paris had been succeeded by London as the centre of ballet and as a meeting-point for dancers and choreographers from all over the world.

The outbreak of war in 1939 disrupted the ballet world. Massine continued to produced new works, however, and staged *Scènes Russes*, to music by Borodin, and *L'Étrange Farandole*, a ballet in four movements to the First Symphony of Shostakovich, depicting a man and woman's struggle

154 Alicia Markova and Igor Youskevich in *Seventh Symphony*

with destiny. Seen against the highly stylized backcloth, the immaculate white tights of Alicia Markova and Igor Youskevich, in contrast with the multicoloured costumes of their partners, designed by Matisse, produced an effect of perfect harmony. *Nobilissima Visione*, based on episodes in the life of St Francis of Assisi, made particular use of hand movements in its choreography.

The Ballets Russes du Colonel de Basil, later known as the Original Ballet Russe, made tours which took them first to Spain, then to London, New York, Australia and New Zealand. In 1936 they presented *Symphonie fantastique* at Covent Garden. In a succession of five scenes Massine recreated the lyrical exaltation of Berlioz's masterpiece, ordering the movement of groups on the stage to harmonize with the powerful sonorities of the music. The grandeur of the choreographic composition was enriched by the masterly décors of Christian Bérard.

The Original Ballet Russe continued its tours in Australia, and then spent some years in the United States and South America. In 1947 it gave a few performances in Paris, and was dissolved shortly afterwards.

CHAPTER FOURTEEN

Ballet in France

The influence of the Ballets Russes began to make itself felt at the Paris Opéra when Jacques Rouché, who became Director in 1914, started to engage the services of well-known musicians such as Stravinsky, Albert Roussel, Jacques Ibert, Paul Dukas, and Gabriel Pierné, and talented painters such as Raoul Dufy, Maurice Brianchon, Yves Brayer, Léon Bakst and Maxime Dethomas. Léo Staats, the choreographer of the Opéra, and Albert Aveline, the 'premier danseur', though not gifted with the genius of a Fokine or a Nijinsky, nevertheless had a true love of their art. Carlotta Zambelli was still the great star who took all the leading roles, supported by Aida Boni and Camille Bos. Clustine, who was to spend eighteen years as choreographer to Pavlova, created *La Roussalka* (1911), with music by Lambert and theme by Pushkin. This was followed by *Suite de danses*, to music by Chopin, and Staats produced *Les Abeilles*, after music by Stravinsky, with décor by Dethomas.

In 1921 Fokine returned to Paris to revive *Daphnis and Chloe*, to Ravel's music, and in 1923 Staats put on *Cydalise et le Chèvre-pied* with the music of Gabriel Pierné, a sylvan décor by Dethomas, and scenario by de Flers and Caillavet. Carlotta Zambelli took the role of Cydalise, and Albert Aveline played the young faun. In 1924 Pavlova made a brief appearance in Paris, and the following year Olga Spessivtzeva (*Ill.* 157) came to the Opéra with the Ballets Russes, dancing *Giselle* partnered by Aveline and Ricaux, and *Soir de fête*, dazzling her audiences with the exquisite purity of her style. After this Bronislava Nijinska passed through with her company, which included the

155 *Corps de ballet*

Yugoslavian ballerina Mia Corak, better known under the name of Mia Slavenska.

In 1929 Rouché engaged George Balanchine as ballet-master at the Opéra. He had decided to mount a new version of *Les Créatures de Prométhée*, the ballet originally created by Vigano in 1801, to commemorate the centenary of Beethoven's death, and asked Balanchine to provide the choreography. Balanchine fell ill, however, and the work was taken over by Serge Lifar, who created a highly individual version of Prometheus, aimed, in his own words, at 'the rehabilitation of male dancing'. The ballet was a great success and Rouché appointed its creator choreographer in 1930. Lifar was then twenty-five; he was to stay at the Opéra another twenty-five years, and produce sixty ballets in the course of his brilliant career. He showed his gifts as a classical dancer in *Le Spectre de la Rose*, in which his style was more virile than Nijinsky's, and *Giselle*, partnered by Spessivtzeva, in which he brought new qualities of depth and lyricism to the role of Albrecht.

1935, for Lifar, was the year of *Icare*. The score—for percussion only—had been written by Szyfer to rhythms laid down in advance by the choreographer, and the neo-classical décor and costumes were created by Larthe. The work was preceded by a manifesto in which Lifar proclaimed that music should be subordinate to dancing in ballet. His aim in re-creating the drama of Icarus was to draw a parallel between the daring experiment of Dedalus and modern aviation, and he himself played the part of Icarus, freeing himself from the bonds of gravity, soaring up, falling again, crashing and finally immobilised in death. Lifar gave a performance of great tragic intensity, suggesting by his powerful mime and play of facial expression the hopes, the struggles, the wonderment and the anguish of the young man.

Harnasie, a ballet in folk-dance style based on peasant life in the Tatras Mountains of Poland, was followed by *Le Roi nu*, a comic ballet whose theme was taken from Andersen's story *The Emperor's Clothes*, with music by Jean Françaix. In *Promenade dans Rome*, an elegant *divertissement*, Serge Lifar, Suzanne Lorcia, Serge Peretti and Geneviève Kergrist danced against a backcloth by Decaris which evoked all the charm of nineteenth-century Rome.

In 1937 and 1938 Lifar produced two ballets with Biblical themes: *David triomphant*, with music by Debussy and Mussorgsky arranged and revised by Rieti and décor by Fernand Léger, which served as a vehicle for the talents of Lycette Darsonval and the young Yvette Chauviré (*Ill.* 159), and *Le Cantique des Cantiques*, which despite Lifar's admirable performance to Honegger's music, was not a success. *Oriane et le Prince d'amour* brought an end to the series of ballets dominated by a single character created by Lifar (*Ill.* 158). In it Lycette Darsonval played the part of the perverse and capricious chatelaine, who is finally conquered by Death, with seductiveness and authority.

In 1941 Lifar created *Istar*, to the symphonic poem by Vincent d'Indy, for Yvette Chauviré. The solo part lasting eighteen minutes, in which the goddess passes through seven gates, divesting herself each time of one of her veils, to set free the Son of Life, won the young dancer promotion

156 Solange Schwartz

157 Olga Spessivtzeva and Serge Lifar in *Bacchus and Ariadne*

to the rank of danseuse étoile at the Paris Opéra and established her reputation. *Entre deux rondes* told the story of how a statue of Apollo (Lifar) and a Degas ballet-dancer (Schwartz) meet in the Louvre, and the choreography—to music by Marcel Samuel-Rousseau—was a lively combination of classical dancing and acrobatics. *Suite en blanc* entered the repertory in 1943. In this ballet the picturesque, colourful music of Edouard Lalo was used as a basis for a

158 *Oriane et le Prince d'amour*. Ballet by Serge Lifar, 1938

series of entrées, primarily designed by Lifar to display the talents of his ballerinas: the lyricism of Yvette Chauviré, the virtuosity of Solange Schwartz (*Ill.* 156), the precision of Lycette Darsonval. The Opéra also had some distinguished male dancers, among them Ritz, René Fenonjois and the young Roland Petit. Delibes' *Sylvia* was revived, with décors by Maurice Brianchon and the leading roles played by Schwartz, Lorcia, Darsonval, Goubé and Lifar, but the work suffered from confusion and lack of style and had only a moderate success.

Le Chevalier et la Damoiselle and *Joan de Zarissa*, however, are undoubtedly Lifar's two masterpieces. The first, which has a medieval setting, tells the story of a fair Damoiselle who is metamorphosed into a doe. The score by Philippe Gaubert perfectly underlines the action, which is by turns poetic and violent; Cassandre's scenery of woodland groves was inspired by medieval illuminated books. The complex role of the doe was danced by Solange Schwartz, who displayed all her range and virtuosity, and Lifar played the wandering knight with great vitality and energy. The cast also included Ritz, Goubé, Peretti, and Roland Petit, and Yvette Chauviré made a memorable appearance in the minor role of a princess. *Joan de Zarissa* (*Ill.* 161), produced at the Opéra in 1942, relates the adventures of a cynical Don Juan whose life of debauchery ends in remorse. The music of Werner Egk and Yves Brayer's sets accentuated the tragic atmosphere of the story, and the choreography, which departed to some extent from the conventions of classical dancing, was one of Lifar's greatest successes. Lifar danced Joan and Solange Schwartz took the part of 'the Fairest One'.

Changes came to the Opéra in 1945 when Maurice Lehmann took over the Directorship. His productions, though possibly overspectacular, had the merit of winning great popularity with the public. The first work to be staged by Lehmann was *Les Mirages*, in which Yvette Chauviré and Michel Renault wandered through a dreamlike landscape, with Madeleine Lafon (*Ill.* 162) in the role of Chimera. Cassandre's set was sober and austere, and Lifar devised a poetic choreography which fitted well with Sauguet's music. In 1950 came *Phèdre*, based on Racine's tragedy, with music by Georges Auric and choreography by Lifar. Tamara Toumanova was an unforgettable Phèdre, tragic and pathetic, and Lifar brought a fine dramatic intensity to the role of Hippolyte.

159 Yvette Chauviré

Other choreographers were now being engaged at the Opéra. In 1952 the Danish ballet-master Harald Lander produced *Les Caprices de Cupidon*, to music by Jens Lolle and with scenery by Chapelain-Midy, a delicate, somewhat mannered work which retained a very eighteenth-century flavour. Maurice Lehmann's revival of *Les Indes galantes* in the same year was a brilliant theatrical and musical event. Rameau's music was given an ingenious choreography by Lifar, Lander and Aveline, and seven different designers—Arbus, Dupont, Chapelain-Midy, Carzou, Fost, Moulène and Wakhevich—worked on the scenery and costumes. The work, which combines opera and ballet, and takes the form of a succession of contrasting scenes, made use of all the latest techniques in stage machinery and lighting.

Also in 1952 Lander produced *Études*, a ballet to the piano suite by Czerny, in which Micheline Bardin, Claude Bessy, Michel Renault and Alexandre Kalioujny gave a masterly exhibition of classical technique (*Ill.* 163). Yet another creation of Lifar's was *Les Noces fantastiques* (1955), a tragic story which ends with a phantom wedding in the depths of the sea between the ghost of a sailor and

160 *Suite en Blanc.* Ballet by Serge Lifar, 1943

161 *Joan de Zarissa*, 1942. Finale

his fiancée, in which Nina Vyroubova (*Ill.* 164) and Peter van Dijk (*Ill.* 167) gave superb performances. Later that year the English choreographer John Cranko produced *La Belle Hélène*, a ballet-bouffe with décor by Marcel Vertès which brought Ancient Greece up to date in a lighthearted style, with Yvette Chauviré, Michel Renault, Max Bozzoni and Claude Bessy as principal dancers. Under the direction of Georges Hirsch, Lifar put on a condensed version of *Romeo and Juliet* in two acts and ten episodes, starring Liane Daydé as Juliet, Michel Renault as Romeo, and Lifar as Brother Lawrence, and with scenery by Wakhevich. 1957 saw a revival of *Le Martyre de Saint Sébastien*, the Debussy mystery play first created by Ida Rubinstein at the Paris Opéra forty-six years before, in which Ludmilla Tchérina established herself as a great dancer and mime in the leading role.

Idylle, which had figured on the bills of the Ballets du Marquis de Cuevas and the Opéra-Comique, was now added to the repertory of the Opéra. *La Dame aux Camélias*, music by Henri Sauguet, was of course inspired by Dumas's novel. Yvette Chauviré was the romantic Marie Duplessis and her partner was George Skibine, who also devised the choreography. Among visiting choreographers were Gene Kelly, who staged the comic ballet *Pas de Dieux* to George Gershwin's Concerto in F, and Vladimir Bourmeister, the Soviet ballet-master, who presented a full-length version of *Swan Lake* at the Opéra. Josette Amiel danced the double role of Odette-Odile, and Peter van Dijk was Prince Siegfried.

A new era opened for the Opéra when Georges Auric became Director. Serge Lifar, now free of all ties with this theatre, pursued his career as choreographer elsewhere, and a new ballet-master, Michel Descombey, brought his youth and lively imagination to the service of the Opéra (*Ill.* 166). He produced for them *Symphonie concer-*

162 Madeleine Lafon

163 *Études*. Ballet by Lander, 1952

tante to Frank Martin's *Petite Symphonie concertante*, with sets by Bernard Daydé, and Claude Bessy and Attilio Labis as the two lovers separated by the crowd. In 1963 Claire Motte and Attilio Labis starred in *But*, an evocation of a basket-ball game with music by Castarède. At the time of writing—the beginning of the 1964 season—Michel Descombey is ballet-master at the Paris Opéra, assisted by two *répétiteurs*, Gérard Mulys and Léone Mail. The new stars, Claude Bessy, Josette Amiel (*Ill.* 170), Claire Motte, Jacqueline Rayet (*Ill.* 167) and Christiane Vlassy share the principal roles, while Yvette Chauviré, artistic and technical adviser, collaborates with Mlle Guillot, Principal of the Opéra Dancing School. The male stars are Attilio Labis, Flemming Flindt (*Ill.* 170), Jean-Paul Andreani, Peter Van Dijk, Cyril Atanassoff; the teachers are Rita Thalia, Robert Blanc, Lucien Legrand, Gérard Mulys, Yves Brieux, Serge Peretti and Madeleine Lafon.

164 Nina Vyroubova

165 Marjorie Tallchief and George Skibine in *Daphnis and Chloe*, 1959

The Opéra, however, does not have a monopoly of ballet in France; several major choreographers, over the years, have left this austere institution to try their wings in the freedom of the outside world. New companies sprang up in Paris and the provinces, producing bold new works, and bringing a new touch of romance to the ballet world. Les Ballets des Champs-Élysées, founded in 1945 by Roger Eudes, then Director of the Théâtre des Champs-Élysées, and Roland Petit's father, revealed many young talents which had come to maturity during the years of occupation: new choreographers (Janine Charrat, Roland Petit, Jean Babilée) and new stars with hitherto unknown names (Renée Jeanmaire—who married Roland Petit

166 Michel Descombey in *Qarrtsiluni*

167 Jacqueline Rayet
and Peter van Dijk
in *Giselle*

168 Claude Bessy
and Attilio Labis
in *Swan Lake*

169 Study for *Swan Lake:* Jacqueline Rayet

170 Josette Amiel and Flemming Flindt

in 1954—Ethery Pagava, Nathalie Philippart, Violette Verdy, Youly Algaroff, Irène Skorik, Nina Vyroubova, Vladimir Skouratoff and Leslie Caron). The company had a brilliant opening with a work which was to prove something of a good-luck charm for Roland Petit: *Les Forains.* Henri Sauguet, who composed the score, wrote:

'I put into the music all my old love of travelling circuses and touring theatre shows, and all my compassion for these wandering artists, who carry a whole world of dream and imagination beneath their faded finery —tawdry rags, in which the gold and the purple still live on.'

Petit's ballet, full of youthful freshness, was a triumph. *Jeu de cartes*, produced in 1945, showed Janine Charrat's talents as a choreographer. The dancers, dressed in white body tights marked with hearts, spades, clubs and diamonds, are enacting a poker game in which the Joker (Jean Babilée) makes and unmakes the 'flushes' and 'straights' as the fancy takes him. A revival of *La Sylphide* in 1946,

171 *Les Liens.* Ballet by Janine Charrat, 1957

arranged by Victor Gsovsky after Taglioni, with Nina Vyroubova and Roland Petit in the principal roles, was a great success, and was followed by a masterpiece—Cocteau's *Le Jeune Homme et la Mort*, with music by Bach and scenery by Wakhevich, starring Nathalie Philippart and Jean Babilée. In this poignant drama a young artist is desperately pursuing an indifferent and cruel girl. He is Love, and she —who in the end crushes her pursuer—is Death. *Le Bal des blanchisseuses* (music by Vernon Duke), *Les Amours de Jupiter* (music by Jacques Ibert), and *La Rencontre ou Œdipe et le Sphinx* (music by Henri Sauguet, starring the enigmatic Leslie Caron) appeared successively on the repertory of this young company, before it was finally disbanded in 1950.

Roland Petit had left the Ballets des Champs-Élysées in 1948 and founded the Ballets de Paris, which opened its first season that same year at the Théâtre Marigny with *Les Demoiselles de la nuit*. The décor was by Fini and the music by Jean Françaix, while Anouilh's enigmatic woman-cat, with her strange feline sensuality, was played by Margot Fonteyn. After *L'Œuf à la coque*, with Colette

Marchand, Petit produced *Carmen* (1949), which definitely established the reputation of Zizi Jeanmaire. In this somewhat revolutionary ballet he altered the emphasis of Mérimée's story and took certain liberties with Bizet's famous score. The brilliant colours of Clavé's scenery and costumes were in perfect harmony with the frenzied, passionate dancing of the two lovers, while the dazzling and seductive Zizi Jeanmaire was queen of the evening, and won an unprecedented triumph (*Ills.* 172, 173). The Ballets de Paris productions of *La Croqueuse de diamants*, *Le Loup*, *Deuil en vingt-quatre heures* (*Ills.* 174, 175) and *La Chambre* also roused enthusiastic interest, and the company's Paris season closed with *Cyrano de Bergerac* in 1959. After a series of long tours in England, Germany and America, Petit, who had been moving in the direction of a new conception of the dance, settled permanently at the Théâtre National Populaire, where he produced a show with Zizi Jeanmaire at the end of 1963.

172 Zizi Jeanmaire in *Carmen*, 1949

Jean Babilée, born of a well-to-do family, devoted his intelligence, energy and wit to the service of ballet. After producing *L'Amour et son amour* and *Till Eulenspiegel* for the Ballets des Champs-Élysées he launched his own company in *Balance à trois* and *Sable*. In 1956 he created *Caméléopard*, to music by Henri Sauguet, in which he moved across the stage in great bounding leaps against a décor which showed a royal city in the last days of a declining civilization.

Janine Charrat was also to form a company and travel the world. Born in Grenoble, she danced the part of the *petit rat* in the film *La Mort du cygne* at the age of twelve, and after partnering Roland Petit in the Ballets des Champs-Élysées emerged at twenty as choreographer in her own right with *Jeu de cartes*. Her creations bear the stamp of her strong personality, her genius for invention, and her courage. She was invited by the Opera of Amsterdam to create the choreography for Weber's *Dance of Oberon*, and in 1949 produced *Abraxas* for the Berlin Opera, followed by Rossini's *Armida* for Florence's May festival. *Abraxas*, based on the story by Goethe, depicts Faust's struggle to escape from the cruel Archisposa and be reunited with the tender Marguerite, and Janine Charrat's choreography, arranged to music by Werner Egk, was a notable

173 Zizi Jeanmaire and Roland Petit in *Carmen*, 1949

174 Set by Clavé for *Deuil en vingt-quatre heures*, 1953

175 Serge Perrault and Colette Marchand *in Deuil en vingt-quatre heures*, 1953

176 Maurice Béjart in *Voilà l'Homme*, 1955

177 *Haut Voltage*. Ballet by Maurice Béjart, 1957

success. Her own ballet company had its début in 1951 in her native town, and included a number of young dynamic talents: Milorad Miskovich, René Bon, Ethery Pagava and Maria Fris. In 1952 she produced *Le Massacre des Amazones*, a work both savage and poetic, which told of the fierce struggle of a group of proud Amazons to master three untameable horses. After *La Danseuse de Degas* the young choreographer created *Algues*, a strange ballet which plunges the spectator into the world of lunacy. The oppressive, dreamlike atmosphere is accentuated by a somewhat confused choreography based on a haunting score that is part music, part sound-effects. The public found the work too unusual to be acceptable, but Janine Charrat had created a new style which may have inspired Béjart in his future creations. She toured many parts of the world and was warmly welcomed everywhere. In 1957, following the trend towards artistic decentralization in France, she founded the Nouveaux Ballets de Janine Charrat, and is at present ballet-mistress and choreographer at the Grand Theatre, Geneva.

Then came Maurice Béjart (*Ill.* 176). Born in Marseilles, he studied at the Paris Opéra School, then founded the Ballets de l'Étoile with Jean Laurent. In 1955 he created *Symphonie pour un homme seul*, finely interpreted by Michèle Seigneuret, to *musique concrète* by Pierre Schaeffer and Pierre Henry, showing modern man, a prisoner of the hectic, noisy life of our age, finally discovering his own solitude. In *Haut Voltage* he returned to much the same theme (*Ill.* 177): a young man seeks to free himself from the spell of a modern sorceress, but she communicates to him a high-tension current destined to kill her rival, his fiancée. This ballet, reminiscent of science fiction, makes use of flashing lights and *musique concrète* to create a kind of mechanized nightmare. In 1956 he presented *Prométhée*, in which Milorad Miskovich, with his great dramatic gifts, made an incomparable God of Fire, and in 1958 *Orphée*, another version of the famous legend, an exotic work in which he again used *musique concrète* by Henry. By now established as an avant-garde choreographer, he produced *Le Sacre du printemps* at the Théâtre des Nations and *La Damnation de Faust* for the Paris Opéra, both of which aroused fierce controversy.

Paris today is one of the world's great centres of ballet. The Théâtre des Nations, directed by M.-A. Julien, and the Festival International de la Danse, organized by J. Robin at the Théâtre des Champs-Élysées, which provide a stage for many famous companies, make a major contribution to French cultural life.

178 Claire Motte in *Swan Lake*

179 Rudolf von Laban

CHAPTER FIFTEEN

German Expressionism and the Classical Dance

We must go back to the nineteenth century to trace the origins of German Expressionism in ballet. Its story begins with three great innovators: François Delsarte, a French teacher who made a complete analysis of the movements and gestures of the human body; Jacques Dalcroze; and Rudolf von Laban.

Émile-Jacques Dalcroze, born in Vienna in 1865, settled in Germany in 1910 where he founded an Institute at Hellerau for the teaching of his system of eurhythmics. He believed that the study of gymnastics, musical theory and rhythm were fundamentally important for physical and moral balance, and his method aimed to develop a sense of rhythm by transposing sounds into bodily movements. It was after a visit to Dalcroze that Diaghilev, clearly influenced by the master's ideas, produced *Rite of Spring*, that somewhat 'sacrilegious' ballet danced with the feet turned inwards.

At the same period a young Hungarian dancer called Rudolf von Laban, born in 1879, a philosopher of music and the dance, had begun working (after a brief period of study in Paris) as a teacher in Munich, Zurich and Hamburg, and eventually as choreographer at the Berlin Opera (*Ill.* 179). For him it was the gesture that determined the feeling, rather than the reverse; he regarded the plastic qualities of rhythm and movement as the source of expressive gesture, and thus of all dancing. Laban put his ideas into practice by producing in a number of different countries ballets such as *Rosario*, *Prometheus*, *Don Juan*, *Cinderella* and *The Enchanter*, but it was in Hamburg, where he settled in 1920, that he created his most important works. At first he wrote ballets with no music whatever (*Agamemnon*, *Night*, *Don Juan*), then for percussion instruments only, going on to music specially composed for his own works and finally descending to scores originally written for other ballets. In this Laban showed his originality by taking the opposite path to most other choreographers. During the Second World War he took refuge in England, where he introduced a system of remedial exercises for factory workers. He was also the inventor of a system of dance notation known as Cinematography, which is applied on a vast scale in America and Russia. Laban's theories are at the root of modern Expressionist dancing.

Mary Wigman was at first a pupil of Dalcroze, but finding that he laid more stress on music than on dancing she went to study under Laban in Munich (*Ills.* 180, 181). In 1912 she appeared as solo dancer in *The Witch*, a ballet which was highly revolutionary for its day and bore the mark of her strong personality. After the Armistice of 1918 teacher and pupil separated to follow their different paths, Laban as theorist and Mary Wigman as dancer. In 1925 she founded her own company and began a series of tours which took her as far afield as America, with Kreutzberg, Georgi, Palucca, and others. She tried to free dancing from music in order to express her feelings with the greatest possible sobriety and purity. Her ideas gained wide acceptance, particularly in Germany, Switzerland and the United States. She now devotes herself to teaching, and divides her time between Switzerland and Germany.

180 Mary Wigman

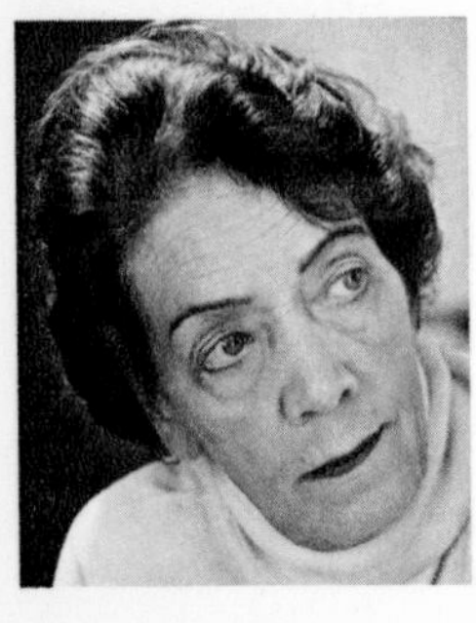

Kurt Jooss, another pupil of Laban, was born in Württemberg, and as a boy entered the Stuttgart Conservatoire, where he studied singing, piano and harmony (*Ill.* 182). In 1920, while attending a course on the art of the drama, he made the acquaintance of Laban, and worked under him for three years as assistant and 'premier danseur'. In June 1924 Jooss was engaged by the Municipal Theatre, Münster, where he met other artists who shared his ideas, among them Aino Siimola, Sigurd Leeder and Fritz Cohen. With

181 Mary Wigman correcting a group

them he formed a dance group known as the 'Neue Tanzbühne'. In 1926 he presented a series of ballets with scenarios written by himself, and a year later founded the Dance Theatre Studio. Soon after he was appointed supervisor of the dancers attached to the Essen Opera, and produced a number of his own works there, with such success that he was offered the post of official ballet-master. In 1932 the Jooss group won first prize at the choreographic competition organized by the Archives Internationales de la Danse in Paris with *The Green Table*, a ballet to music by Cohen which showed a group of bald, bearded diplomats arguing and shouting at each other round a conference

182 Kurt Jooss

table and finally firing their revolvers. The little company, later to take the name of the Ballets Jooss, toured first in Germany, Belgium and Holland and then throughout the world. The style of Kurt Jooss, though strongly influenced by the theories of Laban, does not exclude the classical dance; his works are always built round a theme of social or dramatic interest. Among the most original are *Ball in Old Vienna*, *The Big City* and *The Mirror*. Jooss dissolved his company in 1948, but in 1949 re-opened his school at Essen, which he still directs and which now has nearly seven hundred pupils.

Harald Kreutzberg, born in Bohemia in 1902, was a pupil of Mary Wigman. The ballet-master Max Terpis engaged him to dance at Hanover and then at the Berlin Opera, where he appeared in *Pulcinella*, *The Fox*, *The Toybox*, among others. In 1927 Max Reinhardt gave him a role in *Turandot*, and the following year he took the part of Puck in *A Midsummer Night's Dream* at the Salzburg Festival. After working in close collaboration with Reinhardt in New York he left to tour the United States, then Canada with Ruth Page, subsequently returning to his career of soloist dancer performing his own works. The art of Kreutzberg is essentially dramatic and humorous, but from these two elements he can produce surprising grotesque effects.

Yvonne Georgi, another disciple of Wigman, was born in Saxony. She studied in France, at Besançon, and then at Leipzig before going on to study under Dalcroze, Mary Wigman and the classical teacher Victor Gsovsky. She was a soloist with the Ballets Jooss in 1930, and later gave many recitals and concerts with Harald Kreutzberg in Europe and America. She became a ballet-mistress in Germany and later in the Netherlands, founding a school in Amsterdam in 1936; she also formed a company, which toured the United States in 1939. In 1941 she was attached to the Municipal Opera of Amsterdam, where she produced *Coppélia*, *Pulcinella*, *The Nutcracker* and *Bolero*. She was by now working with well-known choreographers of the classical school such as Victor Gsovsky and Nicolas Orlov, who had an undoubted influence on her creations; she had moved away from German Expressionism towards a more conventional, academic style.

The struggle between the supporters of the classical school and those of the free dance has been a long and bitter one. While it is not easy to be an Expressionist dancer without having studied classical ballet, the reverse is entirely feasible, as is shown when George Balanchine and Jerome Robbins insert passages of free dance into their classical compositions. After World War II in Germany the public had such a hunger for ballet that productions in the classical style were received with enthusiasm, and the pioneers of free dance were obliged to beat a prudent retreat. Nevertheless, the Expressionist style, which is founded more on psychoanalysis than on aesthetics, continued to exert very great influence in Germany, particularly on German opera. Thus Dora Hayer, a dancer who was very popular in Germany, worked in close collaboration with the producer Günther Rennart, interweaving mime and choreography, while Wieland Wagner directed Wagner and Gluck at Bayreuth and Munich in accordance with the concepts of von Laban and Mary Wigman. A characteristic example of his trend in post-war Germany is *Joan of Arc at the Stake (Jeanne d'Arc au Bûcher)*, a poem by Claudel set to music by Honegger, and a number of young producers, among them Oscar Fritz Schuh, Fred Schroer, and Hans Schweikart, are associated with the movement.

The classical ballet in Germany owes much to the untiring efforts of Victor Gsovsky, teacher and ballet-master at the Berlin Opera, and to his wife Tatiana Gsovska. Gsovsky has trained a number of fine dancers, among them Suse Preisser, Gisela Deege, Franz Bauer, Liane Muller, Haill Herber, Lilo Herbert, Nika Sanftleben, Marga Rues, Rainier Höhermann, Gert Reinholm, Ladislav Hansler and Harald Horn, to name only the best-known. All these artists appear in operas and operettas, but they also organize evenings of ballet which are much appreciated by enthusiasts of the dance. Tatiana Gsovska, a choreographer, has produced some remarkable works which fully justify the fame she has acquired both in Germany and abroad, the most outstanding being Handel's *Concerto Grosso*, Berlioz's

Symphonie fantastique, *Till Eulenspiegel*, *Don Juan*, *Hamlet*, *Nobilissima Visione*, *The Pantomime*, *The Chinese Nightingale* and *Joan de Zarissa*.

Thus the Expressionist and Classical schools meet, co-exist, fuse or clash; but though they may sometimes appear to be reconciled, they nevertheless continue to appeal to two equally fervent, but very different publics.

183 *Rite of Spring*. Choreography by Mary Wigman, 1957

184 *Swan Lake*, Act II

CHAPTER SIXTEEN

Ballet in England

The British, in spite of their reputation for imperturbability, have always been passionately devoted to ballet. Gautier speaks of the wild enthusiasm with which London greeted the great Romantic ballerinas Marie Taglioni, Carlotta Grisi and Fanny Cerrito. During the Victorian era two London theatres, the Alhambra and the Empire, regularly featured ballet on their programmes, and famous dancers such as Pierina Legnani, Judith Espinosa, Catherine Geltzer and Tikhomirov appeared there. When Anna Pavlova settled in England in 1912 she found young dancers whom she had no hesitation in recruiting for her troupe. After the Russian Revolution in 1917 a number of foreign artists made their home in Britain; among them were Legat, Astafieva and Cecchetti, three teachers who were to train many excellent dancers such as Vera Savina, Alicia Markova and Anton Dolin, who, at different periods, were to dance in Diaghilev's company.

185 P.J.S. Richardson

But it was Adeline Genée, a Danish dancer married to an Englishman and a star of the Empire Theatre, who gave the first impetus to the growth of ballet in England. With a small group of enthusiasts she founded the Camargo Society and the Royal Academy of Dancing, whose President she remained until 1954. Beside her were three remarkable men who all made notable contributions to the development of British ballet.

The first was P.J.S. Richardson, founder and Director of the *Dancing Times* (*Ill.* 185). From 1910 to 1920 he organized ballet matinées at the West End Theatre at which celebrities like Mary Wigman, Camille Bos, Tamara Karsavina, Vera Trefilova, Alicia Markova and Anton

Dolin appeared. Together with the teacher and ballet authority Edouard Espinosa and Adeline Genée, he brought into being in 1920 the Royal Academy of Dancing. This institution, which received the patronage of the Queen Mother in 1928 and of Queen Elizabeth II in 1953, is today of sufficiently high standard to award diplomas to pupils from all over the world. Richardson was also one of the promoters of the Camargo Society.

186 Cyril Beaumont

Cyril Beaumont, ballet historian, was responsible for making the Cecchetti method more widely known in England through his manual on classical technique, published in 1922 in collaboration with Idzikowsky, a former pupil of Cecchetti (*Ill.* 186). Finally there is Arnold Haskell, author and ballet critic and one of the co-founders of the Camargo Society (*Ill.* 187). This body, composed of ballet-lovers and several organizers of dancing studios such as Marie Rambert and Ninette de Valois, was formed to present performances of ballet to subscription audiences; it was wound up in 1936 and its repertoire incorporated in that of the Vic-Wells Ballet (a company which at that time played alternately at the Old Vic and the Sadler's Wells).

Marie Rambert, whose real name was Myriam Ramberg, was Polish by birth (*Ill.* 188). A former pupil of Jacques Dalcroze and Enrico Cecchetti, she was also a leading apostle of the classical dance, and in 1931 founded the Ballet Club, soon to become the Ballet Rambert. This company, whose aim was to discover and encourage young English dancers and choreographers, started off in the tiny Mercury Theatre, which became a kind of nursery for emerging talents such as Frederick Ashton (*Ill.* 189), Antony Tudor and Andrée Howard. Marie Rambert had herself presented Ashton's *A Tragedy of Fashion* in the revue *Riverside Nights* in 1926, and in 1934 her new company gave a brilliant season which included Ninette de Valois's *Bar aux Folies-Bergère* (inspired by the Manet painting, and starring Alicia Markova), Ashton's *Mephisto Valse*, and *Jardin aux Lilas*, by Antony Tudor, a drama of crossed love set in the Edwardian era.

187 Arnold Haskell

In 1936 London discovered the beautiful Pearl Argyle, June Brae, and Margot Fonteyn; two years later the Ballet Rambert presented two works by Antony Tudor, *The*

Judgment of Paris and *Gala Performance*. The latter is in fact a satire on the ballet, mocking the rivalries between the 'stars' and caricaturing the different styles of the three great schools, those of France, Italy and Russia. During the war the Ballet Rambert joined forces with other troupes and continued its activities as best it could, producing Howard's *The Fugitive* and *Carnival of Animals* in the course of its tours of the provinces. When peace returned the company went back to the Mercury Theatre and resumed its classical repertoire, setting off in 1947 for a tour of Australia and New Zealand sponsored by the British Council. New dancers who were coming to the fore at this time included Belinda Wright, Paula Hinton, and John Gilpin (*Ill.* 190). In 1949 Walter Gore, a pupil of Marie Rambert, presented *Antonia*, to music by Sibelius, followed by *The Life and Death of Lola Montez*, to music by Verdi, and *Variations*, based on a theme by Britten. Today the Ballet Rambert has moved in the direction of a somewhat more modern style, presenting works by such choreographers as Norman Morriss. The most recent 'discoveries' of Marie Rambert are Lucette Aldous and June Sandbrook. The Ballet Rambert appears at various London theatres, principally Sadler's Wells, and performs at Arts Festivals both at home and abroad.

188 Marie Rambert

Ninette de Valois, by birth an Irishwoman named Edris Stannus, was a pupil of Espinosa and Cecchetti and made her début in pantomime in London in 1914 (*Ill.* 194). She danced with Lopokova and Massine in 1922, and joined Diaghilev's company in 1923. In 1925 she partnered Dolin at the Coliseum, and in 1926 rejoined Diaghilev, but finally left the Ballets Russes at the end of that year. She was engaged as producer at the Festival Theatre, Cambridge and later at the Abbey Theatre, Dublin, before returning to London to open her own school of dancing. Lilian Baylis, then Director of the Old Vic, invited her to arrange the dances performed as interludes in the operas that were then given there, and it was now that Ninette de Valois's astonishing career really began. Her first success was *Les Petits Riens* in 1928, followed by *Danse sacrée et Danse profane*, and she was joined between 1932 and 1935 by Alicia Markova, Frederick Ashton and Margot Fonteyn. The Vic-Wells Ballet, of which she was now Director,

189 Sir Frederick Ashton

attracted many young talents: Appleyard, Moreton, Newton, French, Dolin, Judson (as guest-artist), Helpmann (dancer-choreographer and producer), and Ashton (dancer-choreographer). Among ballets arranged by Ninette de Valois were *Checkmate*, a work in the classical style in which a dramatic game of chess is played out between the sinister Black Queen and the bold Red Knight, and *The Rake's Progress*, a mime-ballet inspired by Hogarth's famous series of engravings, a spirited work that was not without moral feeling. Ashton created *Les Patineurs*, a series of *divertissements* at a skating rink enlivened by touches of humour, *Façade*, a witty fantasy, and *Horoscope*. The company was caught on the Continent in 1940, but succeeded in returning to England the following year and

190 John Gilpin and Violette Verdy

191 Nathalie Krassovska

found a temporary home at the New Theatre, where they presented their seasons during the troubled days of the war. It was during this period that Margot Fonteyn and Robert Helpmann emerged as great stars, while Beryl Grey, Moira Shearer, Julia Farron and Margaret Dale also revealed considerable talents. In 1945 the Vic-Wells Ballet divided into two groups, the actors remaining at the Old Vic and the ballet installing itself at Sadler's Wells under the name Sadler's Wells Ballet.

The company re-opened at Covent Garden in 1946 with *The Sleeping Beauty*, to the original choreography by Petipa revised by Frederick Ashton and Ninette de Valois. In this work Margot Fonteyn had one of her greatest roles. The Sadler's Wells Ballet at first kept strictly to classical

192 Svetlana Beriosova in *Giselle*

193 Alicia Markova and Anton Dolin in *The Nutcracker*

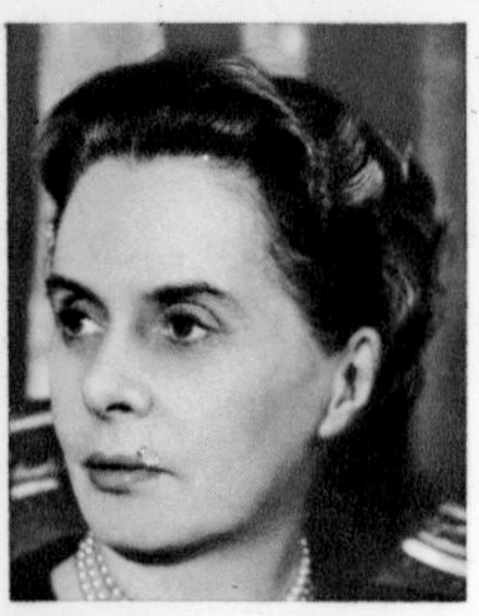

194 Dame Ninette de Valois, founder of the Royal Ballet

works, but gradually adopted a more characteristically 'English' style. In 1946 Ashton presented his masterpiece *Symphonic Variations*, a work of great nobility and purity, with music by César Franck and décors by Sophie Fedorovich. In 1948 came his *Scènes de Ballet*, with music by Stravinsky and a backcloth by Beaurepaire, and ballets to Strauss's *Don Juan* and Prokofiev's *Cinderella*. Ashton played an important part in the ever-growing success of the Sadler's Wells Ballet, and he became artistic director after the departure of Ninette de Valois.

A second English choreographer, Andrée Howard, a former pupil of Preobrajenska and Trefilova, was another talented figure in the company, producing *Assembly Ball* (to music by Bizet) and *A Mirror for Witches*, works which revealed her subtlety and sensitivity. The Sadler's Wells Ballet have had as guest artists Massine, Danilova, Franklin, Dolin and Markova, but Margot Fonteyn remains the undisputed queen of British ballet. Around her are other distinguished stars: Svetlana Beriosova (*Ill.* 192), Doreen Wells, Nadia Nerina, Christopher Gable, Donald Macleary, David Blair, and the latest addition to the company, Rudolph Nureyev (*Ill.* 195), already hailed as a second Nijinsky. In 1957 the granting of a Royal Charter entitled the Sadler's Wells Ballet to take the name 'The Royal Ballet.'

The 'Second Company', the junior company of the Royal Ballet, with its own soloists and repertoire, founded in 1946, was originally based at Sadler's Wells Theatre. It was called first the Sadler's Wells Opera Ballet, then the Sadler's Wells Theatre Ballet. In 1957 all connection was severed with the actual Sadler's Wells Theatre, and the company spends a large part of the year on tour.

Another company that has done much to serve the cause of ballet in England is the Festival Ballet, founded by Anton Dolin and Alicia Markova (*Ill.* 193). Though originally few in number, their troupe rapidly expanded, and gave its first London season at the Stoll Theatre in 1950-51 as part of a Gala Performance of Ballet, to enthusiastic audiences. Anton Dolin invited distinguished guest artists to star in his major productions, among them Alexandra Danilova, Yvette Chauviré, Tamara Toumanova, Mia Slavenska, Colette Marchand, and Janine Charrat.

195 Margot Fonteyn and Rudolph Nureyev in *Swan Lake*

The Festival Ballet appears regularly at the Royal Festival Hall in London, and tours the world with its own young stars, such as Belinda Wright, Toni Lander, Marilyn Burr, Flemming Flindt, John Gilpin, Anita Landa.

All these companies are admirably organized, but remain somewhat isolated, and show—perhaps justifiably—a certain reluctance to admit new ideas from abroad. Though their dancers have real distinction, their scene design for traditional works is often of uncompromising starkness, not so much from a concern for originality as from a certain indifference to artistic effect. The slightly dry, cold style of English classical ballet is now developing towards a more expressive interpretation that is more in keeping with modern ideas.

196 The Ballet Rambert in *Night Shadow*

197 The Ballet Rambert in *Hazana*. Finale

198 *Flames of Paris.* Kirov Theatre, Leningrad, 1932

CHAPTER SEVENTEEN

Soviet Ballet

Even before the Revolution, Alexander Gorsky was an avant-gardiste of Soviet ballet. He began his career as a dancer, and was appointed ballet-master at the Maryinsky Theatre in 1896. A cultivated man with a great love of music and painting and a courageous and independent mind, he introduced a new system of dance notation (evolved in collaboration with Vladimir Stepanoff) to the Imperial Ballet. In 1899 he became ballet-master at the Bolshoi Theatre, where he began to apply his methods, upsetting the conventional rules that were stifling the ballet and introducing life, movement and realism—much to the disapproval of his former teacher, Petipa.

Alexander Gorsky's work in Moscow is closely linked to the development of Stanislavsky's Art Theatre, which revolutionized the stage by insisting on the importance of dramatic expression. Gorsky's creations included an improved version of *Don Quixote*, *Notre-Dame de Paris*, *Salammbô*, and Glazunov's *L'Amour va vite*. In 1911 he produced a new version of *Swan Lake*, allowing greater freedom to the *corps de ballet* and strengthening the character dances in the first and third acts. In 1923 he brought out his last work, a ballet to the music of the Venusberg scene in Wagner's *Tannhäuser*.

After the revolutionary attempt in 1905, the 'wind of change' blowing through Moscow led the Imperial authorities to close down the school of dramatic art attached to the Bolshoi. Despite this setback some distinguished artists emerged from the Moscow School, among them Michel Mordkin and Alexander Volinine, who made their careers outside Russia. Other dancers, grouped around

199 Exercises at the Bolshoi Theatre, with Galina Ulanova *(left)*

Gorsky, were to form the core of the Bolshoi at the time of the Revolution: Vera Karalli, Sofia Fedorova, Victorina Krieger, Vassili Tikhomirov and Catherine Geltzer. In the fateful year of 1917 the Ballet School in Leningrad continued to function, even after the fall of the Winter Palace and the triumph of the Bolsheviks on 7 November. The Maryinsky Theatre now changed its name to the somewhat forbidding title of State Academy of Opera and Ballet, later changing again to Kirov Theatre, after the Soviet leader who was assassinated in 1934. Though its ideology had altered, its *corps de ballet* remained intact, as did its style. Many Russian artists in exile, however, had in these dramatic circumstances to give up all thought of returning home.

Agrippina Vaganova, after studying under great teachers (Ivanov, Gerdt, Legat, Preobrajenska, etc.), herself took up a teaching career. She became a professor (and a severe and exacting one) at the Leningrad Conservatoire, where she stressed the importance of maintaining the link

200 Yuri Zhdanov in *Romeo and Juliet*, 1940

201 Constantin Sergeyev in *Swan Lake*, 1940

with the classical tradition. Among her pupils are Marina Semenova, Galina Ulanova, Nathalie Doudinskaya, Tatiana Betceslova, Alexei Ermolaiev, Vachtang Chaboukiani and Constantin Sergeyev (*Ill.* 201).

Associated with Vaganova's name is that of Kassian Goleizovsky. A teacher at the Kirov Theatre, Leningrad, then at the Bolshoi, Moscow, he enlarged the scope of classical dancing by enriching it with new movements and figures in a vigorous, acrobatic style. He was the teacher of George Balanchine.

The Kirov and the Bolshoi are not really rivals, but the ballets they present are very different in conception. In Moscow the discipline is less strict; in Leningrad they like to claim that Bolshoi dancers sacrifice tradition for the sake of melodramatic effect, while Moscow retorts that those of the Kirov are stiff and expressionless. Both, however, make their own contribution to the greatness of Soviet ballet.

In the nineteen-twenties a number of ultra-modernistic, but somewhat obscure, ballets were produced, following the current trends of Futurism and Constructivism. *The Red Poppy*, produced in Moscow in 1927, however, was a straightforwardly propagandist work, set in the China of that period. It was devised by Tikhomirov and Lashchilin, and the part of the dancing-girl Tao Hoa was played by Catherine Geltzer. *Flames of Paris* (*Ill.* 198), produced at the Kirov in 1932, also had a revolutionary theme, but this time a French one: the victory of the people of Paris in 1792, led by the Carmagnoles. In 1934 came *The Fountain of Bakhtchisarai*, a moving love story enlivened by colourful Tartar dances, based on a lyric by Pushkin, followed a few years later by the supreme achievement of Soviet ballet, *Romeo and Juliet*. This work, which kept closely to Shakespeare's text, had music by Prokofiev and choreography by Lavrovsky, while Galina Ulanova and Constantin Sergeyev took the parts of the doomed lovers. Intimate and poetic episodes alternate with imposing court scenes and those picturesque popular dances which the Russians interpret with such zest and brilliance. This ballet has remained, both in the theatre and in the cinema, a masterpiece of Russian choreography.

202 Inna Zoubkovskaia in *The Stone Flower*

A new choreographer of talent, Vachtang Chaboukiani, came to prominence at this time; his first work of importance, *In the Heart of the Mountains*, was a Georgian ballet to music by André Balanchivadze, brother of George Balanchine. His second great ballet, *Laurencia*, produced in 1939, was based on Lopez de Vega's drama *Fuente Ovejuna*. More popular with the Russian public were Klebanov's *Svetlana* and Khatchaturian's *Gayané*, and above all *The Stone Flower*, Prokofiev's last work, composed shortly before his death, and inspired by the folklore of the Urals. It was produced at the Bolshoi in 1954, with a scenario by Prokofieva and choreography by Lavrovsky, and in 1957 at the Kirov, with choreography by Yuri Grigorivich. Several contemporary Russian ballets take their themes from French literature: works have been built round Balzac's *Les Illusions perdues* and George Sand's *La Petite Fadette*, while Varkovitzky's *Gavroche* (*Ill.* 203), at the Kirov Theatre, Leningrad, recreates Victor Hugo's *Les Misérables*, faithfully reproducing as the finale to one of its scenes Delacroix's picture *Liberty at the Barricades*.

Galina Ulanova is the unchallenged queen of Soviet ballet. Her art developed under the Revolution; she was born in Leningrad, where her father was a producer and her mother a dancer at the Kirov Theatre. After seeing her mother exhausted by hard work during the cold and hungry days of 1920, she obstinately refused to become a dancer, but soon succumbed to her passion for ballet. Among her early roles were the modest ladybird in *Les Caprices du Papillon* and the bird in *Snow White*, to music by Rimsky-Korsakov. After studying under Vaganova she danced Odile in *Swan Lake* at the age of eighteen, but her strict training was still hampering her from expressing her personality to the full. She worked tirelessly to express the feelings of the characters she interpreted, and her

203 *Gavroche*. Kirov Theatre, Leningrad

204 Alexeieva in *The Flight of the Seagull*

205 Anatole Sapogov

206 *The Cape of Good Hope. Scene of the shark hunt*

performance in Vaganova's version of *Swan Lake* marked the beginning of her artistic maturity. *Romeo and Juliet* made her famous. She strove to comprehend and to bring out in her interpretation every shade of meaning both in Shakespeare's play and Prokofiev's music, and confessed later, 'That role cost me ten years of work and study.' She also gave unforgettable performances in *The Sleeping*

207 *Spartacus*. Kirov Theatre, Leningrad, 1956

208 Russian folk dancing company

Beauty and *Giselle*. Her grace, her perfect technique and her acute sensibility have earned her a unique place in the affections of the Russian people. She is now a professor at the Bolshoi.

Other distinguished stars of Soviet ballet are Maia Plissetskaya, Nicolas Fadeyechev, Rimma Karelskaya, Guennadi Liediatk and Boris Khokhlov. The Moscow School of Ballet (founded in 1805), which taught these dancers, is an institution unique of its kind. Children are admitted at the age of nine and the course of study lasts nine years, including both exercises at the bar and training in relaxation, and instruction in the arts. Pupils are taught the literature and history of traditional dances, so that they may restore them to their proper style and see them in their historical context. There are courses on drama and scene design; music is also taught, to develop sense of rhythm and musical responses. Only the very best graduates of the school are engaged at the Bolshoi, the rest being sent to the theatres of Odessa, Riga, Novosibirsk, and so on. Some of them join the State folk-dance companies, notably that of Igor Moiseyev, which tour the great European capitals.

Besides those of the Kirov and the Bolshoi, Russia has a number of other ballet companies in major towns and big industrial cities such as Gorki, Saratov and Odessa. There are no private schools, companies or theatres, but there are as many as nineteen State ballet schools. The company known as the Stanislavsky and Nemirovich-Dantchenko Theatre Ballet deserves special mention. Formed by the well-known dancer Victorina Krieger in 1930, and directed from that date until today by the choreographer Vladimir Bourmeister, it has sixty-six dancers recruited from pupils of the Bolshoi school, of whom Violetta Bovt, Nina Timofeieva, Sofia Vinogradova, Alla Ossipienko and Eleonora Vlassova, with the male dancers Chichinadze and Kouznetsov, are among the most outstanding.

Soviet ballets are totally different from Western ballets, their theme, music, choreography and scenery being conceived according to quite different principles. The Soviet ballet does not aim merely to create something of beauty, but rather to rouse the emotions of its audience and convey definite ideas. The notion of art for art's sake is unknown in Russia. *Spartacus*, produced a few years ago in Moscow, is a faithful account of the life of this revolutionary hero, just as *Flames of Paris* relates a historical episode in the French Revolution. The evocation of moods of dream or fantasy, or the use of symbolism, are frowned on in the U.S.S.R.; everything must be clear, simple, and explicit. Even the classical ballets are treated in this way; the Soviet *Giselle* of the second act is not an unreal phantom, but a resolute young girl who triumphs over obstacles by the sheer force of her love. Great stress is laid on mime in Soviet choreography, and the ballets take the form of a series of lyrical and dramatic episodes, with *pas de deux* remarkable for their athletic, yet smooth, technique. Much use is made of traditional dances in character ballets, while scenery is invariably totally realistic, the Russians claiming that since their productions are essentially popular, abstract art would be out of place. One fact is indisputable, however; whether as soloists or as groups, Soviet dancers are supreme masters of the art of ballet.

209 The American Ballet in *The Sleeping Beauty*

CHAPTER EIGHTEEN

Ballet in the United States

Ballet in the United States was inevitably influenced by the spirit of independence stirred by the innovators who appeared at the beginning of the twentieth century.

It was then that Loie Fuller, originally an actress, danced in costumes of luminous silk that were coloured by new and varied forms of stage lighting. Though hers was primarily an art of spectacle, she reminded her audiences that dance was more than body technique. So did Maude Allan, a Canadian, who danced barefoot and in a loose tunic. Her aim was to recapture the freedom of Greek plastic art.

But the American woman who made most people conscious of the free, Greek-costumes dance was the one who, as a child, had refused to dance on her toes, telling her ballet teacher that she considered the position 'ugly'. 'My art,' wrote Isadora Duncan, 'is just an effort to express my Being.' She sought the 'divine expression of the human spirit', and she felt that it could be found, not through technique, but through inspiration. She found such inspiration in the art of Greece and in the music of Beethoven, Chopin and Wagner.

To Isadora Duncan (*Ill.* 223), the stiff slippers and tight corsets of the ballerina destroyed the natural beauty of the body. She believed the dancer must feel in harmony with nature. The movements she found for herself were simple—running, skipping, leaping; with flowing arm gestures. Her audiences were spellbound. Though her greatest triumphs were achieved in Europe, she eventually conquered America as well. Her art, however, was personal, depending on individual insight and on an innate power to communicate that insight. She founded no school. Yet her feeling for dance as a medium for personal expression permeated many of the manifestations to follow.

In 1906, a young woman from New Jersey made her dance debut as an Indian goddess in a theatre suffused with incense. Ruth St Denis, determined toi nstil dance with the spiritual values she found lacking in her native theatre, turned to the Orient, India, and ancient Egypt for inspiration. She was more concerned with catching the mood and the spirit of a nation than with faithfully reproducing its dance steps. She was not concerned with virtuosity, but she took care to wear theatrical adaptations of native costumes, counting on the appeal of the exotic. With simple movements, she projected the spiritual exaltation of *Radha*, *Eygpta* and *White Jade*.

Most of Miss St Denis' projects were accomplished in cooperation with her husband, Ted Shawn, who, for many years, directed with her a school and a company. So close was the partnership and so prevailing its influence, that the period following the First World War has been called 'the Denishawn Era'.

Like his wife, Shawn was concerned with national dances and with spiritual values. But his chief interests lay in the fields of American Indian and folk material. He pioneered the use of contemporary French and American music for dance. He was also a promoter of the role of the male dancer and, for a number of years, maintained a men's company. After the couple separated, Miss St Denis concentrated on the sacred dance; Shawn on his work as director of a summer school and theatre —Jacob's Pillow in Lee, Mass.

Denishawn aimed for nothing less than obliterating what it considered the prevailingly low standards of American dance and establishing dance as an art capable of expressing, in Miss St Denis' words, 'the whole range of thought and philosophy.' Though stirred by their promise of a new world of dance, their pupils grew dissatisfied with the Denishawn ways of creating that world, and went out to seek ways of their own.

The first to leave the fold was Martha Graham. Where Denishawn had explored foreign lands, Graham explored the human mind. She sought to lay bare the unconscious, the hidden motives and conflicts that determine action. She revealed the psychological validity of early ritual in *Primitive Mysteries* (1931) and *Dark Meadow* (1946); of classic mythology in *Cave of the Heart* (1946) and *Night Journey* (1947) (*Ill.* 210). She did penetrating emotional biographies of poets in *Letter to the World* (1940) and *Deaths and Entrances* (1943). She returned to mythology in her masterpiece *Clytemnestra* (1958), an introspective 'journey of the soul' into the depths of self-discovery—for all its analytic undertones, a work of great theatricality. The probing of the modern mind is present in all Graham choreography. Even the radiantly joyous *Appalachian Spring* (1944), the lyrical *Diversion of Angels* (1948), and the witty *Acrobats of God* (1960), have a tough fibre of conception that never permits them to become romantic or purely comic in feeling.

To communicate her psychological themes, Graham needed a technique that would 'make visible the interior landscape'. The movements she evolved were new and completely individual. At first they were exclusively strong, sharp, and percussive. Later she allowed some

210 Martha Graham and Eric Hawkins in *Night Journey*

flow and gentleness. For Martha Graham, emotion is never superimposed on technique; movements originate in dramatic motivations.

A number of gifted choreographers have emerged from the Graham company. Sophie Maslow has handled folk themes and the contemporary scene with keen perception. Both she and Anna Sokolow have depicted in movement the nervous tensions of jazz, though the latter's strong handling stresses its more serious, even terrifying, aspects of desperation. Pearl Lang has created delicate evocations of musical moods, and the Japanese-American Yuriko has made sensitive dances of distinct femininity.

Like Martha Graham, Doris Humphrey was an apostate from Denishawn and, also like her, she evolved a new technical approach to dance. Humphrey, however, was less concerned with the tortuous problems of the mind of man than she was with his inherent dignity and nobility. She satirized man's follies in *Theatre Piece* 1 and 2 (1936, 1956); she condemned social injustice in *Inquest* (1944); and censored possessive love in *With My Red Fires* (1936). But in *New Dance* (1935) she celebrated the role of the individual in relation to society; in *Day on Earth* (1947) she traced the growth of love in a family; in *Ruins and Visions* (1953) she showed man learning to face reality.

The Humphrey technique derived from her view of human nature; the conflict in man between his desire for progress and his desire for stability, between the peace of equilibrium and the excitement of movement. In physical terms this became the body in balance and the body threatened by the force of gravity. The theory was inherently dramatic, symbolic of man's struggle and ultimate spiritual ascendency over the material world.

Leaving Denishawn with Doris Humphrey was Charles Weidman, who acted as her partner and as co-director of the Humphrey-Weidman company. As a choreographer, his chief gifts were for dramatic story-telling, as in the gripping *Lynchtown* (1936), and for pantomimic comedy, as in his interpretation of James Thurber's *Fables for our Time* (1948).

A member of the Humphrey-Weidman company, who later formed a group of his own, José Limón carried on some of the traditions of his mentors. A powerful and compelling performer, for whom some of the greatest Humphrey works were created, he is also a choreographer. *The Moor's Pavane* (1949) depicted emotional highlights from Shakespeare's *Othello* within a framework of Renaissance court dances. *There is a Time* (1956) was based on the enduring themes of the Book of Ecclesiastes, while *Missa Brevis* (1958) hailed the heroism of a war-ravaged people. Always noble in concept, the works of José Limón reveal deep humility and compassion.

A former member of the Limón company, Pauline Koner has created some powerful dramatic portraits and some poignant lyrical dances of great beauty, culminating in her tribute to the late Doris Hymphrey *The Farewell* (1962).

When the Graham and Humphrey-Weidman companies were being formed in the late 'twenties, American ballet was practically unknown. Apart from a few attempts at the Metropolitan Opera in New York and at the Chicago Opera, ballet was seen in the United States only in performances by foreign companies. In 1910, Anna Pavlova had begun a series of American tours. The Diaghilev company visited the United States in 1916 and 1917. But there were long, barren periods. Then, in 1933,

211 *Till Eulenspiegel.* Choreography by Balanchine, 1951

the Ballets Russes de Monte Carlo began its annual tours, and in 1934, the American Ballet was founded under the direction of George Balanchine.

The initial effect of the Ballets Russes, which had Léonide Massine as its principal choreographer, was to focus attention on ballet as Russian ballet. The glamour attracted large audiences, and natives found it hard to compete. Even with a Russian in charge, the American Ballet was unpopular at first. But the ground was being prepared. In Chicago, Ruth Page was working with the opera company; Catherine Littlefield in Philadelphia and Willam Christensen in San Francisco were forming ballet ensembles. American choreographers were beginning to work in their own way, no longer merely imitating European models. Though they used the established technique of European ballet, they turned to their own country for subject matter. In 1937, Miss Littlefield created *Barn Dance;* in 1938, Eugene Loring composed *Billy the Kid.*

The next two decades marked the emergence of a new era. Through the efforts of Lincoln Kirstein (*Ill.* 212) and Balanchine, the American Ballet developed into the New York City Ballet, becoming one of the world's foremost companies. And the American Ballet Theatre is also widely admired.

Founded in 1939 as Ballet Theatre, the company led by Lucia Chase soon acquired a definite character. Eclectic in its repertory, it preserved the classics, while it gave opportunities to new choreographers. The first to gain prominence through Ballet Theatre was Antony Tudor. Practically unknown in his native England, Tudor was to do his most important work in the United States. *Pillar of Fire* (1942) made history by demonstrating that classical ballet technique could be used to portray the psychological drama of an anguished, frustrated woman. (The idea seemed more suited to Martha Graham.) Tudor's achievement opened the way to a new kind of maturity in ballet. His later works for Ballet Theatre included *Romeo and Juliet* (1943), *Dim Lustre* (1943), and *Undertow* (1945). Each was a kind of experiment—in structure, in nuance of dramatic gesture, in technical manipulation. Though none was a complete, popular success, each enriched the resources of ballet.

212 Lincoln Kirstein

Two years after the première of *Pillar of Fire*, Ballet Theatre scored another success. Jerome Robbins' *Fancy Free* practically established a new genre of ballet—contemporary in rhythm, energetic, light-hearted. Using movements from jazz and tap dance, Robbins showed the adaptability of the ballet idiom to the portrayal of modern, realistic episodes. Later, outside of Ballet Theatre, Robbins was to prove himself equally adept in more serious veins, as in *The Cage* (1951), a portrayal of insect life and death (*Ill.* 214). And he was to triumph in the field of musical comedy, most notably with *West Side Story* (1957). Robbins now is not only a choreographer, but a director with a remarkable grasp of all the elements of total theatre.

Ballet Theatre also used the talents of Agnes de Mille, whose *Fall River Legend* (1948) was acclaimed for its skillful characterizations. Recently, however, the company has leaned more on foreign choreographers such as Birgit Cullberg and Harald Lander.

In its peak period, Ballet Theatre developed such excellent dancers as Nora Kaye and Alicia Alonso. The company is now headed by Lupe Serrano and Royes Fernandez.

213 American Ballet Theatre: Ruth Ann Koesun

214 Nora Kaye and Nicholas Magallanes in *The Cage*, 1951

215 Nina Vyroubova and Serge Golovine in *Tarassiana*, 1951

The New York City Ballet developed in a different direction. Uninterested in dramatic dancing, Balanchine's approach is almost purely musical. But his range of styles is wide, for his taste in music is catholic and his choreography reflects the varied structures and moods of the scores he selects. Consequently, the repertory of the New York City Ballet includes such diverse works as the romantic *Scotch Symphony* of Mendelssohn (1952) and *Liebeslieder Walzer* of Brahms (1960); the purely classical *Symphony in C* of Bizet (1947) and *Divertimento No. 15* of Mozart (1956); the spritely *Stars and Stripes* of Souza (1958); and the complex abstractions of Stravinsky's *Agon* (1957) and Webern's *Episodes* (1959).

Balanchine claims that it is easy to choreograph: one simply listens to the music. Generally, he likes the kind of music that he calls 'pure and heartless'. Like a rose, it is there to be admired but not to excite emotion. To such music, Balanchine sets 'pure and heartless' choreography—beautiful but intentionally without meaning beyond itself. The movement he sets to classical music is elegant and refined; that for romantic scores is full and flowing. When he deals with contemporary atonal music, Balanchine choreographs in spasmodic, disconnected

216 André Eglevsky
217 Maria Tallchief III *Four Temperaments*
218 Marjorie Tallchief and George Skibine in *Idylle*

phrases, as sparse and concentrated as a twelve-tone score. On occasion, Balanchine has used plots, as in *Orpheus* (1948), but the story is never dominant, the dramatic element never approaches the literalness of pantomime. As Kirstein once remarked, 'He has no interest in any effect that is not danced'.

The performing style of the New York City Ballet is crisp, precise, brilliant and impersonal. Slim and long-legged, its ballerinas are known for their virtuosic fleetness. Among them have been Diana Adams, Jillana, Allegra Kent, Melissa Hayden, Maria Tallchief (*Ill.* 217), Violette Verdy and Patricia Wilde. Balanchine choreography is less favourable to male dancers, but at least three outtanding ones—Jacques d'Amboise, Arthur Mitchell, and Edward Villella—have developed within the company.

Balanchine also forms a curious link between the ballet and the modern dance in America. Since—with a few exceptions—his ballets are devoid of plot and characterization, he belongs to a school of thought that is now common in the field of the modern dance; the school that believes that the subject matter of dance is dancing. Leader of the group (which really has only this one belief in common) is Merce Cunningham, a former member

219 *Age of Anxiety.* New York City Ballet

of the Martha Graham company. Utilizing the factor of chance, Cunningham strips his dances of any semblance of logical order and coherence. Chance determines movements, their placement, and even the duration of the dance. This, he feels, results in something far more interesting than what he could contrive deliberately.

Another former Graham dancer, Paul Taylor, has experimented in various styles. In the beginning, he stood motionless on stage while electronic music was played on a tape recorder. Then he tried a wild, frantic kind of movement. Then he did a type of 'ballet blanc' to music by Handel. No one, least of all Taylor, knows what he will do next.

Then there is Alwin Nikolais, who calls his compositions 'theatre pieces of movement, sound, light, and color'. Using a variety of stage properties—capes, poles, hoops, wires, and oddly shaped forms of fabric and plastic—he turns his performers into weird and fascinating apparitions, who move through a startling array of lighting effects to strange, electronic sounds.

In the United States there is far more variety in the scene of modern dance than there is in ballet, where—

220 The Marquis de Cuevas Company in *Le Mal du Siècle*

despite his versatility—Balanchine dominates the entire field, setting a standard of style that has become a model to most young American choreographers. Since few of them are gifted with Balanchine's musicality, few ballets of consequence are being choreographed by anyone else.

One of the rare, creative talents to emerge in ballet in the 1960s is Robert Joffrey, whose young company seems equally adept in the classics and in the modern dramatic or jazz ballets that their director and his guest choreographers devise for them. And other groups are developing. There is the Boston Ballet of E. Virginia Williams, reared in the Balanchine tradition but with a freshness of its own. And there is promise in the Washington Ballet, directed by Frederic Franklin. Most encouraging is the growth of the regional ballet movement, companies of rigidly selected student-dancers, who perform for communities within their own area. Beginning with Dorothy Alexander's Atlanta Civic Ballet and now embracing some 150 companies, the regional movement serves as an excellent place of apprenticeship for future dancers and choreographers.

But there is an audience for more major professional

221 The Chicago Opera Ballet in *L'Amour Sorcier*

ballet companies than now exist. And the only large company trying to challenge the established groups is the Harkness Ballet, which is European-oriented and is led by two former stars of the French company of the Marquis de Cuevas, Marjorie Tallchief and George Skibine (*Ill.* 218).

222 Sonia Arova and Rudolph Nureyev in *The Merry Widow*

CHAPTER NINETEEN

Ballet around the World

The rediscovery of the dance is one of the most striking artistic phenomena of the first half of the twentieth century.

With Isadora Duncan, the 'young bacchante' whose dancing thrilled and scandalized the world, free dance came into being (*Ill.* 223). Her ideal was to liberate the dance from its fetters, and through movement to rediscover joy and freedom. At the opposite pole to Isadora Duncan stood Serge de Diaghilev; while one preached the free dance, the other was the great apostle of classical ballet. They pursued their separate aims with equal faith, like

223 Isadora Duncan

two rockets set upon different paths, but aimed at the same goal. Isadora Duncan's influence soon began to reach even those strongholds of tradition, the Russian Imperial Theatres, and gradually spread also to the Swedish and American ballets.

At the same time as it was being influenced by this movement of liberation, the dance became a subject for study and research; ethnographers now began to make the public familiar with the exotic dances of Africa and Asia. We owe this development to the great German philosopher Nietzsche, whose works include many references to the dance. For him dancing symbolised a way of thinking, a mode of being; thus he claims that the philosopher's spiritual food should be as frugal as that of a dancer,

'For it is not fatness, but greater suppleness and greater vigour that a good dancer demands of his food, and I do not know what better the mind of a philosopher could wish for than to become a good dancer, for the dance is its ideal, its own peculiar art, and in the end its sole creed, its religion.'

Elsewhere he says:

'To judge the worth of a book, a man, or a work of music, the essential thing to know is whether it has rhythm, or better still, whether it "dances".'

And *Zarathustra* ends with a hymn to the dance:

'Beyond, in that distant future never glimpsed even in dreams, where the gods in their dances are ashamed to cover themselves, where all Becoming seems to be dancing and divine mirth... there, may every day on which we have not danced at least once be lost for us!'

Isadora Duncan came into the world just as Nietzsche was leaving Bâle and his chair of Philology to become a wanderer through the Engadine and Italy, dreaming of the Dance, the supreme revelation.

Today ballet continues its search for different forms, and tomorrow it may even combine with speech and song in its attempt to express the tragedy of modern man. It has now conquered the entire world; as some countries retire from the central maelstrom of its activity, others take their place. Ballet is an art as various and as constantly changing as life itself, and after the ages of Noverre and Blasis the twentieth century has undoubtedly been the most fertile in invention. Ballet lives in many countries, but everywhere with a different character and emphasis, shaped by national history, climate, customs, temperament: in France that character is grace, in Germany Expressionism, in Russia realism, in Africa mysticism. There are as many manners as there are masterpieces; the romantic grace of *Les Sylphides*, the tragedy of *Icare*, the contrast of impassioned dancing and serene music in *Le Jeune Homme et la Mort*, the subtle allegory of Stravinsky's *Serenade*, the grandiose choreographic orchestration of *Symphonie fantastique*, the primitive savagery of *Rite of Spring*, the psychological insights of *Age of Anxiety*. But the ideal ballet is undoubtedly the one in which music, dancing and scenery are perfectly balanced and blended to form an integrated whole. *Les Demoiselles de la Nuit*, in which Jean Françaix's score,

224 Giulio Perugini and Violetta Elvin in *Swan Lake*, 1952

Roland Petit's choreography and Léonor Fini's sets combine to create one complete and harmonious spectacle, is the perfect example.

Though France, Germany, England, Russia and the United States now reign supreme in the ballet world, the art also flourishes in many other countries.

Italy, once the spiritual home of ballet, has since unfortunately grown sterile and produced no works of real interest. Diaghilev's influence never touched Italy, although Cecchetti did his best to stem the decline by training pupils who are now the country's leading ballet-masters: Corbo, Caorsi, Gallizia, Radice, Poli, Battaggi, Fornaroli, and so on. The Hungarian choreographer Aurel Milloss, an ex-pupil of Laban, worked for several years in Italy, first at La Scala, Milan, then at the Rome Opera and at the San Carlo Theatre, Naples. His varied and fertile talent produced several interesting works—*Les Créatures de Prométhée* after Vigano, Bartók's *Miraculous Mandarin*, *Allegra Piazzetta*, Gershwin's *Rhapsody in Blue*—but had no lasting influence on Italian ballet. Important reforms have recently been introduced by the Academy of Dancing, making it compulsory for all ballet teachers to sit an examination.

Bianca Gallizia's school at the San Carlo Theatre, Naples, is undoubtedly one of the most representative in Italy. A former star ballerina, she has created a number of interesting works, and her pupils include Sonia Del Gindice, Maria Pia Tommasini, and Antonio Greco. The school of La Scala, Milan, which is under the direction of an Englishwoman, Esmée Bulnes, has produced some fine artists, among them Carla Fracci, Mario Pistoni, Roberto Fascilla, Bruno Telloli, Walter Venditti, Vera Colombo, Fiorella Cova and Luciana Novaro—the latter a particularly beautiful, intelligent and spirited dancer, who specialized in character roles and is today herself one of the directors of the school. The Rome Opera School has also had its moment of glory; among its ex-pupils are Giulio Perugini (*Ill.* 224) and Ugo Dell'Ara, who became ballet-masters at La Scala, Milan, and Maria Dalba. The Rome Opera itself has three 'premiers danseurs', Marisa Matteini, Giovanni Perugini and Walter Zappolini, and each season produces three or four ballets, but no original works.

In Brussels, Maurice Béjart, after a lapse of a century and a half, took up the mantle of Jean-Antoine Petipa. The history of Belgian ballet began in 1700 with the choreographer La Gomme, then declined until 1826, when it was given new life by Jean-Antoine Petipa (father of the celebrated Lucien and Marius), who brought a number of famous stars, including leading Italian ballerinas, to the Théâtre Royal de la Monnaie. In 1927 Katchourovsky was engaged as ballet-master, followed by Nicolas Zverev, Jean-Jacques Etchevery and Maurice Béjart (*Ill.* 225). The stars of the company are Laga, Lagan, Berdel and Simon, while Tania Bari is the leading soloist of the Twentieth Century Ballet, a troupe created by Béjart which has done much to stimulate the development of Belgian ballet.

The Netherlands has at present two ballet companies, the Het National Ballet and the Netherlands Dance Theatre. The former was founded in Amsterdam in 1961 by Sonia Gaskell, and has a repertoire of both classical and modern works, including *The Four Temperaments* (Balanchine-Hindemith), *Caprichos* (Ross-Stravinsky), *Shirah* (Lang), *Jungle* (van Dantzig) (*Ill.* 227), *Contrasts* (Kaesen), *The Miraculous Mandarin* and *La Rencontre*. The soloists are Marianna Hilarides, Sonja van Beers, Leonie Kramer, Panchita de Peri and Billy Wilson. The Netherlands Dance Theatre is under the artistic direction of Benjamin Harkavry, Job Sanders and Hamy Bourmann, and most of the works on its repertoire are modern, created by, for example, Hans van Manen, Benjamin Harkavry, Rudi van Dantzig, Aart Verstegen, Jaan Flier. Some of its soloists are also its directors or choreographers, such as Willy de la Bye, Hannie van Leeuwen, Alexandra von Rhijn, Hans van Manen, Jaan Flier and Job Sanders.

Auguste Bournonville died in Copenhagen in 1878, after a brilliant career as choreographer and ballet-master in Denmark. Michel Fokine was engaged in 1925 as guest-choreographer and produced many of the great masterpieces of the Ballets Russes, but the Danish ballet had its great flowering under his pupil Harald Lander, ballet-master from 1932 to 1951. Among his works were *Qarrtsiluni* (1942), inspired by the Danish explorer Knud Rasmussen's expedition to Greenland, Galeotti's *The*

225 *(above left)*
Michèle Seigneuret
and Maurice Béjart
in *Haut Voltage*

226 *(above right)*
Henning Kronslam,
Mette Mollerup,
Kirsten Bundgaard,
Kirsten Simone
in *Apollo Musagetes*

227 Maria Koppers
and Billy Wilson
in *Jungle*

Whims of Cupid and the Ballet-Master, with its quaint period charm, and *Etudes*. In 1943 the great ballerina Margot Lander, his first wife, left the stage, and Harald Lander later went to Paris to direct the ballet of the Opéra. Toni Lander, his second wife, is now internationally famous. Today the ballet-masters at Copenhagen, Henning Kronslam and Niels Bjórn Larsen, share their fame with Margrethe Shanne, Inge Sand, Tuth Andersen, Mette Mollerup, Svend Erik Jensen, and Frank Schaufuss. A number of visiting choreographers—Ashton, Balanchine, Cullberg, Petit, Robbins, Taras, de Valois—have produced works at the Copenhagen Opera, while noted Danish choreographers include Erik Bruhn *(Concertette)*, Biger Bartholin (Prokofiev's *Classical Symphony*), Borge Ralov *(The Courtesan)*, and Kirsten Ralov *(La Dame aux Camélias)*. Flemming Flindt and Erik Bruhn are today leading exponents of the style of the great Danish school.

The Stockholm Opera Ballet was founded in 1773 by the French choreographer Louis Gallodier. Filippo Taglioni

228 Margareta von Bahr and Klaus Salin in *Miss Julie*

229 Antonio, the great Spanish contemporary dancer

was for a time in charge of Swedish ballet and introdupec some far-reaching reforms; his daughter Marie was born in Stockholm in 1804. The first Swedish ballet-master was Anders Selinder; he was succeeded by Robert Sijablom from 1887-90, after which Michel Fokine made an important contribution to Swedish ballet. In 1920 the wealthy Rolf de Maré founded the Ballets Suédois with Jean Borlin and some of the best artists of the Stockholm Opera, but Jean Borlin did not long survive the disbanding of the company. A disciple of German Expressionism, Julian Algo, introduced the works of Diaghilev to Sweden, and his successor Georges Gué, who was Finnish by origin, trained its dancers in the best Russian tradition. Expressionism made its appearance in Sweden with the First World War; Birgit Akesson, who developed free dance to its furthest limit, created some interesting works, using designs by leading Cubist painters. Birgit Cullberg, an ex-pupil of Jooss, produced a number of important works for the Stockholm Opera, one of the best-known being

230 *Mazeppa*. Warsaw Ballet

Miss Julie, based on the bitter, cynical drama by Strindberg (*Ill.* 228). Another young dancer, Ivo Cramer, influenced by Cullberg, composed *Biblical Pictures* and *The Emperor of Portugal.*

Austria could be said to be the cradle of Opera ballet, for here its history goes back to the seventeenth century, when Maria Theresa incorporated the Court ballet into the State Opera. After that day all the famous names of European ballet appeared at one time or another on the stage of the Viennese Opera, beginning with Hilferding, Angiolini, Noverre and Taglioni. The despotic reign of Italian ballerinas was brought to an end by Joseph Hallsreiter, who brought Viennese dancers—Gusti Pichler, Julia Draper, and, nearer our own time, Edeltraut Brexner—into the limelight. Between the wars Austrian ballet went through a time of crisis; Richard Strauss endeavoured to mount *Crème fouettée* with the ballet-master Heinrich Kroller. Some noted modern choreographers, however, among them Bronislava Nijinska and Marguerite Wallmann came to the assistance of the Vienna Opera, and after World War II Willy Franz and Dimitri Parlich were succeeded by Aurel Milloss. Today the Viennese Ballet is proud to number among its ranks Edeltraut Brexner, Christi Zimmerl, Willy Dirtl, Karl Musil and Paul Vondrak.

231 *Giselle.* Ballet of the Finnish National Opera

The Budapest Opera Ballet dates from 1829. At first Italian choreographers—Smeraldi, Mazzantini, Guerra—held the field, but in the twentieth century it was the turn of the Russian school. Jyulia Harangozo staged *Czardas*, Gershwin's *Rhapsody in Blue* (choreography by Gyorgy Tabor) and Sandor Jemmiz's *Divertissement*. In 1948 the Soviet choreographer Vainonen was invited to take over the direction of the Budapest company, and later Harangozo became Director of the *corps de ballet*, which included Zsuzsa Kun, Gabrielle Lakatos, Adele Orosz, Victor Rona, Victor Fulop and Ferenc Havas. Among ballets they have performed are *The Miraculous Mandarin*, *The Wooden Prince*, *Swan Lake*, *Giselle*, *Scheherazade*, *The Fountain of Bakhtchisarai* and *Flames of Paris*.

In Yugoslavia the Belgrade Ballet was formed in 1921 for the original purpose of performing opera *divertissements*, but it was not long before they became an independent section of the Yugoslav National Opera. A number of Russian artists brought their distinctive personality to the company, and the repertoire came to include Delibes's *Coppélia*, Prokofiev's *Romeo and Juliet*, Hirstich's *Legend of Ohrid*, Lotka's *Ballad of a Medieval Love Story*, Baranovich and Parlich's *Cœur de Pain d'épice*, Stravinsky's *Orpheus*, and Kalomiris's *Yolanda*. Among the stars of the Yugoslav

Ballet are Ruth Parnel, Vera Kostich, Mira Sanfina, and Milica Jovanovich, while Milorad Miskovich, Douska Sifnios and Dimitri Parlich have reached international status. Parlich has established himself as one of the greatest Yugoslav choreographers.

The first Polish ballet company come into being two hundred years ago, when Stanislas II Poniatowski and Augustus III were disputing the throne of Poland, and was called His Majesty's Dancers. It was directed by a Frenchman, Le Doux, but his work was cut short by the overrunning of Poland. Round about 1820, however, cultural interchange resumed; French dancers visited Poland and Polish dancers travelled abroad to perfect their art. Under the imperial régime, ballets were performed once more, now on the vast stage of the New Grand Theatre, and included the full Romantic repertoire, from *La Sylphide* and *Giselle* to *Le Diable boiteux* and *La Esmeralda*. The *corps de ballet* was directed first by Filippo Taglioni and the dancer Roman Turczynowicz, then by some of the

232 The Komaki Company. Japanese classical ballet

greatest Italian masters, including Enrico Cecchetti. After the recovery of independence early in the twentieth century, Piotr Zalicha and Felix Parnell were in charge of the Warsaw Ballet, and endeavoured to build up a national repertoire. In the inter-war period a number of ballets with popular themes and with scores by Polish composers were created, and Arnold Szyfman, Bronislava Nijinska and Léon Woizikowsky were working in this distinctively Polish idiom when war cut short their efforts in 1940. After the war a new theatre rose out of the ruins of Warsaw and the ballet returned, with a repertoire of both classical and modern works and some distinguished stars, among them Olga Sawicka, Marta Bokota, Vitold Borkowsky, Stanislas Szymanky and Bogdan Bulder.

Canada's National Ballet was founded fairly late, in 1950 in Toronto, under the direction of the ballerina Celia Franca, who has played a large part in the development of Canadian ballet. The Montreal Ballet, founded by Ludmilla Chiriaeff, with Rosella Hightower and Anton Dolin as guest artists, has recently undertaken a long tour. It was the Canadian National Ballet which gave the great Soviet ballerina Galina Samsova her chance by letting her dance, triumphantly, in Raymundo Larrain's production of *Cinderella*, at the Théâtre des Champs-Élysées, Paris.

In Mexico, it is modern dancing that is popular with young audiences and appears in theatres all over the country. The dancer Guillermina Bravo, born in Veracruz, had studied with Waldeen before being invited by Charles Chavez, Director of the National Institute of Fine Arts, to direct the Mexican Academy of Dancing. She subsequently founded the National Ballet of Mexico, creating works with predominantly social themes, and dancing not only on stages but also at meetings and in public squares. Among the ballets she has created are *El Zanate* by Galindo, *Recuerdo a Zapata* by Mabarak, *The Sterile Cloud* by Noriega, and *Cuauhnàhuac* by Revueldas.

Roger Fenongeois, a French dancer from the Opéra, has given a great spur to ballet in Montevideo with the leading dancers Tola Leef, Raoul Severo and Eduardo Ramirez.

Cuba boasts an internationally famous star, Alicia Alonso. After studying with Fedorova and Vilzak and with the professor Vera Volkova, she was engaged with the American Ballet Theatre, and one night took over, at short notice, Alicia Markova's role in *Giselle*. Her performance was a triumph, and she went on to star in both classical and modern ballets, eventually founding a company. In 1947 she was decorated by the Cuban Government for her services to the arts in Cuba, and in 1950 gave up her dancing career for teaching, opening a school in Havana.

The Colon Theatre Ballet in Buenos Aires was created in 1925, and today numbers ninety strong. Dancers and choreographers work alternately in the theatre and in the vast amphitheatre situated close to the capital. A number of celebrities from abroad—Adolphe Bolm, George Skibine, Janine Charrat, John Taras, Serge Lifar—have made guest appearances in Buenos Aires to produce their works. The Colon Theatre's repertoire includes both classics and avant-garde ballets: *Swan Lake*, *Coppélia*, *Giselle*, but also *Agon*, Harrild y Moriana's *Usher*, Constantino Gaito's *The Town with the Golden Gates*, Ginestera's *Panambi*, *Estancia*, and *Variations Concertantes*, Gianneo's *Snow White*. Among its stars are Maria Ruanova, Dora del Grande, Lida Martinoli, Irina Borovska, Esmeralda Agoglia, Olga Ferri, Norma Fontenla, Enrique Lommi, Jorge Tomin, and Antonio Trujol. Argentina has also attracted international stars of the first rank such as Olga Spessivtzeva, Serge Lifar, Margot Fonteyn, Yvette Chauviré, Alicia Markova, Tamara Toumanova, Marjorie Tallchief and George Skibine.

The visit of the Ballets Jooss to Chile in 1940 provided the stimulus for the growth of ballet in that country. Ernst Uthoff was a member of the company when he was invited, with his wife Lola Botka and Rudolph Pescht, to open a school of dancing at the Music Institute of the University of Santiago. Today he is Director of the National Ballet of Chile, which has visited Argentina and appeared at Rio de Janeiro for the music festival held there in 1963. Its repertoire is entirely modern and consists mainly of works by Uthoff himself, such as *The Prodigal*, *Miracle at Almeda*, *The Tumbler*, *Images of Chile*.

It was a Czech, Edward Borovansky, who was responsible for the birth of ballet in Australia. This dancer-choreographer, born in Prerov in 1902, had danced with

Pavlova and then with the Ballets Russes de Monte Carlo before a tour took him to Sydney in 1939. Here he founded the Borovansky Australian Ballet, and in 1952 became Director of the new Borovansky Ballet Company. A number of Australian dancers have now joined companies abroad and have earned themselves a high reputation.

Ballet arrived in Tokyo after the First World War, when the Komaki Ballet was founded, based on the teaching of Eliane Pavlova, a Russian ballerina who had settled in Japan. Its first production was *Swan Lake* with Moniko Tani, the great Japanese star. In 1950, Sakiko Hirosi and Naoto Seki emerged as 'premiers danseurs', and two years later Sonia Arova (*Ill.* 222), Serge Lifar, Lycette Darsonval, then Nora Kaye, Antony Tudor, Margot Fonteyn, Barbara Steel and Nadia Grey were invited to Japan to perform classical ballets.

The history of ballet does not end here. It will undergo further transformations, responsive to all the external influences of our day, and international exchanges, ever more numerous and more effective, will shape it in the image of our modern world.

Without rejecting the rich legacy of the past, ballet will open up wider horizons, and vision, technique and artistry will combine to give us yet more young and original works. But it will always be, in the words of Paul Valéry, 'a grove whose lovely branches are forever tossing on the winds of music'.

List of Illustrations

Basse-Dance accompanied by viol and lute. Wood. Musée de Douai. Frontispiece.

1 Court dance. Treatise by Guglielmo Ebreo. 15th century. Paris, Bibliothèque Nationale 11

2 Rustic dance with a musician playing the bagpipes. Print Tuscany, Wolfenbüttel, Bibliothek 12

3 Illuminated frontispiece. Treatise by Guglielmo Ebreo, dedicated to Duke Galeazzo Sforza. 15th century. Paris, Bibliothèque Nationale 13

4 Marriage of Boccaccio Adimari and Lisa Ricasoli. Chest. Florence, Accademia 14-15

5 Dance with two men, a woman and musicians. Theatrum Sanitatis. Rome, Bibliotheca Casanatense..... 16

6 Dance of the Theological Virtues. Detail of fresco of the Church Militant by Andrea da Firenze. Florence, Santa Maria Novella (Photo Alinari).................... 17

7 Open-air dancing in Florence. Lorenzo the Magnificent and Poliziano. After 'le canzoni a ballo composte dal Magnifico Lorenzo de Medici'. (Photo Bibliothèque Nationale)...................................... 18

8 Fabritio Caroso, author of the treatise 'Il Ballarino'. Venice, 1581. Paris, Bibliothèque Nationale........ 20

9 Cesare Negri, author of the treatise 'Le Grazie d'Amore', 1602. Paris, Bibliothèque Nationale............... 21

10 The Battle. *Ballet à quatre* by Cesare Negri. Treatise 'Le Grazie d'Amore'. Paris, Bibliothèque Nationale. 23

11-14 *Saut du nœud. Fioretto.* First position for *double tour en l'air. Contre-pas* to verses by Ovid. Treatise of Fabritio Caroso, 'Il Ballarino', 1581. Paris, Bibliothèque Nationale 24

15 Preparation. From 'Il Ballarino'. Paris, Bibliothèque Nationale 25

16 Open-air dancing in Venice. Anonymous print in Pompeo Molmenti, 'Storia di Venezia nella vita privata', vol. 2. (Photo Rigal).......................... 25

17 Ballet put on by Catherine de 'Medici in honour of the Polish ambassadors, 1573. J. Daurat, 'Magnificentissimi spectaculi'. (Photo Bibliothèque Nationale)........ 26

18 Bracelli: design for ballet costume. (Photo Bibliothèque Nationale) 28

19 Bracelli: design for ballet costume. (Photo Bibliothèque Nationale) 29

20 Dancing at the court of Henri III. 16th century. Paris, Louvre 30

21 *Ballet comique de la Reine*, 1581. Entry and dance of the satyrs. From 'Le Ballet comique de la Royne', Balthasar de Beaujoyeux (1582). Paris, Bibliothèque Nationale 31

22 *Ballet comique de la Reine*, 1581. Entry and dance of the satyrs. From 'Le Ballet comique de la Royne', Balthasar de Beaujoyeux (1582). Paris, Bibliothèque Nationale 32

23 *Ballet comique de la Reine*, 1581. *Entrée.* From 'Le Ballet comique de la Royne', Balthasar de Beaujoyeux (1582). Paris, Bibliothèque Nationale..................... 33

24 *Ballet du Noël des Fleurs.* Florence, 1618. (Photo Bibliothèque Nationale).......................... 34

25 *Le Nozze dei Dei.* Dance of naiads and tritons. Florence, 1603. (Photo Bibliothèque Nationale)....... 36-7

26 Scene from *Les Dons du Roi des Alpes à Madame Royale.* Turin, Biblioteca del Re.................. 38

27 Scene from *Le Gris de Lin.* Illumination. Turin, Biblioteca del Re............................... 38

28 Ballet on horseback at the court of Turin. Illumination. Turin, Biblioteca del Re......................... 39

29 *Les Dons du Roi des Alpes à Madame Royale.* First tableau. Illumination. Turin, Biblioteca del Re..... 39

30 Ballet inspired by the Orient. Illumination. Turin, Biblioteca del Re............................... 40

31 Ballet inspired by the Orient. Illumination. Turin, Biblioteca del Re............................... 40

32 Choreography for ballet on horseback. Florence, 1615. (Photo Bibliothèque Nationale)............. 41

33 Choreography for ballet on horseback. Florence, 1615. (Photo Bibliothèque Nationale)............. 42

34 Choreography for ballet on horseback. Florence, 1615. (Photo Bibliothèque Nationale)............. 43

35 *Hercule à Thèbes*, Finale Opera by J. Melani. Florence, 1661. Paris, Bibliothèque Nationale.............. 44-5

36 *La Délivrance de Renaud*, 1617. The Duke of Luynes as Renaud. 'Discours au vray du ballet dansé par le Roy'. Paris, 1617. (Paris, Bibliothèque Nationale)........ 46

37 *La Délivrance de Renaud.* The King as a Fire Demon. 'Discours au vray du ballet dansé par le Roy'. Paris, 1617. (Paris, Bibliothèque Nationale) 46

38 Sixteenth - century masque. Detail of *Portrait of Henry Hunton.* (Photo National Gallery, London)... 47

39 *La Délivrance de Renaud.* Monsieur de Monpoullan as a Spirit of Air. 'Discours au vray du ballet dansé par le Roy'. Paris, 1617. Paris, Bibliothèque Nationale..... 48

40 *La Délivrance de Renaud.* 'Discours au vray du ballet dansé par le Roy'. Paris, 1617. Paris, Bibliothèque Nationale 49

41 *Hercule à Thèbes*, Act II. Dance of the young girls at Samos. Opera by J. Melani, 1661. Venice, Biblioteca Marciana 51

42 *Ballet de la Jeunesse.* Paris, Bibliothèque de l'Opéra. 52

43 Charles-Louis Beauchamp (1636-1719). Paris, Bibliothèque de l'Opéra.............................. 54

44 Jean-Baptiste Lully (1632-1687). Paris, Bibliothèque de l'Opéra 54

45 Louis Pécourt (1655-1729). Paris, Bibliothèque de l'Opéra 55

46 Jean Ballon (1676-1739). Paris, Bibliothèque de l'Opéra 55

47 Marie-Thérèse de Subligny (1666-1736). Paris, Bibliothèque de l'Opéra......................... 55

48 Translation of Feuillet's treatise by John Weaver. Paris, Bibliothèque de l'Opéra..................... 56

49 German translation of Feuillet's treatise. Paris, Bibliothèque de l'Opéra 56

50 The three arts of a gentleman: fencing, dancing and horsemanship. Frontispiece of the Ritter Lexikon, 1742. Paris, Bibliothèque de l'Opéra 56

51 Molière (1622-1673). Paris, Bibliothèque de l'Opéra 57

52 *La Nuit*, 1653. Louis XIV as the Sun. Paris, Bibliothèque Nationale, Print Collection 57

53 Jean-Georges Noverre. Paris, Bibliothèque de l'Opéra 58

54 Marie-Madeleine Guimard (1743-1816). Paris, Bibliothèque de l'Opéra 61

55 Marie-Anne de Camargo, by Vigée-Lebrun, *c.* 1780 (Photo Bulloz) 63

56 *Pas de deux* from *Sylvie*. Dauberval and Marie Allard. Paris, Bibliothèque de l'Opéra 64

57 Marie Sallé. Paris, Bibliothèque de l'Opéra. (Photo Somogy) 65

58 Ballet headdress. Drawing by Boquet. Paris, Bibliothèque de l'Opéra 66

59 Dauberval in *La Reine de Jolconde*. Paris, Bibliothèque de l'Opéra 67

60 Auguste Vestris. By Romany (Adèle de Romance). Paris, Bibliothèque de l'Opéra 68

61 La Campilli in *Zoraida* at La Scala. Paris, Bibliothèque de l'Opéra, Collection Silvestri 70

62 Michele Fabiani. Milan, Collection Bertarelli ... 73

63 Décor for *Les Cannibales vaincus*. Moscow, Bakhruchine Museum 75

64 Pierre Gardel (1758-1840). Munich, Theatrical Museum 76

65 La Barbarina in a *ballet champêtre*. Munich, Theatrical Museum. 76

66 Peter Crux. Munich, Theatrical Museum 77

67 Antoine Bournonville. (Photo Royal Opera Theatre, Copenhagen) 78

68 Vincenzo Galeotti. (Photo Royal Opera Theatre, Copenhagen) 79

69 Costume design. Watercolour by G.A. Braganza. 18th century. Milan, Theatrical Museum of La Scala. 80

70-71 Maria de Caro. Engravings by G. Lasinio, 1797. Milan, Theatrical Museum of La Scala 82

72 Rehearsal of a pastoral ballet by Pietro Longhi. Oil painting. Milan, Theatrical Museum of La Scala 84

73 Antonio Muzzarelli. Milan, Collection Bertarelli. 85

74 Gaetano Gioja. Milan, Theatrical Museum of La Scala 86

75, 77 The Viganos. Drawings by Shadow. Berlin, Wissenschaftliche Bibliothek 88-9

76 The elder Vigano. Drawing by Cherubino Cornienti, 1835. Milan, Theatrical Museum of La Scala 88

78 Salvatore Vigano (1769-1821). Paris, Bibliothèque de l'Opéra 89

79 The Viganos. Drawings by Shadow. Berlin, Wissenschaftliche Bibliothek 90

80 Maria Medina Vigano. Milan, Theatrical Museum of La Scala 91

81 *The Vestal Virgin*. La Scala, 1818. Ballet by Salvatore Vigano. Décor: A. Sanquirico. Munich, Theatrical Museum 92

82 Samengo and Amalia Brugnoli in *The Magic Ring*. Drawing by Levasseur, 1832. Milan, Collection Bertarelli 94

83 Maximilien Gardel (1741-1787). Paris, Bibliothèque de l'Opéra 96

84 Jean-Pierre Aumer. Paris, Bibliothèque de l'Opéra 97

85 Emilia Bigottini (1784-1858). Paris, Bibliothèque de l'Opéra 97

86 Marie Taglioni. Paris, Bibliothèque de l'Opéra .. 98

87 *Pas de deux* from *Giselle*. Romantic lithograph. (Photo Rigal) 99

88 Carlotta Grisi in *La Péri*. Paris, Opéra, 1843. Lithograph. Paris, Bibliothèque de l'Opéra 100

89 Lucile Grahn in *La Esmeralda*. Munich, Theatrical Museum 100

90 Poster for the première of *Giselle*, at the Opéra, 1841 101

91 Marie Taglioni in *La Sylphide*. Paris, Bibliothèque de l'Opéra 102

92 Carlotta Grisi and Jules Perrot dancing the Polka. Munich, Theatrical Museum 103

93 Fanny Elssler in *La Esmeralda* at the Theatre of St Petersburg. Moscow, Bakhruchine Museum 104

94 Set for *La Fille du Danube*. Moscow, Bakhruchine Museum. 105

95 Carlotta Grisi, Marie Taglioni, Fanny Cerrito and Lucile Grahn in Jules Perrot's *Pas de Quatre*, 1845. Milan, Theatrical Museum of La Scala 106

96 Jean Coralli. Milan, Theatrical Museum of La Scala 107

97 Marie Taglioni in *Joko, le Singe brésilien*. Paris, Bibliothèque de l'Opéra 108

98 Carlotta Grisi and Lucien Petipa in *Giselle*. 'Pas des Vendanges'. Paris, Bibliothèque de l'Opéra 109

99 Nathalie Fitzjames (b. 1819). Paris, Bibliothèque de l'Opéra 109

100 Jules Perrot's *Pas de Quatre*. Marie Taglioni's curtain call. Paris, Bibliothèque de l'Opéra 109

101 Carlo Blasis (b.1795). Paris, Bibliothèque de l'Opéra 110

102 Sofia Fuoco (1830-1916), in *La Rosière*. Paris, Bibliothèque de l'Opéra 112

103 Olimpia Priora (b. 1836). Paris, Bibliothèque de l'Opéra 113

104 Elena Andreianova. (Photo Bakhruchine Museum) 114

105 Carolina Rosati. Paris, Bibliothèque de l'Opéra. 114

106 Amalia Ferraris (1830-1904). Paris, Bibliothèque de l'Opéra 115

107 Set for the original *Coppélia* at the Paris Opéra, 28th May 1870. Paris, Bibliothèque de l'Opéra 116

108 Arthur de Saint-Léon (1821-1870). Paris, Bibliothèque de l'Opéra 118

109 Fanny Cerrito and Antonio Guerra in *Le Lac des Fées*. Paris, Opéra, 1839. Music: Auber. Paris, Bibliothèque de l'Opéra. (Photo Somogy) 119

110 The Eden Theatre. 'Monde Illustré', 1894. Paris, Bibliothèque Nationale 120

111 Carolina Pochini. Milan, Collection Bertarelli. 122

112 *Excelsior*. Ballet by Manzotti, at the Jovellanos Theatre, Madrid. Paris, Bibliothèque de l'Opéra 123

113 *Amor*. Ballet by Manzotti. La Scala, 1886. 'Teatro Illustrato', 1886. Paris, Bibliothèque de l'Opéra 124

114 Caterina Beretta. Milan, Collection Bertarelli. 124

115 Louis Mérante (1828-1877). Paris, Bibliothèque de l'Opéra 125

116 Zina Richard. Paris, Bibliothèque de l'Opéra .. 125

117 *Korrigane*, performed at the Paris Opéra. (Photo Pic) 126

118 Virginia Zucchi, by Clairin. (Photo Pic) 127

119 Carlotta Brianza in *La Esmeralda*. Moscow, Bakhruchine Museum 128

120 Pierina Legnani in *Le Corsaire*. Moscow, Bakhruchine Museum 128

121 *The Sleeping Beauty*. Olga Preobrajenska in the role of the White Cat. Moscow, Bakhruchine Museum 129

122 Enrico Cecchetti (1850-1928). (Photo Private Collection) 129

123 Rostavleva (*centre*) in *The Sleeping Beauty* at the Bolshoi. Moscow, 1899, Production by Gorsky after Petipa. Moscow, Bakhruchine Museum 130

124 Marius Petipa. Paris, Bibliothèque de l'Opéra. 131

125 Marie Petipa in *Le Marché des Innocents*, ballet of Marius Petipa. Paris, Opéra, 1861. Paris, Bibliothèque de l'Opéra 131

126 *The Nutcracker* at the Maryinsky Theatre, St Petersburg. Moscow, Bakhruchine Museum 133

127 *Swan Lake* at the Maryinsky Theatre, St Petersburg. Moscow, Bakhruchine Museum 133

128 Serge de Diaghilev. Sculpture by Gurdjan. (Photo Markevich) 134

129 Costume by Alexandre Benois for *Petrouchka*. Paris, Bibliothèque de l'Opéra. (Photo Giraudon) 137

130 Anna Pavlova in *The Dying Swan*. Choreography: Fokine; music: Saint-Saëns. (Photo Private Collection) 139

131 Vera Trefilova. Moscow, Bakhruchine Museum 140

132 Catherine Geltzer in *La Bayadère*. Moscow, Bakhruchine Museum 140

133 Tamara Karsavina in *The Firebird*. Moscow, Bakhruchine Museum 140

134 Tamara Karsavina, by Jacques-Émile Blanche. 141

135 Michel Fokine. (Photo Pic) 142

136 Nijinsky, Tamara Karsavina and Ludmilla Schollar in *Jeux*. (Photo Pic) 142

137 Costume by Léon Bakst for *Cléopâtre*. (Photo Pic) 143

138 Vaslav Nijinsky in *Giselle*. Paris, Bibliothèque de l'Opéra 143

139 Léonide Massine in *Soleil de Nuit*. (Photo Pic) .. 144

140 Tamara Toumanova and Léonide Massine in *The Three-Cornered Hat*. (Photo Ballets Russes de Monte Carlo) 145

141 Backcloth by André Derain for *La Boutique Fantasque*. (Photo Pic) 146

142 Design by Picasso for a Chinese costume in *Parade*, 1917. Paris, Bibliothèque de l'Opéra 147

143 Curtain for *Parade*, designed by Picasso, 1917. Paris, Musée des Arts Décoratifs 150

144 Costumes by Larionov for *Renard*, 1922. (Photo Bibliothèque de l'Opéra) 151

145 Design by Marie Laurencin for *Les Biches*, 1924. (Photo Giraudon) 151

146 *Les Mariés de la Tour Eiffel*. The Ballets Suédois at the Théâtre des Champs-Élysées in 1921 152

147 Curtain by Irène Lagut for *Les Mariés de la Tour Eiffel*. (Photo Pic) 154

148 René Blum (1878-1942). (Photo Private Collection) 155

149 Colonel de Basil (d. 1951). (Photo Private Collection) 155

150 Costume by André Derain for *Concurrence* 156

151 Costumes designed by Christian Bérard 156

152 Alexandra Danilova. Paris, Bibliothèque de l'Opéra 157

153 Tamara Toumanova. (Photo Ballets Russes de Monte Carlo) 157

154 Alicia Markova and Igor Youskevich in *Seventh Symphony*, 1938. Ballets de Monte Carlo. Choreography: Léonide Massine; music: Beethoven; décor and costumes: Christian Bérard 158

155 *Corps de ballet*. (Photo Studio Iris) 160

156 Solange Schwartz. (Photo Liptnitzky) 163

157 Olga Spessivtzeva and Serge Lifar in *Bacchus and Ariadne* by A. Roussel. Costumes: de Chirico. (Photo Liptnitzky) 163

158 *Oriane et le Prince d'amour*, Paris, Opéra, 1938. Book: Claude Séran; choreography: Serge Lifar; music: F. Schmitt; décor and costumes: P. Pruna. (Photo Liptnitzky). 164

159 Yvette Chauviré. (Photo Bibliothèque de l'Opéra) 165

160 *Suite en Blanc*, Paris, Opéra, 1943. Choreography: Serge Lifar; Score arranged by Namouna, after music by Lalo; décor: Dignimont. (Photo Lido) 166

161 *Joan de Zarissa*. Finale at the Paris Opéra in 1942. Choreography: Serge Lifar; music: Werner Egk; décor: Yves Brayer. (Photo Bibliothèque de l'Opéra) 167

162 Madeleine Lafon. (Photo Liseg) 168

163 *Études*. Paris, Opéra, 1952. Choreography: H. Lander; music: Czerny, arr. K. Riisager; décor: Moulène. Created in 1948 at the Royal Opera, Copenhagen. (Photo Lido) 168

164 Nina Vyroubova. (Photo Lido) 169

165 Marjorie Tallchief and George Skibine in *Daphnis and Chloe.* Paris, Opéra, 1959. Choreography: George Skibine; music: Ravel; décor and costumes: Marc Chagall. (Photo Liptnitzky) 169

166 Michel Descombey in *Qarrtsiluni,* 1940. Chor.: H. Lander; music: K. Riisager; décor: Bernard Daydé. Created at the Royal Opera, Copenhagen in 1942. Revised at the Paris Opéra in 1960. (Photo Pic) 170

167 Jacqueline Rayet and Peter van Dijk in *Giselle.* Leading dancers of the Paris Opéra. Décor: Carzou. (Photo Pic) 171

168 Claude Bessy and Attilio Labis in *Swan Lake.* Leading dancers of the Paris Opéra. (Photo Pic) 171

169 Study for *Swan Lake.* Jacqueline Rayet. (Photo Pic) 172

170 Josette Amiel and Flemming Flindt. Leading dancers of the Paris Opéra in a *pas de deux.* (Photo Koruna) 172

171 *Les Liens.* Toulouse, 1957. Choreography: Janine Charrat; music: J. Semenoff; décor and costumes: Bernard Daydé. (Photo Lido) 173

172 Zizi Jeanmaire in *Carmen.* London, Prince's Theatre, 1949. Choreography: Roland Petit; music: Bizet; décor and costumes: A. Clavé. (Photo Lido) 174

173 Zizi Jeanmaire and Roland Petit in *Carmen.* London, Prince's Theatre, 1949. Choreography: Roland Petit; music: Bizet; décor and costumes: A. Clavé. (Photo Baron Studios) 175

174 Set by Clavé for *Deuil en vingt-quatre heures.* Paris, Théâtre de l'Empire, 1953. Choreography: Roland Petit; music: Thiriet; décor: A. Clavé. (Photo Liptnitzky). 175

175 Serge Perrault and Colette Marchand in *Deuil en vingt-quatre heures.* Paris, Théâtre de l'Empire, 1953. Choreography: Roland Petit; music: Thiriet; décor: A. Clavé. (Photo Lido) 175

176 Maurice Béjart in *Voilà l'Homme.* Paris, Théâtre Fontaine, des Quatre Saisons, 1955. Choreography: Maurice Béjart; music: Philippe Arthuys; décor: Jean Desvilles; costumes: A. Fabra. (Photo Khiel) 176

177 *Haut Voltage.* The Janine Charrat Company at the Théâtre Marigny, Paris, in 1957. Book: Pierre Rallys; choreography: Maurice Béjart; décor: Abel Rillard. (Photo Khiel) 176

178 Claire Motte in *Swan Lake.* A leading dancer at the Opéra. (Photo Studio Iris) 178

179 Rudolf von Laban (b. 1879). (Photo Private Collection) 180

180 Mary Wigman. (Photo Orgel-Köhne) 182

181 Mary Wigman correcting a group. (Photo Orgel-Köhne) 183

182 Kurt Jooss. (Photo Enkelmann) 184

183 *Rite of Spring.* Berlin, State Opera House, 1957. Choreography: Mary Wigman. (Photo Enkelmann) 187

184 *Swan Lake,* Act II. Royal Ballet Company, Covent Garden. (Photo Houston Rogers) 188

185 P.J.S. Richardson (b. 1875). (Photo Private Collection) 189

186 Cyril Beaumont. (Photo Paul Welson) 190

187 Arnold Haskell (b. 1903). (Photo Private Collection) 190

188 Marie Rambert (b. 1888). (Photo B.B.C.) . 191

189 Sir Frederick Ashton, director of the Royal Ballet Company, Covent Garden. (Photo Royal Ballet) . 191

190 John Gilpin and Violette Verdy. (Photo Seymour). 192

191 Nathalie Krassovska. (Photo Festival Ballet). 192

192 Svetlana Beriosova in *Giselle.* (Photo Royal Ballet). 193

193 Alicia Markova and Anton Dolin in *The Nutcracker.* (Photo Festival Ballet) 193

194 Dame Ninette de Valois, founder of the Royal Ballet. (Photo Royal Ballet) 194

195 Margot Fonteyn and Rudolph Nureyev in *Swan Lake.* (Photo Studio Iris) 195

196 June Sandbook and ensemble in *Night Shadow.* Choreography: George Balanchine; music: Bellini-Rieti; décor and costumes: Alix Stone. Ballet Rambert. (Photo Blomfield) 197

197 Finale from *Hazana.* Choreography: Norman Morrice; music: Surmach; décor and costumes: Ralph Koltai. Ballet Rambert. (Photo Blomfield) 197

198 *Flames of Paris.* Kirov Theatre, Leningrad, 1932. Choreography: V. Vainonen; music: A. Safiev. (Photo Off. Cult. Sov.) 198

199 Exercises, Bolshoi Theatre, Moscow *(left to right)* Galina Ulanova, Eugenia Farmaniantz and Erina Tikhomirova 200

200 Yuri Zhdanov in *Romeo and Juliet.* Ballet of Prokofiev. Choreography: Lavrovsky; décor: Williams. Kirov Theatre, Leningrad, 1940. (Photo A. Vororinsky). 201

201 Constantin Sergeyev in *Swan Lake.* Kirov Theatre, Leningrad, 1940. (Photo A. Vorotinsky) 201

202 Inna Zoubkovskaia in *The Stone Flower.* (Photo B. Riabinine) 202

203 *Gavroche.* Kirov Theatre, Leningrad. Ballet by Varkovitzky. (Photo Off. Cult. Sov.) 203

204 L. Alexeieva in *The Flight of the Seagull.* (Photo Off. Cult. Sov.) 204

205 Anatole Sapogov. (Photo Vorotinsky) 204

206 *The Cape of Good Hope.* Scene of the shark hunt. (Photo Riabinine) 204

207 *Spartacus.* Kirov Theatre, Leningrad, 1956. Choreography: Yacobson; music: Khatchaturian; décor: Khodasievich. (Photo Vorotinsky) 204

208 The Russian ballet. Folk dancing company.. 205

209 The American ballet in *The Sleeping Beauty.* (Photo Studio Iris) 208

210 Martha Graham and Eric Hawkins in *Night Journey.* 211

211 *Till Eulenspiegel.* New York City Ballet, New York City Center, 1951. Choreography: George Balanchine. (Photo New York City Ballet) 213

212 Lincoln Kirstein. (Photo New York City Ballet) 214

213 American Ballet Theatre. Ruth Ann Koesun. (Photo American Ballet) 215

214 Nora Kaye and Nicholas Magallanes in *The Cage*. New York City Ballet, New York City Center, 1951. Choreography: J. Robbins; music: Stravinsky; costumes: R. Sobotka. (Photo New York City Ballet) 215

215 Nina Vyroubova and Serge Golovine in *Tarassiana*. Marquis de Cuevas Company, 1951. Choreography: John Taras. (Photo Marquis de Cuevas Company) 215

216 André Eglevsky. (Photo New York City Ballet) 216

217 Maria Tallchief in *Four Temperaments*. (Photo New York City Ballet) 216

218 Marjorie Tallchief and George Skibine in *Idylle*. (Photo Lido) 216

219 *Age of Anxiety*. New York City Ballet. (Photo New York City Ballet) 217

220 The Marquis de Cuevas Company in *Le Mal du Siècle*. Choreography: James Starbuch; music: Alex North. (Photo Lido) 218

221 The Chicago Opera Ballet in *L'Amour Sorcier*. Chicago Opera Ballet. Choreography: Ruth Page. (Photo Ruth Page) 219

222 Sonia Arova and Rudolph Nureyev in *The Merry Widow*. Chicago Opera Ballet. Choreography: Ruth Page. (Photo Ruth Page) 220-1

223 Isadora Duncan. Lithograph by Bourdelle.. 222

224 Giulio Perugini and Violetta Elvin in *Swan Lake*. La Scala, Milan, 1952. (Photo Piccagliani)....... 224

225 Michèle Seigneuret and Maurice Béjart in *Haut Voltage*. (Photo Khiel) 227

226 Henning Kronslam, Mette Mollerup, Kirsten Bundgaard, Kirsten Simone in *Apollo Musagetes*. Royal Opera Theatre, Copenhagen. Choreography: George Balanchine; music: Igor Stravinsky. (Photo Royal Opera Copenhagen) 227

227 Maria Koppers and Billy Wilson in *Jungle*. Het National Ballet, The Hague. Choreography: Rudi van Dantzig; electronic music: Hens Badings. (Photo Joop Gans) 227

228 Margareta von Bahr and Klaus Salin in *Miss Julie*. At the Finnish National Opera. Choreography: Birgitt Cullberg. (Photo Taisto Tuomi)................ 228

229 Antonio (b. 1923). (Photo Private Collection) 228

230 *Mazeppa*. Warsaw Ballet. Book: Irena Turska; music: Tadeuz Szeligowski. (Photo Off. Cult. Pol.). 229

231 *Giselle*. Production of the Finnish National Opera. (Photo Taisto Tuomi)........................ 230-1

232 The Komaki Company. Japanese classical ballet 232

Index of Ballets

The following abbreviations are employed: chor.: choreography; scen.: scenario; mus.: music; déc.: décor; cost.: costumes; prem.: première; cast.: principal members of the cast; Th.: Theatre/Théâtre; rev. prod.: revised production; Cov. Gdn.: Covent Garden; Royal Opera House, Ballets de M.C.: Ballets Russes de Monte-Carlo; Ballets Russes: Ballets Russes de Diaghilev; Ballets des Ch.-E.: Ballets des Champs-Élysées; N.Y. City Ballet: New York City Ballet; Ballets du Basil: Ballets Russes du Colonel de Basil (later, the Original Ballet Russe); Ballet de Cuevas: Grand Ballet du Marquis de Cuevas. Number in italic refer to the illustrations.

Abducted Wife, The (C. Taglioni), 85
Abeilles, Les (Staats/Stravinsky), 161
Abraxas. 5 tableaux. Chor.: Charrat; mus. and book: Egk; déc. and cost.: Fenneker; 1st perf.: 8 Oct. 1949, Berlin, Städtische Oper; cast: Charrat, Orban, 174
Achille à Scyros (Achilles in Scyros) (M. Gardel), 68; (Metastasio), 83
Acrobats of God (Graham), 211
Adam and Eve Driven from Paradise, 20
Adèle de Ponthieu (Noverre), 86
Aeneas in Italy (Hilferding), 83
Agamemnon (Laban), 182
Age of Anxiety. Chor.: Robbins; mus.: Bernstein; déc.: Smith; book: after poem by W.H. Auden; 1st perf.: 26 Feb. 1950, N.Y. City Center, N.Y. City Ballet; cast: Leclerq, Bolender, Moncio, Robbins, **224**, *219*
Aglaé ou l'élève de l'amour (F. Taglioni), 101
Agon, 216, 234
Aladdin or the Wonderful Lamp (Hoguet), 77
Alceste (Beauchamp), 57
Alcidiane (Beauchamp), 57
Alcine, 46
Algues. 4 acts. Chor.: Charrat; mus.: Bernard; déc. and cost.: Castelli; 1st perf.: 20 April 1953, Paris, Th. des Ch.-E.; Ballets de Janine Charrat; cast: Charrat, van Dijk, Fris, Piéral, 177
Allegra Piazzetta (Milloss), 225
Alma ou la Fille de Feu (Perrot), 100
Alzire (Voltaire/Hilferding), 71
Amor. Chor.: Manzotti; mus.: Marenco; déc. and cost.: Edel; 1st perf.: 17 Feb. 1886, La Scala, Milan, *113*
Amour et l'hymen au village, L' (Coralli), 103
Amour et son amour, L'. 1 act. Chor.: Babilée; mus.: Franck; déc. and cost.: Cocteau; 1st perf.: Paris, Th. des Ch.-E.; cast: Babilée, Philippart, 174
Amour plus fort que la Mort, L' (Sacco), 79
Amour Sorcier, L' (Page), *221*
Amour va vite, L' (Gorsky), 199
Amours de Cupidon, Les (Galeotti/Lander), 79
Amours de Jupiter, Les 5 tableaux. Chor.: Petit; mus. Ibert; book: Kochno, after Ovid 'Metamorphoses'; déc. and cost.: Hugo; 1st perf.: 5 March 1946, Paris, Th. des Ch.-E., Ballets des Ch.-E.; cast: Schwartz, Skorik, Philippart, Pagava, Nevada, Petit, Babilée, 173
Amours Déguisées, Les (Beauchamp), 57
Amphion (Rubinstein/Valéry), 154
Antigone, 81
Antoine et Cléopâtre (Noverre), 62; (Aumer) 96
Antonia (Gore/Sibelius), 191
Apollo Musagetes. 2 tableaux. Arg. and mus.: Stravinsky; chor.: Bolm; 1st perf.: 27 April 1928, Washington, Library of Congress; cast: Bolm, Page, Holmes, Reiman. Chor.: Balanchine; déc.: Bauchant; cost.: Chanel; 1st perf.: 12 June 1928, Paris, Th. Sarah-Bernhardt, Ballets Russes; cast: Lifar, Tchernicheva, Doubrovska, 149, *226*
Apollo Placato (Canziani), 86
Apollon, 48
Apothéose d'Hercule (Noverre), 77
Appalachian Spring (Graham), 211
Après-midi d'un Faune, Prélude à l' (Debussy/Mallarmé), 140, 142
Armida (e), 50; (Coralli) 103; (Charrat/Rossini), 174
Art Conquered by Nature, 85
Assembly Ball (Howard/Bizet), 194
Astuzie Femminili (Massine), 146
Ataxerxes (Rinaldi), 74
Atys (Beauchamp), 57
Aurora's Wedding. Chor.: Petipa, additional dances by Nijinska; mus.: Tchaikovsky; déc.: Benois; cost.: Benois, Goncharova; 1st perf.: 18 May 1922, Paris, Opéra, Ballets Russes; cast: Trefilova, Vladimirov, 148
Aventure de Tancrède dans la forêt enchantée, L', 48

Bacchanales, Les, 50
Bacchus and Ariadne (Roussel), *157*
Baiser de la fée, Le. 4 acts. Chor.: Nijinska; mus.: Stravinsky; déc. and cost.: Benois; 1st perf.: 27 Nov. 1928, Paris, Opéra, Ida Rubinstein Co; cast: Rubinstein, Schollar, Vilzak, 154
Bal, Le. 2 tableaux. Chor.: Balanchine; mus.: Rieti; déc. and cost.: de Chirico; book: Kochno; 1st perf.: 7 May 1929, Monte Carlo, Ballets Russes; cast: Danilova, Dolin, 149
Bal des Ardents, 42
Bal des blanchisseuses, Le. Chor.: Petit; mus.: Duke; déc. and cost.: Lepu; book: Kochno; 1st perf.: 19 Déc. 1946, Paris, Th. des Ch.-E., Ballets des Ch.-E.; cast: Darmance, Petit, 173
Bal masqué, Le (Henry), 95
Balance à trois. 1 act. Chor.: Babilée; mus.: Damase; déc. and cost.: Keogh; book: Nepo and Babilée; 1st perf.: 25 April 1955, Th. de M.C., Ballets Jean Babilée; cast: Chauviré, Kaliougny, Babilée, 174
Ball in Old Vienna. 1 act. Chor.: Jooss; mus.: Lanner; déc. and cost.: Sumola; 1st perf.: Essen, 1932, Ballets Jooss, 184
Ballad of a Medieval Love Story (Lotka), 231
Ballet comique de la Reine, Le. Chor.: Beaujoyeux; mus.: de Beaulieu and Thibault de Courville; déc.: Patin; book: La Chesnay; 1st perf.: 15 Oct. 1581; Paris, Hôtel de Bourbon, Louvre, 31, 33, 42, *21*, *23*
Ballet de la Jeunesse, *42*
Ballet de la Reine représentant la beauté, Le, 43
Ballet des Arts, Le (Beauchamp), 57
Ballet des Effets de la Nature (Morel), 50
Ballet des Saisons, Le (Beauchamp), 57
Ballet du Château de Bicêtre (Corneille), 50
Ballet du Noël des Fleurs, *24*
Ballo dell'ingrate, Il (Rinuccini/Monteverdi), 35
Bar aux Folies-Bergère (de Valois), 190
Barabau (Balanchine), 149
Barbier de Séville (S. Taglioni), 103
Barbieri, I, 21

Barn Dance (Littlefield), 214
Bayadère, La, *132*, 140
Beach. 3 tableaux. Chor.: Massine; mus.: Françaix; déc. and cost.: Dufy; book: Herdyk; 1st perf.: 18 April 1933, Monte Carlo, Ballets de M.C.; cast: Lichine, Riabouchinska, Baronova, 155
Beau Danube, Le. Chor.: Massine; mus.: J. Strauss, orch. Désormière; déc. after Guys; cost.: Beaumont; 1st perf.: 17 May 1924. Paris, Th. de la Cigale; cast: Lopokova, Massine. Rev. prod.: 1 act, 2 tableaux; 15 April 1933, Ballets de M.C.; cast: Massine, Danilova, Lichine, 154, 155
Belle Hélène, La. 4 tableaux. Chor.: Cranko; mus.: Offenbach, arr. Aubert and Rosenthal; déc. and cost.: Vertès; book: Achard and Manuel; 1st perf.: 6 April 1955, Paris, Opéra; cast: Chauviré, Renault, Bozzoni, Bessy, 167
Berger et la Fée, Le (Galeotti), 79
Biblical Pictures (Cramer), 230
Biches, Les. 1 act. Chor.: Nijinska; mus.: Poulenc; déc. and cost.: Laurencin; 1st perf.: 6 Jan. 1924, Th. de M.C., Ballets Russes; cast: Nemchinova, Tchernicheva, Nijinska, Woizikowsky, Vilzak, Zvereff, Rev. prod.: Nijinska, London, Cov. Gdn, 1964, 148, 151, *145*
Big City, The. 3 tableaux. Chor.: Jooss; mus.: Tansman; déc. and cost.: Heckroth; 1st perf.: 21 Nov. 1932, Cologne, Opera, Ballets Jooss; cast: Leeder, 184
Billy the Kid (Loring), 214
Blacks and Whites (Rota), 121
Bluebeard. 2 prologues, 4 acts, 3 interludes. Book and chor.: Fokine; mus.: Offenbach; déc.: Vertès; 1st perf.: 27 Oct. 1941, Mexico, Palacio de Bellas Artes, Ballet Theatre Co.; cast: Dolin, Markova, Borona, Chase, 157
Boemi, 1 (Ricci), 38
Bolero. 1 act. Chor.: Nijinska; mus.: Ravel; déc.: Benois; 1st perf.: 22 Nov. 1928; Paris, Opéra; cast: Rubinstein, Vilzak, 154, 184
Boris Godunov, 135
Bourgeois Gentilhomme, Le. 2 tableaux, after Molière. Chor.: Balanchine; mus.: Strauss; curtain, déc. and cost.: Benois; 1st perf.: 3 May 1932, Monte Carlo, Ballets de M.C.; cast: Lichine, 57
Boutique Fantasque, La. Chor.: Massine; mus.: Rossini, arr. Respighi; curtain, déc. and cost.: Derain; 1st perf. 5 June 1919, London, Alhambra Th., Ballets Russes; cast: Lopokova, Massine, Nemchinova, Tchernicheva, Nijinska, Woizikowsky, Vilzak, Zvereff, 146, *141*
Brésilia (F. Taglioni), 101
Brigands, Les (M. Petipa), 131
Britannicus (Racine/Hilferding), 71
But, 169

Cadmus et Hermione (Beauchamp), 57
Caesar in Egypt (Gioja), 87
Cage, The. Chor.: Robbins; mus.: Stravinsky; cost.: Sobotka; 1st perf.: 14 June 1951, N.Y. City Center, N.Y. City Ballet; cast: Kaye, Mounsey, Magallanes, 215, *214*
Caméléopard (Babilée/Sauguet), 174
Cannibales Vaincus, Les, *63*
Cantique des Cantiques, Le (Lifar/Honegger), 163
Cape of Good Hope, The, 206
Caprices de Cupidon, Les (Lander/Lolle), 165
Caprices de Galatée (Noverre), 66
Caprices de l'Amour et du Maître de Danse (Galeotti), 79
Caprices du Papillon, Les, 203
Caprichos (Ross/Stravinsky), 226
Captain Cook in the Indies (Muzzarelli), 87
Carmen. 5 tableaux. Chor.: Petit; mus.: Bizet; déc. and cost.: Clavé; 1st perf.: 21 Feb. 1949, London, Prince's Th., Ballets de Paris; cast: Jeanmaire, Petit, Perrault, Hamilton, 174, *172*, *173*
Carnival of Animals. 1 act. Chor. and déc.: Howard; mus.: Saint-Saëns; 1st perf.: 26 March 1943, London, Mercury Th., Ballet Rambert, 191
Cato (J.C. Bach), 83
Cave of the Heart (Graham), 211
Cefalo (Caccini and Rinuccini), 43
Cendrillon, see Cinderella
Chambre, La. 1 act. Chor.: Petit; mus.: Auric; déc. and cost.: Buffet; book: Simenon; 1st perf.: 20 Dec. 1955, Paris, Th. des Ch.-E., Ballets de Paris; cast: Mlakar, Miller, 174
Charm of Love, The, 40
Château des esprits, Le (Bonnachon), 95
Chatte, La. 1 act. Chor.: Balanchine; mus.: Sauguet; déc. and cost.: Gabo and Pevsner; book: Kochno; 1st perf.: 30 April 1927, Monte Carlo, Ballets Russes, cast: Spessivtzeva, Lifar, 149
Checkmate (de Valois), 192
Chercheuse d'Esprit, La. Ballet-pantomime, 1 act. Chor.: M. Gardel; perf.: Choisy; Fontainebleau, 1777; Paris, Acad. Royale de Musique, 1 March 1778; cast: Guimard, Allard, Dauberval, Despréaux, M. and P. Gardel, 68
Chevalier et la Damoiselle, Le. 2 act. Chor.: Lifar; mus.: Gaubert; déc. and cost.: Cassandre; 1st perf.: 2 July 1941, Paris, Opéra; cast: Schwartz, Chauviré, Lifar, Peretti, Coubé, Jeanmaire, 165
Chinese in Europe, The (Angiolini), 73
Chinese Nightingale, The (Gsovska), 186
Christine de Suède (S. Taglioni), 103
Cinderella (Cendrillon), (Decombe) 96; 127; Ballet in 3 acts, after tale by Perrault; (Laban), 182; 3 acts. Chor.: Ashton; mus.: Prokofiev; déc.: Malclès; 1st perf.: 23 Dec. 1948, London, Cov. Gdn, Sadler's Wells; cast: Shearer, Somes, 194; Perf. 1963, Paris, Th. des Ch.-E.; chor.: Orlikowski; mus.: Prokofiev; prod.: Orlikowski and Larrain; déc. and cost.: Larrain, 233
Cinq Sens de la Nature, Les (Morel), 50
Circé (d'Agliè), 38
Circe's Enchanted Island (Salomoni), 85
Classical Symphony (Bartholin/Prokofiev), 228
Cleopatra (Cléopâtre), (Angiolini), 73; 1 act. Chor.: Fokine; mus.: Arensky, with additions by Taneev, Rimsky-Korsakov, Glinka, Mussorgsky and Glazunov; déc. and cost.: Bakst; 1st perf.: 2 June 1909, Paris, Th. du Châtelet, Ballets Russes; cast: Pavlova, Rubinstein, Karsavina, Nijinsky, Fokine, 136, *137*
Cleopatra's Feast, 75
Clytemnestra (Graham), 211
Code of Terpsichor, 111
Cœur de Pain d'épice (Baranovich and Parlich), 231
Comédiens jaloux, Les (Nijinska), 155
Concertette (Bruhn), 228
Concerto Grosso (Gsovska/Handel), 185
Concurrence. 1 act. Chor.: Balanchine; mus.: Auric; book, déc. and cost.: Derain; 1st perf.: 12 April 1932, Monte Carlo, Ballets de M.C.; cast: Baronova, Toumanova, Woizikowsky, 155, *150*
Conqueror of the Centaurs, The, 42
Conquête de Malacca (S. Taglioni), 103
Contes russes, Les (Massine), 145
Contrasts (Kaesen), 226
Conversations of Diana and Apollo, 40
Coppélia. Ballet-pantomime, 2 acts, 3 tableaux. Chor.: Saint-Léon; mus.: Delibes; déc.: Cambon, Deplechin, Lavastre; cost.: Lormier; book: Nuitter, Saint-Léon after Hoffmann's 'Le Marchand de Sable'; 1st perf.: 25 May 1870, Paris, Opéra; cast: Bozzacchi, Fiocre, Dauty, 117, 136, 184, 231, 234, *107*
Coq d'Or, Le. 1 act. Chor.: Fokine; mus.: Rimsky-Korsakov; curtain, déc. and cost.: Goncharova; book:

Bielsky/Benois; 1st perf.: 24 May 1914, Paris, Opéra, Ballets Russes; cast: Karsavina, Bougakov, Cecchetti, 144
Coriolanus (Vigano), 90
Corsaire, Le. 3 acts, 5 tableaux. Chor.: Magillier; mus.: Adam; déc. and cost.: Deplechin, Cambon, Thierry and Martin; 1st perf.: 23 Jan. 1856, Paris, Opéra; cast: Rosati, *120*
Cosaque Jaloux, Le (Sacco), 79
Cotillon. 1 act. Chor.: Balanchine; mus.: Chabrier; déc. and cost.: Bérard; book: Kochno; 1st perf.: 12 April 1932, Monte-Carlo, Ballets de M.C.; cast: Toumanova, Lichine, Woizikowsky, 155
Count of Monte Cristo, The (Rota), 121
Countess of Egmont, The (Rota), 121
Courtesan, The (B. Ralov), 228
Création du Monde, La. 1 act. Chor.: Borlin; mus.: Milhaud; déc. and cost.: Léger; book: Cendrars; 1st perf.: 25 Oct. 1923, Paris, Th. des Ch.-E.; Ballets Suédois; cast: Borlin, Strandin, 153
Creation of Adam, The, 20
Creatures of Prometheus, The (Les Créatures de Prométhée). Chor.: Vigano; mus.: Beethoven; 1st perf.: 28 March 1801, Vienna; cast: Cosentini, Vigano, 90. Rev. prod.: Chor.: Lifar; déc.: Quelvée; 1st perf.: 30 Dec. 1929, Paris, Opéra; cast: Lifar, Spessivtzeva, Peretti, Lorcia, 162. Rev. prod.: Chor.: Milloss; 1st perf.: 1940, Rome, Opera; cast: Radice, Dell'Ara, 225
Crème fouettée (R. Strauss-Kroller), 230
Croqueuse de diamants, La. 4 tableaux. Chor.: Petit; mus.: Damase; déc. and cost.: Wakhevich; 1st perf.: 25 Sep. 1950, Paris, Th. Marigny, Ballets de Paris; cast: Jeanmaire, Petit, Hamilton, 174
Cuauhnàhuac (Bravo/Revueldas), 233
Cupid and Psyche (Rinaldi), 75
Cydalise et le Chèvre-pied. 2 acts, 3 tableaux. Chor.: Staats; mus.: Pierné; déc.: Dethomas; book; de Flers and Caillavet; 1st perf.: 15 Jan. 1923, Paris, Opéra; cast: Zambelli, Aveline, 161
Cyrano de Bergerac. Chor.: Petit; mus.: Constant; déc.: Basarte; cost.: Saint-Laurent; 1st perf.: 17 April 1959, Paris, Alhambra, Ballets de Paris; cast: Jeanmaire, Beaumont, Jossi, Ferran, Mars, Reich, Petit, 174
Czardas (Harangozo), 231

Daedalus, 92
Dafne (Caccini and Rinuccini), 43
Dame aux Camélias, La. 2 acts. Chor.: Gsovsky; mus.: Sauguet; 1st perf.: 30 Sep. 1957, Berlin Festival; cast: Chauviré, Reinholm. Rev. prod.: 3 Feb. 1960, Paris, Opéra; chor.: Skibine; déc. and. cost.: Dupont; cast: Chauviré, Skibine, 168; (Ralov) 228
Damnation de Faust, La (Béjart), 177
Danaïdes, Les (Noverre), 62
Dance of Oberon (Charrat/Weber), 174
Danse sacrée et Danse profane (de Valois), 191
Danseuse de Degas, La (Charrat), 177
Dansomanie, La (P. Gardel), 68
Daphnis et Céphyse (Decombe), 96
Daphnis and Chloe. Chor. and book: Fokine; mus.: Ravel; déc.: Bakst; 1st perf.: 8 June 1912, Paris, Th. du Châtelet, Ballets Russes; cast: Nijinsky, Karsavina, 142, 161. Rev. prod.: Chor.: Skibine; déc. and cost.: Chagall; 1st perf.: 3 June 1959, Paris, Opéra; cast: Marjorie Tallchief, Rayet, Skibine, Bozzoni, Descombey, *165*
Daphnis et Pandrose ou la Vengeance de l'Amour (P. Gardel), 68
Dark Meadow (Graham), 211
Daughter of Satan (Rota), 121
Daughters of War (Casati), 121
David triomphant. Chor.: Lifar; mus.: Debussy/Mussorgsky, arr. Rieti; déc.: Léger; cast: Chauviré, Darsonval, 163
Day on Earth, A (Humphrey/Britten), 212
Death of Hercules (Clerico), 87
Deaths and Entrances (Graham), 211
Defeat of Prejudice, The (Angiolini), 73
Défense du Paradis, La, 28
Délivrance de Renaud, La, 39, 40, 46, 48, *36*, *37*, *40*
Demoiselles de la Nuit, Les. 3 tableaux. Chor.: Petit; mus.-Françaix; déc. and cost.: Fini; book: Anouilh; 1st perf. 21 May 1948, Paris, Th. Marigny, Ballets de Paris; cast: Fonteyn, Petit, Hamilton, 173, 224
Departure of Aeneas, The, 85
Dernier jour de Missolonghi ou la mort de Byron (Cortesi), 107
Déserteur, Le (Dauberval), 96, 107
Destruction of Carthage, The (D. Ballon), 85
Deuil en vingt-quatre heures. 5 tableaux. Chor.: Petit; mus.: Thiriet; déc. and cost.: Clavé; 1st perf.: 17 March 1953, Paris, Th. de l'Empire, Ballets de Paris; cast: Marchand, Perrault, 174, *174*, *175*
Deux Créoles, Les (Aumer), 96
Deux Etoiles, Les (M. Petipa), 131
Deux Pigeons, Les. 3 acts. Chor.: Mérante; mus.: Messager; déc. and. cost.; Rubé, Chaperon, Lavastre, Bianchini; 1st perf.: 18 Oct. 1886, Paris, Opéra; cast: Mauri, Mérante, Sanlaville, 124
Diable à Quatre, Le, 98
Diable boiteux. Le, 3 acts. Chor.: Coralli; mus.: Gide; déc. and cost.: Feuchères, Séchan, Dieterlé, Philastre, Cambon; 1st perf.: 1 June 1836, Paris, Opéra; cast: Elssler, Mazillier, 98, 103, 232
Diane de Poitiers (Fokine), 156
Diavolina (Saint-Léon), 117
Dido (Angiolini), 73; (Vigano), 92
Dim Lustre (Tudor), 214
Discovery of America, The, 81
Diversion of Angels (Graham), 211
Divertimento N° 15 (Balanchine), 216
Divertissement (Harangozo/Jemmiz), 231
Don Juan. Chor.: Fokine; mus.: Gluck; déc.: Andreu; 1st perf.: 23 June 1936, London, Alhambra, Ballets de M.C.; cast: Vilzak, Lauret, Eglevsky, 157, 182, 186. Rev. prod.: Chor.: Ashton; mus.: R. Strauss; déc.: Burra; 1st perf.: 25 Nov. 1948, London, Cov. Gdn, Sadler's Wells; cast: Fonteyn, Shearer, Helpmann, 194
Don Juan or the Stone Feast. Chor.: Angiolini; mus.: Gluck; 1st perf.: 17 Oct. 1761, Vienna, 72
Don Quixote, 5 tableaux. Chor.: de Valois; mus.: Gerhard; déc.: Burra; 1st perf.: 20 Feb. 1950, London, Cov. Gdn, Sadler's Wells; cast: Helpmann, Fonteyn, Grant. (Gorsky), 199
Dons du Roi des Alpes à Madame Royale, *26*, *29*
Douairière de Billebahaut, La, 50
Dutch Fair, The (C. Taglioni), 85
Dying Swan, The. 1 act. Chor.: Fokine; mus.: Saint-Saëns; cost.: Bakst; 1st perf.: 1905, St Petersburg, by Anna Pavlova, 135, 138, *139*

Eagle of Virtue (Angiolini), 73
Eglogue de Versailles, L', 57
Egypta (St Denis), 210
Electre ou la Pléiade perdue (P. Taglioni), 103
Elfes, Les, 3 acts, 4 tableaux. Chor.: Mazillier; mus.: Gabrielli; déc.: Deplechin, Nolau, Rubre, Thierry and Martin; 1st perf.: 11 Aug. 1856, Paris, Opéra; cast: Ferraris, L. Petipa; 115. Rev. prod.: 1 act; Chor.: Fokine; mus.: Mendelssohn; déc.: Visconti; cost.: Violet; 1st perf.: 26 Feb. 1924, N. Y. Metropolitan, 157
Emperor of Portugal, The (Cramer), 230

Enchanted Garland, The (Fabiani), 85
Enchanter, The (Laban), 182
Enfant prodigue, L', see Prodigal Son
Enlèvement des Sabines, L', 95
Entre deux rondes (Lifar/Samuel-Rousseau), 164
Eoline ou la Dryade (Perrot), 100
Episodes (Balanchine), 216
Epreuve d'amour, L'. Chor.: Fokine; mus.: Mozart; déc.: Derain; 1st perf.: 1936, Ballets de M. C., 156
Esmeralda, La (Perrot), 98, 122, 232, *89*, *93*, *119*
Estancia (Ginestera), 234
Esther, 20
Età d'Oro, L', 38
Etoile, L' (Hansen), 125
Etoile de Messine, L'. Ballet-pantomime, 2 acts, 6 tableaux. Chor.: Borri; mus.: Gabrielli; book: Foucher; 1st perf.: 20 Nov. 1861, Paris, Opéra; cast: Ferraris, Marquet, Mérante, Coralli, Berthier, Chapuy, 117
Etrange Farandole, L'. 1 act, 4 tableaux. Chor.: Massine; mus.: Shostakovich; déc.: Matisse; 1st perf.: 11 May 1939, Monte Carlo, Ballets de M. C.; cast: Markova, Youskevich, 158
Etudes. 1 act. Chor.: Lander; mus.: Czerny, arr. Riisager; déc.: Moulène; 1st perf.: 1948, Copenhagen, Royal Opera. Rev. prod.: 19 Nov. 1952, Paris, Opéra; cast: Bardin, Renault, Kalioujny, 166, 228, *163*
Etudes choréographiques. Chor.: Nijinska; mus.: Bach; déc. and cost.; Bilinsky; 1st perf.: 27 Jan. 1931, Paris, Th. des Ch.-E., Opéra Russe, 155
Euridice (Caccini and Rinuccini), 43
Europa Riconosciuta, L' (Salieri/Legrand), 86
Excelsior. 12 tableaux. Chor.: Manzotti; mus.: Marenco; déc.: Edel; 1st perf.: 11 Jan. 1881, Milan, La Scala; cast: Vergani, Montenara, 122, 124, *112*

Fable of Bacchus and Ariadne, The, 86
Fables for our Time (Weidman), 212
Façade (Ashton), 192
Fâcheux, Les (Molière), 57; Chor.: Nijinska; mus.: Auric; curtain, déc. and. cost.: Braque; book: Kochno; 1st perf.: 19 Jan. 1924, Th. de M. C., Ballets Russes; cast: Dolin, Tchernicheva, Vilzak, Nijinska, 148
Fair of London, The, 75
Fair Zoraida (de Rossi), 87
Fall of Troy, The (Clerico), 87
Fall River Legend. 1 act. Book and chor.: de Mille; mus.: Gould; déc.: Smith; cost.: White; 1st perf.: 22 April 1948, N. Y. Metropolitan, Ballet Theatre; cast:Alonso, Kaye, Adams, Bentley, Kriza, 215
False Nino (Rinaldi), 74
Fancy Free. 1 act. Chor.: Robbins; mus.: Bernstein, déc.: Smith; cost.: Love; 1st perf.: 18 April 1944, Ballet Theatre; cast: Reed, Bentley, Lang, Kriza, Robbins, Eckl, 215
Fandango, Le (Mérante), 124
Farewell, The (Koner), 213
Faust (S. Taglioni), 100, 103
Fées de la Forêt de Saint-Germain, 50
Femmes de bonne humeur, Les. 1 act. Chor.: Massine; mus.: Scarlatti, arr. Tommassini; déc. and cost.: Bakst, 145
Festin, Le, 136, 140
Fête de Mars, La, 95
Fêtes chinoises, Les (Noverre), 61
Fêtes du Sérail, Les (Noverre), 62
Fêtes vénitiennes, Les (Campra), 56
Fiancés, Les (S. Taglioni), 103
Fille des Neiges, La (Snow White), (M. Petipa), 131
Fille du Danube, La (F. Taglioni), 101, *94*, 107
Fille du Pharaon, La (M. Petipa), 127, 130
Fille mal gardée, La. Ballet-pantomime, 2 acts. Chor. Dauberval; 1st perf. 1 July 1789, Bordeaux, 69, 88
Firebird, The (L'Oiseau de Feu), 3 tableaux. Chor.: Fokine; mus.: Stravinsky; déc. and cost.: Golovine and Bakst; 1st perf.: 25 June 1910, Paris, Opéra, Ballets Russes; cast: Karsavina, Fokine, Cecchetti, Fokina, 138, *133*
Flames of Paris. 4 acts, 7 tableaux. Chor.: Vainonen; mus.: Asafiev; déc. and cost.: Dimikiev; 1st perf.: 7 Nov. 1932, Leningrad, Bolshoi Co.; cast: Ulanova, 202, 207, 231, *198*
Flemish Peasant Dance in an Inn, 81
Flight of the Seagull, The, *204*
Flick et Flock (P. Taglioni), 103
Flûte enchantée, La (S. Taglioni), 103
Foire d'Amsterdam, La (Galeotti), 79
Folie de la Danse, La (Coralli), 103
Folle Feinte, La (La Finta Pazza), (Torelli/Sacrati), 53
Fontaine de Jouvence, La (Noverre), 61
Forains, Les. 1 act. Chor.: Petit; mus.: Sauguet; book: Kochno; 1st perf.: 2 March 1945, Paris, Th. des Ch.-E.-Ballets des Ch.-E.; cast: Vyroubova, Pagava, de Berg, Sadovska, Petit, Foye, 172
Force de l'Amour, La (d'Agliè), 38
Force of Love and Hate, The (Rinaldi), 74
Fountain of Bakhtchisarai, The. 4 acts, prologue. Chor.: Zakharov; mus.: Asafiev; déc. and cost.: Khodasevich; book; Volkov, after Pushkin; 1st perf.: 22 Sep. 1934, Leningrad, Kirov Th.; cast: Ulanova, 202, 231
Four Temperaments. Chor.: Balanchine; mus.: Hindemith; déc. and cost.: Seligmann; 1st perf.: 20 Nov. 1946, N. Y., Ballet Society; cast: Caccialanza, Leclerq, Moylan, Reiman, Bolender, Christensen, Dollar, Moncion. 216, 226, *217*
Fox, The, 184
Fugitive, The. 1 act. Chor.: Howard; mus.: Salzedo; déc, and cost.: Stevenson; 1st perf.: 16 Nov. 1944, Bedford, Royal Country Theatre, Ballet Rambert; cast: Gilmour: Gore, 191

Gala Performance. 1 act, 2 tableaux. Chor.: Tudor; mus.. Prokofiev; déc. and cost.: Stevenson; 1st perf.: 5 Dec: 1938, London, Toynbee Hall, Ballet Rambert; cast: van Praagh, Lloyd, Larsen, 191
Gambler, The (Rota), 121
Gavroche (Varkovitzky), 202, *203*
Gayané. Chor.: Anisimova; mus.: Khatchaturian; déc.: Altman; 1st perf.: 1942, Mololov, Kirov Theatre Co.; cast: Doudinskaya, Sergeyev, Anisimova, 202
Gemma, 114
General Colli in Rome, or the Pope's Ballet. Chor.: Franchi; mus.: Pontelibero; scen.: Salfi, 86, 87
Giselle, 2 acts. Chor.: Coralli/Perrot; mus.: Adam; déc.: Ciceri; book: Gautier/Coralli; 1st perf.: 28 June 1841. Paris, Académie Royale de Musique; cast: Grisi, L. Petipa, Dumilâtre, 97, 103, 105, *87*, *90*, *98*, 107, 108, 117. Rev. prod.: 1910, Ballets Russes; déc. and. cost.: Benois; cast: Karsavina, Nijinsky, *138*. Rev. prod.: 1924, Paris, Opéra; déc. and. cost.: Benois; cast: Spessivtzeva, Aveline/Ricaux, 161, 162, 206, 207, 214, 219, 232, 234, *167*, *192*, *231*
Gitane, La (F. Taglioni), 101
Gloria d'Amore, La, 38
Goddess of Valhalla (Borri), 122
Gods Go a-Begging, The. Mus.: Handel, orch. Beecham; déc.: Bakst; cast: Danilova, Woizikowsky, 149
Grand Ballet de la Reine, Le, 48
Green Table, The. 1 act, 8 tableaux. Chor.: Jooss; mus.: Cohen; déc. and. cost.: Heckroth; 1st perf.: 3 July 1932, Paris, Th. des Ch.-E.; cast: Jooss, Uthoff, Pescht, Czobel, 183

Gris de Lin, Le (d'Aglié), 38, *27*

Hamlet (Henry), 95; (Gsovska), 186
Harnasie (Lifar), 162
Haut Voltage. Chor.: Béjart; mus.: Constant and Henry; déc.: Rillard; book: Rallys; 1st perf.: 27 March 1956, Metz; cast: Trailine, Miskovich, 177, *177*, *225*
Hazana. Chor.: Morrice; mus.: Surinach; déc. and. cost.: Koltai, *197*
Hercule à Thèbes (Melani), *35*, *41*
Hercule amoureux (Ercole Amante), (Cavalli), 53
Herodiad. Chor.: Charrat; mus.: Sunderland; 1st perf.: 30 Nov. 1949, Paris, Th. des Ch.-E., Ballets des Ch.-E.; cast: Philippart, Constantine
Hesione (Lully), 56
Homme et son désir, L. 3 tableaux. Chor.: Borlin; mus.: Milhaud; déc. and cost.: Parr; arg.: Claudel; 1st perf.: 6 June 1921, Paris, Th. des Ch.-E., Ballets Suédois; cast: Johanson, Borlin, Stejerner, Smith, Ari, 153
Horaces et les Curiaces, Les (Noverre), 86
Horoscope (S. Taglioni), 100. 1 act. Chor.: Ashton; mus. Lambert; déc.: Fedorovich; 1st perf.: 27 Jan. 1938 London, Sadler's Wells Th., Sadler's Wells Ballet; cast: Fonteyn, Somes, 192
Hunt of Diana, The, 40

Icare. Chor.: Lifar; mus.: rhythms by Lifar, orch. Szyfer; déc. and cost.: Larthe; 1st perf.: 9 July 1935, Paris, Opéra; cast: Lifar, 162, 224
Idoménée (Crébillon/Hilferding), 71
Idylle. 1 act. Chor.: Skibine; mus.: Serette; book, déc. and cost.: Camble; 1st perf.: 2 Jan. 1954, Paris, Th. de l'Empire, Ballet de Cuevas; cast: Marjorie Tallchief, Skibine, Skouratoff, 167, 168, *218*
Images of Chile (Uthoff), 234
Imaginaires, Les (Lichine/Auric), 156
Impatience, L' (Beauchamp), 57
In the Heart of the Mountains (Chaboukiani/Balanchivadze), 202
Incendie de Ninive, L' (P. Taglioni), 103
Indes galantes, Les. 1st perf.: 23 Aug. 1734, Paris, Académie Royale de Musique, 64. Rev. prod.: Opera-ballet in prologue, 4 *entrées*, epilogue, spoken preludes by Fauchois; mus.: Rameau; review: Dukas, Busser. Prologue: 'Le palais d'Hébé': chor.: Aveline; setting: Arbus; déc. and cost. Dupont. 1st *entrée* 'Le Turc généreux': Chor.: Aveline; déc. and cost.: Wakhevich. 2nd *entrée* 'Les Incas': chor.: Lifar; déc. and cost.: Carzou, 3rd *entrée* 'Les Fleurs': chor.: Lander; déc. and cost.: Fost and Moulène. 4th *entrée* 'Les Sauvages': chor.: Lifar; déc. and cost.: Chapelain-Midy. Epilogue: chor.: Lifar. 1st perf.: 18 June 1952, Paris, Opéra, 166
Ines de Castro (S. Taglioni), 103
Inquest (Humphrey), 212
Iphigenia (Angiolini), 73
Isaeus (Duberval), 81
Isis (Beauchamp), 57
Isolde of Normandy (Casati), 121
Istar. Chor.: Lifar; mus.: d'Indy; déc.: Bakst; 1st perf.: 31 Dec. 1941, Paris, Opéra; cast: Chauviré, 163

Jack-in-the-Box. Chor.: Balanchine; mus.: Satie, orch. Milhaud; déc. and cost.: Derain; Ist perf.: 3 July 1926, Paris, Th. Sarah-Bernhardt, Ballets Russes; cast: Idzikowsky, Danilova, 149
Jardin aux Lilas. 1 act. Chor.: Tudor; mus.: Chausson; déc. and. cost.: Stevenson; 1st perf.: 26 Jan. 1936, London, Mercury Th., Ballet Rambert; cast: Lloyd, van Praagh, Laing, Tudor, 190
Jarre. 1 act. Chor.: Borlin; mus.: Casella; déc. and. cost.: de Chirico; 1st perf.: 19 Nov. 1924, Paris, Th. des Ch.-E., Ballets Suédois; cast: Bolin, Friis, Viber, 153
Jason, 21
Jason et Médée, 66
Jenny ou le Mariage secret (Aumer), 96
Jeu de Cartes. 3 'deals'. Chor.: Charrat; mus.: Stravinsky; déc.: Roy; 1st perf.: 12 Oct. 1945, Paris, Th. des Ch.-E., Ballets des Ch.-E.; cast: Babilée, 172, 174
Jeune Homme et la Mort, Le. 2 tableaux. Chor.: Petit; mus.: Bach, orch. Respighi; déc.: Wakhevich; book: Cocteau; 1st perf.: 25 June 1946, Paris, Rh. des Ch.-E., Ballets des Ch.-E.; cast: Philippart, Babilée, 173, 224
Jeux. 1 act. Chor.: Nijinsky; mus.: Debussy; déc. and cost.: Bakst; 1st perf.: 15 May 1913, Paris, Th. des Ch.-E.: Ballets Russes; cast; Karsavina, Schollar, Nijinsky, 142, *136*
Jeux d'enfants. 1 act. Chor.: Massine; mus.: Bizet; curtain, déc. and cost.: Miró; book: Kochno; 1st perf.: 14 April 1932, Monte Carlo, Ballets de M. C.; cast: Riabouchinska, Toumanova, Baronova, Lichine, 155
Joan de Zarissa. Chor.: Lifar; mus.: Egk; déc.: Brayer; 1st perf.: 1942, Paris, Opéra; cast: Lifar, Schwartz, 165, *161* (Gsovska), 186
Joan of Arc at the Stake (Jeanne d'Arc au Bûcher) (Claudel/Honegger), 185.
Joko, le Singe brésilien (S. Taglioni), *97*
Jolie Fille de Gand, La. Ballet-pantomime, 3 acts. Chor.: Albert; mus.: Adam; déc.: Ciceri, Philastre, Cambon; 1st perf.: 22 June 1942, Paris, Opéra; cast: Grisi, L. Petipa, Coralli, 98, 107
Jongleuse, La, 122
Jovita ou les Boucaniers. 3 tableaux. Chor.: Mazillier; mus.: Labarre; déc. and cost.: Deplechin, Thierry, Cambon; 1st perf.: 11 Nov. 1853, Paris, Opéra; cast: Rosati, Mérante, Petipa, 115
Judgment of Paris (Tudor), 191
Jugement de Paris, Le (P. Gardel), 68
Jungle (van Dantzig/Badings), 226, *227*

Korrigane, La. 2 acts. Chor.: Mérante; mus.: Vidor; déc. Lavastre, Rubé, Chaperon; cost.: Lacoste; book: Coppée; 1st perf.: 1 Dec. 1880, Paris, Opéra; cast: Mauri, Sanlaville, Mérante, 124, *117*

Lac des Fées, Le (Auber), *109*
Ladies of the Seraglio, The, 75
Laurencia (Chaboukiani), 202
Legend of Joseph, The. 1 act. Chor.: Fokine; mus.: R. Strauss; déc.: Sert; cost.: Bakst; book: Kessler and Hofmannsthal; 1st perf.: 14 May 1914, Paris, Opéra, Ballets Russes; cast: Kouznetsova, Boulgakov, Massine, 144
Legend of Ohrid (Hirstich), 231
Letter to the World. Chor.: Graham; mus.: Johnson; déc.: Lauterer; cost.: Gilfond; 1st perf.: 11 Aug. 1940, Vermont, Bennington College, Martha Graham Co., 211
Liebeslieder Walzer (Balanchine), 216
Liens, Les. Chor.: Charrat; mus.: Semenoff; déc. and. cost.: Daydé; 1st perf.: 1957, Toulouse, *171*
Lieutenant Kije (Fokine), 157
Life and Death of Lola Montez, The (Gore/Verdi), 191
Lodovico il Moro (Clerico), 87
Loup, Le, 174
Loves of Igor, The (Muzzarelli), 87
Loves of Rinaldo and Armida (Rota), 121
Loves of Zephyr, The (Fabiani), 85
Lynchtown (Weidman), 212

Madame, 50
Magic Ring, The, *82*

Magician, The (Salomoni), 85
Mal du Siècle, Le (Starbuch/North), *220*
Maladetta, La (Hansen), 125
Manon (Casati), 121
Marché des Innocents, Le, 125
Marco-Spada ou la Fille du Bandit, 116
Mariage Forcé, Le (Beauchamp, after Molière), 57
Mariés de la Tour Eiffel, Les. 1 act. Chor.: Borlin; mus.: Tailleferre, Auric, Honegger, Milhaud, Poulenc; déc.: Lagut; cost.: Hugo; book: Cocteau; 1st perf.: 18 June 1921, Paris, Th. des Ch.-E., Ballets Suédois; cast: Ari, Figoni, Smith, Wahlander, Eltrop, 153, *146*, *147*
Mars et Vénus, ou les Filets de Vulcain (Blache), 96
Martyre de Saint-Sébastien, Le. Mystery play, 5 acts. Chor.: Rubinstein; mus.: Debussy; déc. and. cost.: Bakst; book: d'Annunzio; 1st perf.: 22 May, 1911, Paris, Th. du Châtelet; cast: Rubinstein, 167
Maschera ou Les Nuits de Venise, La, 117
Massacre des Amazones, Le. Chor.: Charrat; mus.: Semenoff; déc. and. cost.: Bazaine; book: Charrat and Sarrazin; 1st perf.: 24 Dec. 1951, Grenoble, Th. municipal, Ballets de Janine Charrat; cast: Charrat, Bon, Lhotka, Oukhtomsky, 177
Matelots, Les. 5 tableaux. Chor.: Massine; mus.: Auric; déc. and cost.: Pruna; book: Kochno; 1st perf.: 17 June 1925, Paris, Th. de la Gaîté-Lyrique, Ballets Russes cast: Lifar, Woizikowsky, Slavinsky, Sokolova, Nemchinova, 148
Mavra, 148
Mazeppa, 230
Médée et Jason (Noverre), 62, 86
Mephisto Valse (Ashton), 190
Mercure. 3 tableaux. Chor. and. arg.: Massine; mus.: Satie; curtain, déc. and cost.: Picasso; 1st perf.: 15 June 1924, Paris, Th. de la Cigale, 154
Mercury and Mars (Monteverdi), 42
Merlaison, La (Louis XIII), 50
Merry Widow, The (Page), *222*
Métamorphoses chinoises, Les (Noverre), 62
Michelangelo (Manzotti), 122
Midsummer Night's Dream, A. (Casati), 121, 184
Miracle at Almeda (Uthoff), 234
Miraculous Mandarin (Milloss/Bartók), 225, 226, 231
Mirages, Les. 1 act, 2 tableaux. Chor.: Lifar; mus.: Sauguet; déc. and. cost.: Cassandre; book: Cassandre and Lifar; 1st perf.: 15 Dec. 1947, Paris, Opéra; cast: Chauviré, Renault, Bardin, Dynalix, Lafon, 165.
Mirra (Vigano), 92
Mirror, The (Jooss), 184
Mirror for Witches, A. Prologue and 5 tableaux. Chor.: Howard; mus.: Ivor; déc.: Adams; cost.: Howard and Adams; 1st perf.: 4 March 1952, London, Cov. Gdn., Sadler's Wells Ballet; cast: Heaton, Farron, Edwards, Hart, Chatfield, 194
Missa Brevis (Humphrey/Limón), 213
Miss Julie. 4 tableaux, after Strindberg. Chor.: Cullberg; mus.: Rangström; déc. and. cost.: Fridericia; 1st perf.: 1 March 1950, Stockholm, Rickstеatern; cast: Rosen, Mengarelli, 230, *228*
Mondo Festeggiante, Il, 42
Montagnards, Les (d'Agliè), 38
Moor of the Antilles, The (Manzotti), 122
Moor's Pavane, The (Limón), 213
Mort d'Ajax, La (Noverre), 62
Mort d'Orphée, La, 66
Muette de Portici, La (Auber), 107
Mystères de Paris (Cortesi/Sue), 107

Naissance de la Paix, La (Descartes), 39
Néméa ou l'Amour vengé (Saint-Léon), 117
New Dance (Humphrey), 212
Night (Laban), 182
Night Journey (Graham), 211, *210*
Night Shadow (La Somnambula), Chor.: Balanchine; mus.: Rieti/Bellini; déc. and. cost.: Stone; 1946, Monte Carlo; 1961, Sadler's Wells Theatre, Ballet Rambert, *196*
Ninette à la Cour (M. Gardel), 68
Nobilissima Visione (Massine), 159; (Gsovska), 186
Noces, Les. 4 tableaux. Chor.: Nijinska; mus. and book: Stravinsky; déc. and. cost.: Goncharova; 1st perf.: 14 June 1923, Paris, Th. de la Gaîté-Lyrique, Ballets Russes; cast: Doubrovska, Ignatov, 148
Noces fantastiques, Les. 2 acts, 4 tableaux. Chor.: Lifar; mus.: Delannoy; déc.: Chastel; cost.: Levasseur; 1st perf.: 9 Feb. 1955, Paris, Opéra; cast: Vyroubova, van Dijk, 166
Notre-Dame de Paris (Gorsky), 199
Notte d'Amore, La (Ricci), 38
Nozze dei Dei, Le, 38, *25*
Nuit, La (Benserade), 57, *52*
Nutcracker, The (Casse-Noisette). 2 acts, 3 tableaux. Chor.: L. Ivanov; mus.: Tchaikovsky; déc.: Botcharov and K.M. Ivanov; cost.: Vsevolojsky and Ponomarev; book: M. Petipa, after Dumas's version of a tale by Hoffmann; 1st perf.: 18 Dec. 1892, St Petersburg, Maryinsky Th., 127, 132, *126*. Rev. prod.: 1934, London, Sadler's Wells; 1947, Paris, Opéra-Comique; 1954, N.Y. City Center; 184, *193*

Ode. 2 acts. Chor.: Massine; mus.: Nabokov; déc.: Tchelichev and Charbonnier; book: Kochno; 1st perf.: 6 June 1928, Paris, Th. Sarah-Bernhardt, Ballets Russes; cast: Beliamina, Doubrovska, Lifar, 149
Œdipus Rex (Cocteau), 149
Œuf à la coque, L'. 1 act. Chor. and book: Petit; mus.: Thiriet; déc. and cost.: Lepri; 1st perf.: 16 Feb. 1949, London, Prince's Th., Ballets de Paris; cast: Marchand, Jeanmaire, Vyroubova, Petit, Perrault, Hamilton, Skouratoff, 173
Olympiad (Metastasio), 74, 85
Ombre, L'. 3 tableaux. Chor.: F. Taglioni; mus.: Maurer; déc.: Serkov; cost.: Matieu; 1st perf.: 28 Nov. 1839, St Petersburg; cast: M. Taglioni, 101
Ondine (Perrot), 100
Orfeo (Poliziano), 21
Oriane et le prince d'amour. 2 acts. Chor.: Lifar; mus.: Schmitt; déc. and. cost.: Pruna; book: Séran; 1st perf.: 7 Jan. 1938, Paris, Opéra; cast: Darsonval, Lifar, Goubé, 163, *158*
Orphan of China (Angiolini), 73
Orphée. Chor. drama, 2 acts, 8 tableaux. Chor.: Béjart; mus.: Henry; déc. and cost.: Küfner; 1st perf.: 17 Sep. 1958, Liège, Th. Royal, Ballet Théâtre de Paris de Béjart; cast: Béjart, Seigneuret, Belda, Maubert, Cano, Monin, Bari, 177, *217*
Orpheus (Gluck/Angiolini), 73; (Balanchine/Stravinsky), 231
Othello (Vigano), 90

Pafio e Mirra (Legrand), 86
Pages du Duc de Vendôme, les, 107
Palais d'Alcine, Le (Beauchamp), 57
Panambi (Ginestera), 234
Pantomime, The (Gsovska), 186
Papillon, Le (M. Petitpa), 131
Paquita, 98
Parade. 1 act. Chor.: Massine; mus.: Satie; curtain, déc. and cost.: Picasso; book: Cocteau; 1st perf.: 18 May 1917, Paris, Th. du Châtelet, Ballets Russes; cast: Lopokova, Massine, Zvereff, Woizikowsky, Chabelska, 145, *142*, *143*

Pas d'Acier. 2 tableaux. Chor.: Massine; mus.: Prokofiev; constructions and cost.: Jaculov; 1st perf.: 8 June 1927, Paris, Th. Sarah-Bernhardt; cast: Doubrovska, Thernicheva, Nikitina, Massine, Lifar, Woizikowsky, 149
Pas de Deux. Chor.: Kelly; mus.: Gershwin; déc. and cost.: François; 1st perf.: 6 July 1960, Paris, Opéra; cast: Bessy, Labis, Descombey, 168
Pas de Quatre (Perrot), *95*, *100*
Pas de Trois, 103
Patineurs, Les. 1 act. Chor.: Ashton; mus.: Meyerbeer; déc. and cost.: Chappell; 1st perf.: 16 Feb. 1937, London, Sadler's Wells; cast: Fonteyn, Helpmann, Honer, Turner, 192
Paul et Virginie, 107
Pavillon d'Armide, Le. 1 act, 3 tableaux. Chor.: Fokine; mus.: Tcherepnine; book, déc. and cost.: Benois; 1st perf.: 25 Nov. 1907, St Petersburg, Maryinsky Th.; cast Pavlova, Nijinsky, Gerdt. Rev. prod.: 1909, Paris, Karsavina, Nijinsky, 136, 140
Peace, 38
Peleus and Thetis (Angiolini), 73
Pellegrina, La, 35
Péri, La (Coralli), 98, 103, *88*
Persée et Andromède, 95
Perséphone (Rubinstein/Gide), 154
Petits Riens, Les (Noverre), 62; (de Valois), 191
Petite Symphonie concertante (Martin), 169
Petrouchka. 4 tableaux. Chor.: Fokine; mus.: Stravinsky; déc. and cost.: Benois; 1st perf.: 13 June 1911, Paris, Th. du Châtelet, Ballets Russes; cast: Nijinsky, Karsavina, 140, 213, *129*
Phèdre (Lifar/Auric), 165
Pietro Micca (Manzotti), 122
Pillar of Fire (Tudor), 214, 215
Plaisirs de l'Ile Enchantée, Les (Beauchamp), 57
Polovtsian Dances, see Prince Igor
Pomme d'Or, La (Il Pomo d'Oro) (Cesti), 53
Poor Yourka (Cesare/Starzer), 72
Porzia (Beretti), 87
Présages, Les. 4 parts. Chor.: Massine; mus.: Tchaikovsky, 5th Symphony; déc. and. cost.: Masson; 1st perf.: 13 April 1933, Monte Carlo, Ballets de M. C.; cast: Verchinina, Baronova, Riabouchinska, Lichine, Woizikowsky, 155
Primitive Mysteries (Graham), 211
Prince Igor, Polovtsian Dances of. Chor.: Fokine; mus.: Borodin; déc. and cost.: Roerich; 1st perf.: 19 May 1909, Paris, Th. du Châtelet, Ballets Russes; cast: Smirnova, Bolm, Fedorova, 136, 140
Prodigal, The (Uthoff), 234
Prodigal Son, The (L'Enfant prodigue), 96; (Borri), 122. 3 tableaux. Chor.: Balanchine; book: Kochno; mus.: Prokofiev; déc. and. cost.: Rouault; 1st perf.: 21 May 1929, Paris, Th. Sarah-Bernhardt, Ballets Russes de Diaghilev; cast: Lifar, Doubrovska, 149
Promenade dans Rome. 4 tableaux. Chor.: Lifar; mus. Samuel-Rousseau; déc. and cost.: Decaris; book: Vaudoyer; 1st perf.: 14 Dec. 1936, Paris; cast: Lifar, Lorcia, Peretti, Kergrist, 162
Prométhée (Béjart), 177
Prométhée, voleur du feu céleste (d'Agliè), 38
Prometheus (Vigano; Haydn/Beethoven), 90; (Laban), 182
Psyché (Beauchamp), 57; (P. Gardel), 68; (Hilferding), 71
Puissance de l'Amour, La (Morel), 50
Pulcinella (Massine), 184
Pygmalion (Angiolini), 73

Qarrtsiluni. 1 act. Chor.: Lander; mus.: Riisager; déc. and cost.: Johansen; 1st perf.: 21 Feb. 1942, Copenhagen, Royal Theatre, Danish Royal Ballet. Rev. prod.: déc.: Daydé; Paris, Opéra, 1960, 226, *166*
Quatre Monarchies Chrétiennes, Les, 50, 51

Radha (St Denis), 210
Raillerie, La (Beauchamp), 57
Rake's Progress, The (de Valois), 192
Raoul (Vigano), 88
Rape of Proserpine (Hilferding), 71
Réception d'une jeune nymphe à la cour de Terpsichore (F. Taglioni), 97
Recuerdo a Zapata (Bravo/Marabak), 233
Red Poppy, The (Tikhomirov and Lashchilin), 202
Refuge of Cupid, The (Angiolini), 73
Reine de Jolconde, La, 59
Réjouissances flamandes, Les (Noverre), 61
Relâche (Picabia/Satie), 153
Renard (The Fox). 1 act. Chor.: Nijinska; mus.: Stravinsky; déc. and cost.: Larionov; 1st perf.: 18 May 1922, Paris, Opéra; cast: Nijinska, Idzikowsky, 148. Rev. prod.: 21 May 1929, Paris, Th. Sarah-Bernhardt; chor.: Lifar, 149, *144*
Renaud et Armide (Noverre), 62, 86
Rencontre ou Œdipe et le Sphinx, La. 1 act. Chor.: Lichine; mus.: Sauguet; déc. and cost.: Bérard; 1st perf.: 8 Nov. 1948, Paris, Th. des Ch.-E.; Ballets de Ch.-E.; cast: Caron, Babilée, 173, 226
Rendez-vous des plaisirs, Le, 40
Rêve, Le (Hansen), 125
Révolte dans le sérail (F. Taglioni), 101
Rhapsody in Blue (Milloss/Gershwin), 225; (Tabor/Harangozo), 231
Richard Cœur de Lion (Vigano/Sedaine and Grétry), 88
Rinaldo and Armida (Angiolini), 73
Rite of Spring (Sacre du Printemps). 2 acts. Chor.: Nijinsky; mus.: Stravinsky; déc.: Roerich; 1st perf.: 29 May 1913, Paris, Th. des Ch.-E., Ballets Russes; cast: Marie Piltz, 143, 181. Rev. prod.: Chor.: Massine; déc.: Roerich; 1st perf.: 1920, Oct. Paris, Th. des Ch.-E., Ballets Russes. Rev. prod.: Chor.: Béjart; déc.: P. Caille; 1st perf.: 9 Dec. 1959, Brussels, Th. Royal de la Monnaie; cast: Bari, Casado, 177 (Graham), 210; (Wigman), *183*, 224
Riverside Nights (revue), 190
Robert and Bertram (Hoguet), 77
Robert le Diable, Chor.: Coralli; mus.: Meyerbeer; déc.: Ciceri, 96
Rodolphe (Borri/Sue), 122
Roi des fêtes de Bacchus, Le, 57
Roi nu, Le. 4 tableaux. Chor.: Lifar; mus.: Françaix; déc, and cost.: Pruna; 1st perf.: 15 June 1936, Paris, Opéra; cast: Chauviré, Lifar, Goubé, 162
Rolla (Manzotti), 122
Romeo and Juliet. Chor.: Lavrovsky; mus.: Prokofiev; cast: Ulanova, Sergeyev, 202, 204, 87, 149, 154, 167, 231, *200*
Ronde des Saisons, La (Hansen), 125
Rosario (Laban), 182
Rosière, La, *102*
Rossignol, Le (Stravinsky), 144
Roumanoff (S. Taglioni), 103
Roussalka, La (Clustine/Lambert), 161
Rübezahl, 122
Ruins and Visions (Humphrey), 212

Sable. Chor.: Babilée; mus.: Le Roux; déc. and cost.: de Nobili; 1st perf.: 19 June 1956, Paris, Th. des Ch.-E., Ballets Jean Babilée; cast: Biegovich, Kalioujny, Sombert, Sanders, Masson, 174
Sacre du Printemps, see Rite of Spring
Sailors' Return, The, 75
Saint Cecilia, 20

Salade. Choreographic counterpoint, 2 acts. Chor.: Massine; mus.: Milhaud; book: Flamant; déc. and cost: Braque; 1st perf.: 1924, Paris, Th. de la Cigale, 154
Salammbô (Gorsky), 199
Sammete and Tamiri (Vigano), 90
Sardanapalus (Casati), 121
Scènes de Ballet. Chor.: Ashton; mus.: Stravinsky; déc.: Beaurepaire; 1st perf.: 1948, London, Cov. Gdn, Sadler's Wells Ballet, 195
Scènes Russes (Massine/Borodin), 158
Scheherazade. 1 act. Chor.: Fokine; mus.: Rimsky-Korsakov; déc. and cost.: Bakst; book: Bakst 1st perf.: 4 June 1910, Paris, Opéra, Ballets Russes; cast: Rubinstein, Nijinsky, Cecchetti, Boulgakov, 139, 231
Scipio, 75
Scotch Symphony. Chor.: Balanchine; mus.: Mendelssohn; déc.: Armistead; cost.: Karinska and D. Folkes; 1st perf.: 11 Nov. 1952, N.Y. City Center, N.Y. City Ballet; cast.: Maria Tallchief, Eglevsky, 216
Séducteur au village, Le (Decombe), 96
Seleuco (Rinaldi), 75
Semiramis (Voltaire/Angiolini); 73, (Rubinstein/Valéry), 154; (Blum/Fokine), 156
Serenade. 3 movements. Chor.: Balanchine; mus.: Tchaikovsky; déc. and cost.: Lurçat; 1st perf.: 6 Dec. 1934, Hartford, Avery Memorial Th., 224
Seventh Symphony. 4 parts. Chor.: Massine; mus.: Beethoven; déc. and cost.: Bérard; 1st perf.: 5 May 1938, Monte Carlo, Ballets de M. C.; cast: Markova, Francklin, Theilade, Youskevich, *154*
Shirah (Lang), 226
Sieba (Manzotti), 122
Siege of Cythera, The (Favart/Angiolini), 72
Sleeping Beauty, The. Chor.: M. Petipa; mus.: Tchaikovsky; déc.: Levogt, Bocharov, Shilov, Ivanov; cost.: Svevolojsky; 1st perf.: 3 Jan. 1890, St Petersburg, Maryinsky Theatre; cast: Brianza, Gerdt, Cecchetti, Marie Petipa, Nikitina, 132, *121*, *123*. Rev. prod.: Diaghilev, déc. Bakst, 148; London, Royal Ballet, 193, *209*; 204
Snow White. 3 acts, 6 tableaux. Chor.: Lifar; mus.: Yvain; déc.: Bouchène; 1st perf.: 14 Nov. 1951, Paris, Opéra; cast: Daydé, Vyroubova, Lifar, Bozzoni, Andréani. (Rimsky-Korsakov), 203; (Gianneo), 234
Soleil de Nuit (Massine), *139*, 145
Soir de fête. Chor.: Staats; mus.: Delibes; 1st perf.: 30 June 1925, Paris, Opéra; cast: Spessivtzeva, Ricaux, 161
Somnambule, ou l'Arrivée d'un nouveau Seigneur, La (Aumer), 96
Somnambula, La, see Night Shadow
Sophonisbe (Trissino), 28; (Gioja) 87
Source, La. 3 acts, 4 tableaux. Chor.: Saint-Léon; mus. Minkus/Delibes; déc. and cost.: Deplechin, Rube, Lavastre, Chaperon; 1st perf.: 12 Nov. 1866, Paris, Opéra; cast: Salvioni, Mérante, Fiocre, 117
Spartacus. Chor.: Yacobson; mus.: Khatchaturian; déc.: Khodasievich, 207, *207*
Spectre de la Rose, Le. 1 act. Chor.: Fokine; mus.: Weber; déc. ans cost.: Bakst; book: Vaudoyer; 1st perf.: 19 April 1911, Monte Carlo, Ballets Russes; cast: Karsavina, Nijinsky, 162
Sport (Manzotti), 124
Star of the North, The (Casati), 121
Stars and Stripes (Balanchine), 216
Statue de Vénus (Coralli), 103
Sterile Cloud, The (Bravo/Noriega), 233
Stone Flower, The. Chor.: Lavrovsky; mus.: Prokofiev; déc.: Starzhentsky; book: Prokofieva; 1st perf.: Feb. 1954, Moscow, Bolshoi; cast: Plissetskaya, Chorokhova, Ermolaiev, 202, *202*
Strelitz, The (Vigano), 90
Strenght of Blood, The (Hilferding), 71
Suite de danses (Clustine/Chopin), 161
Suite en blanc. Chor.: Lifar; mus.: Lalo; déc.: Dignimont; 1st perf.: 23 July 1943, Paris, Opéra; cast: Schwartz, Darsonval, Chauviré, Ritz, Fenonjois, Lifar, 164, *160*
Svetlana. Chor.: Radunsky, Posspekhine, Popko; mus.: Klebanov; 1st perf.: 1939, Moscow, Bolshoi; cast: Lepechinskaya, Kondratov, 202
Swan Lake (Le Lac des Cygnes). 4 acts. Book: Bigichev, Geltzer; chor.; M. Petipa, Ivanov; mus.: Tchaikovsky; déc.: Bocharov, Levogt; 1st perf.: 15-27 Jan. 1895, St Petersburg, Maryinsky Th.; cast: Legnani, Gerdt, 127, 132, *127*. Rev. prod.: Bourmeister, 1953; 168. Gorsky, 1896, 1906, 1920; 199. 20 Nov. 1934, London, Sadler's Wells Th., Vic Wells Ballet; cast: Markova, Helpmann. (Ulanova) 203, 204; (Lifar), 231, 234, 235; *168*, *169*, *178*, *184*, *195*, *201*, *224*
Sylphide, La. Ballet-pantomime, 2 acts. Chor.: F. Taglioni; book: Nourrit; mus.: Schneitzhoeffer; déc.: Ciceri; cost.: Lami, or Lormier; 1st perf.: 12 March 1832, Paris, Académie Royale de Musique; cast: M. Taglioni, Mazillier, Noblet, Elie. Perf.: 26 July 1832, London, Cov. Gdn; 18 Sep. 1837, St Petersburg, Maryinsky Th.; 29 May 1841, Milan, La Scala. Rev. prod.: Chor.: Gsovsky; déc.: Serebriakoff; cost.: Bérard; 1st perf.: 15, June: 1946, Paris, Th. des Ch.-E., Ballets des Ch.-E.; cast, Vyroubova, Petit, 97, 98, 100, 101, 103, 107, 108, 112. 172, 232, *91*
Sylphides, Les. 1 act. Chor.: Fokine; mus.: Chopin, arr. Stravinsky; déc. and cost.: Benois; 1st perf.: 2 June 1909, Paris, Th. du Châtelet, Ballets Russes; cast: Pavlova, Karsavina, Baldina, Nijinsky, 136, 224
Sylvia, the Nymph of Diana. 3 acts, 4 tableaux. Chor.: Mérante; mus.: Delibes; book: Barbier, Reinach; déc.. Chéret, Rubé, Chaperon; cost.: Lacoste; 1st perf.: 14 June 1876, Paris, Opéra; cast: Sangalli, Mérante, 124: Rev. prod.: Chor.: Lifar; déc. and cost.: Brianchon; 1st perf.: Feb. 1941, Paris, Opéra; cast: Darsonval, Schwartz, Lorcia, Lifar, 164
Sylvie, 66, *56*
Symphonic Variations. 1 act. Chor.: Ashton; mus.: Franck; déc.: Fedorovich; 1st perf.: 24 April 1946, London, Cov. Gdn, Sadler's Wells Ballet; cast: Fonteyn, Shearer, May, Somes, Shaw, Danton, 194
Symphonie concertante. 4 movements. Chor.: Descombey; mus.: Martin; déc. and cost.: Daydé; 1st perf.: 14 March 1962, Paris, Opéra; cast: Bessy, Labis, 168
Symphonie Fantastique, 5 tableaux. Chor.: Massine; mus.: Berlioz; déc. and cost.: Bérard; 1st perf.: 24 July 1936, London, Cov. Gdn, Ballets du Basil; cast: Toumanova, Massine, Verchinina, Zorich, 156, 159, 186, 224
Symphonie pour un homme seul. Chor.: Béjart; mus.: Henry and Schaeffer; 1st perf.: 30 July 1955, Paris, Th. de l'Étoile, Ballets de l'Étoile; cast: Béjart, Seigneuret, 177
Symphony in C (Balanchine/Bizet), 216

Tannhäuser (chor.: Gorsky), 199
Tarassiana (Taras), *215*
Tarentule, La (Coralli), 103
Tempête, La (Hansen), 98, 125
Tentation de la bergère, La. 1 act. Chor.: Nijinska; mus.: Monteclair, orch. Casadessus; déc. and cost.: Gris; 1st perf.: 3 Jan. 1924, Th. de M. C., Ballets Russes; cast: Nemchinova, Slavinsky, Woizikowsky, Vilzak, 148
Théa ou la fée des fleurs (P. Taglioni), 103
Theatre Piece, 1 and 2 (Humphrey), 212
There is a Time (Humphrey/Limón), 213
Thésée (Beauchamp), 57
Theseus and Ariadne (Angiolini), 73
Three-Cornered Hat, The. 1 act. Chor.: Massine; mus.: de

Falla; déc. and cost.: Picasso; tech. adviser: Felix; book: Sierra; 1st perf.: 22 July 1919, London, Alhambra, Ballets Russes; cast: Danilova, Lifar, 145, *140*
Till Eulenspiegel (Babilée), 174; (Gsovska) 186; (Balanchine), *211*
Titans, The (Vigano), 92
Toilette de Vénus, La (Noverre), 62
Tournament of the Winds, The, 42
Town with the Golden Gates, The (Gaito), 234
Toybox, The, 184
Tragedy of Fashion, A. Chor.: Ashton; mus.: E. Goossens; déc.: Fedorovich; 1st perf.: 15 June 1926, Hammersmith, Lyric, Ballet Rambert; cast: Rambert, Ashton, 190
Train bleu, Le. 1 act. Scen.: Cocteau; chor.: Nijinska; mus.: Milhaud; curtain: Picasso; décor: Laurens; cost.: Chanel; 1st perf.: 20 June 1924, Paris, Th. des Ch.-E., Ballets Russes; cast: Nijinska, Sokolova, Dolin, Woizikowsky: 148
Triomphe de l'Amour, Le. Scen.: Benserade and Quinault; déc.: Bérain, 56, 57
Triomphe de Minerve, Le, 46
Triomphes, Les, 50
Triumph of Neptune, The. 2 acts. Chor.: Balanchine; mus., Berners; book: S. Sitwell; 1st perf.: 3 Dec. 1926, London, Lyceum, Ballets Russes; cast: Danilova, Lifar, 149
Tumbler, The (Uthoff), 234
Turandot, 184

Undertow (Tudor), 214
Union de Flore et de Zéphyr, L' (Coralli), 103
Union Pacific. 1 act, 4 tableaux. Chor.: Massine; mus.: Nabokov; déc.: Johnson; cost.: Sharaff; 1st perf.: 6 April 1934, Philadelphia, Forrest Th., Ballets de M. C.; cast: Massine, Delarova, Osato, Toumanova, Eglevsky, 156
Usher (Harrild y Moriana), 234

Valse, La. 1 act. Chor.: Fokine; mus.: Ravel; 1st perf.: 25 June 1931, Paris, Opéra, Ida Rubinstein Co. 1936, Ballets de M. C., 156
Vampire (Rota), 121
Variations (Nijinska/Beethoven), 155; (Gore/Britten) 191
Variations concertantes (Ginestera), 234
Vert-Vert. 3 acts. Chor.: Mazillier; mus.: Deldevez/Tolbecque; déc.: Cambon/Thierry; cost.: Lormier; 1st perf.: 25 Nov. 1851, Paris, Opéra; cast: Plunkett, Priora, 113
Vertu, ennemie des apparences, La (d'Agliè), 38
Vertumne et Pomone, 66
Vestal Virgin, The. Chor.: Vigano; déc.: Sanquirico; 1818, Milan, La Scala, 92, *81*
Vicissitudini del Tempo, Le, 38
Voilà l'Homme. Chor.: Béjart; mus.: Arthuys; déc.: Desvilles; cost.: Fabra; book: Kenan; 1955, Paris, Th. Fontaine des Quatre-Saisons, *176*
Voleurs, Les, 50

Walnut of Benevento, The (Vigano), 90
War of Beauty, The, 42
West Side Story (Robbins) 215
Whims of Cupid and the Ballet-Master, The (Lander), 228
White Jade (St Denis), 210
Witch, The (Laban), 182
With My Red Fires (Humphrey), 212
Wooden Prince, The, 231
World, The, 40

Xerxes (Cavalli), 53

Yedda (Mérante), 124
Yolanda (Kalomiris), 231

Zémir et Azor, 101
Zénate, El (Bravo/Galindo), 233
Zéphire et Flore. 1 act. Chor.: Massine; mus.: Dukelsky; déc. and cost.: Braque; book: Kochno; 1st perf.: 28 April 1925, Monte Carlo, Ballets Russes; cast: Nikitina, Dolin, Lifar, 148
Zoraida, *61*

Index of Names

Numbers in italic refer to the illustrations

Adam, Adolphe, 98, 103
Adams, Diana, 217
Adimari, Boccaccio, 9, *4*
Agata, Michel de, 78
Agliè, Count Filippo San Martino d', 38
Agoglia, Esmeralda, 234
Akesson, Birgit, 229
Aldous, Lucette, 191
Aldridge, Robert, 78
Alembert, Jean Le Rond d', 61
Alessandro, Barbetta, 23
Alexander, Dorothy, 219
Alexeieva, L., *204*
Algaroff, Youly, 172
Algo, Julian, 229
Allan, Maude, 209
Allard, Marie, 66, 69, 81, *56*
Alonso, Alicia, 215, 233
Amboise, Jacques d', 217
Amiel, Josette, 168, 169, *170*
Ancre, Maréchal d', 48
Andersen, Tuth, 228
Andreani, Jean-Paul, 169
Andreianova, Elena, *104*
Andreu, Mariano, 157
Angiolini, Gasparo, 72-75, 77, 79, 81, 85, 157, 230
Angiolini, Pietro, 81
Anjou, Duke of, 29
Anne of Austria, 53
Anouilh, Jean, 173
Antonio, *229*
Appleyard, 192
Aquilanti, 83
Ara, Ugo Dell', 225
Aranda, Marquis d', 107
Araya, 75
Arbus, 166
Argyle, Pearl, 190
Arova, Sonia, 235, *222*
Ashton, Sir Frederick, 155, 190, 191-194, 228, *189*
Astafieva, Serafina, 189
Atanassoff, Cyril, 169
Aubigné, Agrippa d', 31
Aubry, Santina, 71, 72
Auden, W.H. 216
Aumer, Jean-Pierre, 96, *84*
Aurevilly, Barbey d', 98, 156
Auric, Georges, 153-55, 165, 168
Aveline, Albert, 161, 166

Babilée, Jean, 170, 172-74
Baccelli, 79
Bach, Johann Christian, 83
Bach, Johann Sebastian, 135, 155, 173
Bahr, Margaretta, von, *228*
Baïf, Antoine du, 25, 27
Bajetti, 108
Bakst, Léon, 135, 149, 161, *137*
Balanchine, George, 138, 149, 155, 162, 185, 201, 202, 211, 213-17, 219, 226, 228
Balanchivadzé, André, 202
Balbi, 53
Ballon, Dominique, 85
Ballon (Balon), Jean, 56
Ballon, Thérèse, 85
Balzac, Honoré de, 202
Barbarina, La, 77, *65*
Bardi, Count Giovanni di, 35, 43
Bardin, Micheline, 166
Bari, Tania, 226
Baronova, Irina, 155
Baranovich, 231
Bartholin, Biger, 228
Bartók, Béla, 225
Bartoli, 85
Basil, Wassili, Colonel de, 155, 156, 159, *149*
Baskakova, Axinia, 75
Bassi, Giovanna, 79
Battaggi, 225
Baudelaire, Charles, 107, 117
Bauer, Franz, 185
Baylis, Lilian, 191
Beauchamp, Charles-Louis, 54-56, 43
Beaujoyeux, Balthasar de, 23, 24, 29, 31-33, 35, 43
Beaulieu, Sire de, 31
Beaumont, Cyril, 190, *186*
Beaumont, Count Etienne de, 154
Beccari, Colombe, 83
Beaurepaire 194
Beccari, Filippo, 83
Beers, Sonja van, 226
Beethoven, Ludwig von, 90, 155, 162, 209
Béjart, Maurice, 177, 226, *176*, *177*, *225*
Belgiojoso, Baldassarino de, *see* Beaujoyeux
Belloni, 108
Benois, Alexandre, 126, 135, 136, 138, *129*
Benserade, 54, 57
Bentivoglio, Annibale, 20
Bérain, Jean, 57
Bérard, Christian, 155, 159, *151*
Berdel, 226
Beretta, Caterina, 127, *114*
Beretti, Filippo, 87
Beriosova, Svetlana, 194, *192*
Berlioz, Hector, 159, 185
Bernardo, Tettoni, 23
Bessonne, Emma, 127
Bessy, Claude, 166, 167, 169, *168*
Betceslova, Tatiana, 201
Bias, Fanny, 96
Bigottini, Emilia, 96, *85*
Binetti, Anna Ramoni, 78, 83
Bizet, Georges, 155, 174, 194, 216
Blache, Jean-Baptiste, 96
Blair, David, 194
Blanc, Robert, 169
Blanche, Jacques-Émile, *134*
Blasis, Carlo, 98, 112, 117, 224, *101*
Blasis, Virginia, 111
Blondi, 56, 71
Blum, René, 148, 155-57
Bogdanova, Nadejda, 114
Bokota, Marta, 233
Bolm, Adolphe, 135, 136, 234
Bologna, Gian, 35
Bon, René, 177
Bonesi, 122
Boni, Aida, 161
Bonnachon, Henri, *see* Henry
Boquet, Louis, *58*
Borkowsky, Vitold, 233
Borlin, Jean, 153, 229
Borodin, Alexandre, 136, 158
Borovansky, Edward, 234
Borovska, Irina, 234
Borri, Pasquale, 113, 117, 121, 122
Bos, Camille, 161, 189
Boschetti, Amina, 103, 117
Botka, Lola, 234
Botticelli, Sandro, 21
Bourmann, Hamy, 226
Bourmeister, Vladimir, 168, 206
Bournonville, Antoine, 79, *67*
Bournonville, Auguste, 79, 98, 108, 226
Bovt, Violetta, 206
Bozzachi, Giuseppina, 117
Bozzoni, Max, 167
Bracelli, *18*, *19*
Brae, June, 190
Brahms, Johannes, 216
Brantôme, 24, 28
Bravo, Guillermina, 233
Brayer, Yves, 161, 165
Brexner, Edeltraut, 230
Brianchon, Maurice, 161, 165
Brianza, Carlotta, 127, 148, *119*
Brieux, Yves, 169
Brissac, Maréchal de, 23
Britten, Benjamin, 191, 212
Bronzino, 35
Brugnoli, Amalia, 85, 97, *82*
Bruhn, Erik, 68, 79, 228
Buffequin, 51
Bulder, Bogdan, 233
Bulnes, Esmée, 225
Bundgaard, Kirtsen, *226*
Buranello, 74
Burgioni, La, 85
Burr, Marilyn, 196
Burton, John, 212
Bye, Willy de la, 226

Caccini, Giulio, 35, 43
Caillavet, 161
Camargo, Marie-Anne de Cupis de, 66, *55*
Cambon, 115
Campanini, Barbarina, 74
Campilli, La, *61*
Campioni, Ancilla, 85
Campioni, Anna, 81, 85
Campioni, Antonio, 78, 85
Campioni, Giuseppe, 85

Campra, 56
Camprubi, 107
Canziani, 86
Caorsi, 225
Carlo, Beccaria, 23
Caro, Maria de, 83, *70*, *71*
Caron, Leslie, 172, 173
Caroso, Fabritio, 25, 27, *8*
Carzou, Jean, 166
Casanova, Giacomo, 72, 74, 76, 78, 83, 107
Casati, Giovanni, 112, 121
Castarède, 169
Castiglione, 22
Cataï, 78
Catherine the Great, 72, 74, 76
Cavalieri, 35
Cavalli, 53
Cecchetti, Enrico, 122, 127, 138, 189, 190, 191, 225, 233, *122*
Cendrars, Blaise, 153
Cerrito, Fanny, 100, 112, 114, 117, 189, *106*, *109*
Cesare, Agosto, 22
Cesare, Gaetano, 72
Cesari, 90
Cesti, 53
Chaboukiani, Vachtang, 201, 202
Chabrier, Emmanuel, 155
Chaliapin, 135
Chameroy, Clotilde, 96
Chapelain-Midy, R., 166
Charles III, 81
Charles V, 20, 23
Charles VIII, 27
Charles IX, 23, 28, 29
Charles XII, 60
Charrat, Janine, 170, 172, 174, 177, 194, 234
Chase, Lucia, 214
Chauviré, Yvette, 163-65, *159*, 167-69, 194, 234
Chavez, Charles, 233
Cheremetief, Prince, 76
Cherubini, Luigi, 68
Chesnay, 31
Chichinadze, 206
Chilovski, 126
Chiriaeff, Ludmilla, 233
Chirico, Giorgio de, 149
Chitroff, Mlle, 76
Chopin, Frédéric, 135, 136, 161, 209
Christensen, Willam, 214
Ciceri, 97, 98
Clair, René, 153
Clairin, *118*
Claudel, Paul, 153, 185
Clavé, Antoni, 174, *174*
Clerico, Francesco, 87
Clustine, Ivan, 161
Cocteau, Jean, 136, 145, 149, 153, 154, 173
Cohen, Fritz, 182, 183
Colombo, Vera, 225
Colonna, Teresa, 71, 72
Conti, Anna, 85
Corak, Mia, *see* Slavenska
Coralli, Jean (Peracini), 90, 97, 103, 107, *96*
Coralli, Teresa, 90
Corbo, 225
Cornalba, Elena, 127
Cornazzano, Antonio, 16, 25
Corneille, Pierre, 50, 57
Cortesi, Antonio, 107
Cosentini, Maria, 90
Coulon, Antoine, 96, 103, 108
Coulon, Jean-François, 95, 96, 98
Courtelle, 40
Cova, Fiorella, 225
Cramer, Ivo, 230
Cranko, John, 167
Crébillon, 71
Crux, Peter, 77, *66*
Cucchi, Claudine, 112
Cuevas, Marquis de, 167, 220
Cullberg, Birgit, 215, 228-30
Cunningham, Merce, 217, 218
Czerny, Charles, 166

Dalba, Maria, 225
Dalcroze, Émile-Jacques, 181, 182, 184, 190
Dale, Margaret, 193
Danilova, Alexandra, 149, 155, 157, 194, *152*
Dantzig, Rudi van, 226
Darsonval, Lycette, 163-65, 235
Dauberval, Jean Bercher, 66, 69, 78, 81, 88, 96, *56*, *59*
Daydé, Bernard, 169, 218
Daydé, Liane, 167
Debussy, Claude, 132, 140, 163, 167
Decaris, 162
Decombe, François-Albert, 95
Deege, Gisela, 185
Delacroix, Eugène, 203
Delibes, Léo, 117, 124, 164, 231
Delphin, 48
Delsarte, François, 181
Deplechin, 115
Derain, André, 146, 155, 157, *141*, *150*
Descartes, 39, 95
Deschars, 56
Descombey, Michel, 168, 169, *166*
Desmartins, 56
Dethomas, Maxime, 161
Diaghilev, Serge de, 105, 121, 127, 132, 135, 136, 138, 139, 142, 144, 146, 148, 149, 151, 153, 155-57, 181, 189, 191, 213, 221, 225, 229, *128*
Didelot, 118
Diderot, 61
Dijk, Peter van, 167, 168, *167*
Diobono of Milan, 23, 24
Dirtl, Willy, 230
Dolin, Anton, 100, 148, 155, 157, 189, 191, 192, 194, 233, *193*
Doubrovska, Felia, 148
Doudinskaya, Nathalie, 201
Doukoudovsky, 158
Draper, Julia, 230
Dufy, Raoul, 155, 161
Dukas, Paul, 161
Duke, Vernon, 173
Dumas, Alexandre, 168
Dumont, 55
Dumoulin, 60
Duncan, Isadora, 135, 209, 210, 221, 223, *223*
Dupont, 166
Dupré, 60, 68
Dutarque, 111

Ebreo, Guglielmo, 15-17, 25, *1*, *3*
Ebreo, Isacchino, 38
Egk, Werner, 165, 174
Eglevsky, André, *216*
Elisabeth Petrovna, Empress of Russia, 71
Elssler, Fanny, 97, 98, 101, 107, 122, 129, *93*
Elvin, Violetta, *224*
Era, Antonietta Dell', 127
Ermolaiev, Alexei, 201
Ernst, Max, 149
Espinosa, Édouard, 190, 191
Espinosa, Judith, 189
Este, Lucrezia d', 20
Etchevery, Jean-Jacques, 226
Eudes, Roger, 170

Fabiani, Michele, 85, *62*
Fadeyechev, Nicolas, 206
Falla, Manuel, de, 145
Farron, Julia, 193
Farrufino, 22
Fascilla, Roberto, 225
Favart, 73
Fedorova, Sofia (Sophie Fedorovich), 194, 200, 233
Fenongeois, Roger, 233
Fenonjois, René, 164
Fernandez, Royes, 215
Ferrara, Domenico da, *see* Piacenza
Ferraris, Amalia, 107, 112, 115, 116, *106*
Ferri, Olga, 234
Feuillet, Raoul, 56, 78, *48*, *49*
Fini, Léonor, 173, 225
Fitzjames, Nathalie, 107, *99*
Flers, de, 161
Flier, Jaan, 226
Flindt, Flemming, 68, 79, 169, 196, 228, *170*
Fogliazzi, Teresa, 81
Fokine, Michel, 132, 135, 136, 138, 140, 142, 144, 156, 157, 161, 226, 229, *135*
Fontenelle, 57
Fontenla, Norma, 234
Fonteyn, Dame Margot, 173, 190, 191, 193, 194, 234, 235, *195*
Fornaroli, 225
Fost, 166
Fracci, Carla, 225
Fraincine, 55
Franca, Celia, 233
Françaix, Jean, 155, 162, 173, 224
Franchi, Paolino, 86
Francis II, 72
Franck, César, 194
François II, 23
Franklin, Frederic, 158, 194, 219
Franz, Willy, 230
French, 192
Fris, Maria, 177
Frossard, Louis, 79
Fuchs, Caroline, 107
Fuller, Loie, 209

Fulop, Victor, 231
Fuoco, Sofia, 112, *102*
Fusi, Margherita, 85

Gable, Christopher, 194
Gabrielli, 117
Gaito, Constantino, 234
Galeotti, Vincenzo, 79, 85, 226, *68*
Galindo, 233
Galliari brothers, 86
Gallini, Andrea Giovanni, 79
Gallino, Giovan, 24
Gallizia, Bianca, 225
Gallodier, Louis, 79, 228
Galster, Amalia, 101
Galuppi, 77
Gardel, Maximilien, 62, 68, 77, 78, *83*
Gardel, Pierre, 68, 95, 96, 103, 111, *64*
Garrick, David, 61
Gaskell, Sonia, 226
Gaubert, Philippe, 165
Gautier, Théophile, 96-98, 100, 114, 189
Gelosi, 29
Geltzer, Catherine, 138, 140, 189, 200, 202
Genée, Adeline, 189, 190
George II, 61
Georgi, Yvonne, 182, 184
Gerdt, Paul, 200
Gershwin, George, 168, 225, 231
Gianneo, 234
Gide, André, 154
Giera, Francesco, 59
Gilpin, John, 191, 196, *190*
Gindice, Sonia Del, 225
Ginestera, 234
Gioja, Gaetano, 87, *74*
Glazunov, Alexander, 199
Gluck, Christoph Willibald, 62, 72, 73, 157, 185, 211
Goethe, 103, 174
Goleizovsky, Kassian, 201
Golovine, Serge, 135, *215*
Gomme, La, 226
Goncharova, Natalia, 144
Gonzaga, Elisabetta, 20
Gore, Walter, 191
Gorsky, Alexander, 132, 199, 200
Gosselin, Geneviève, 96
Goubé, 165
Goudar, Sarah, 85
Graham, Martha, 210, 211-14, 218, *210*
Grahn, Lucile, 98, 100, 108, *89*, *106*
Grande, Dora del, 234
Greco, Antonio, 225
Grétry, 88
Grey, Beryl, 193
Grey, Nadia, 235
Grigorivich, Yuri, 202
Grisi, Carlotta, 97, 98, 100, 103, 114, 128, 189, *88*, *92*, *95*, *98*
Grossatesta, Gaetano, 81, 83
Gsovska, Tatiana, 185
Gsovsky, Victor, 173, 184, 185
Gué, Georges, 229
Guedeonoff, M., 129
Guerra, Antonio, 231, *109*
Guillot, Mlle. 169
Guimard, Marie-Madeleine, 61, 66
Gurdjan, *128*

Hallsreiter, Joseph, 230
Handel, George-Frideric, 149, 185, 218
Hanover, Duke of, 40
Hansen, 125
Hansler, Ladislav, 185
Harangozo, Jyulia, 231
Harkavry, Benjamin, 226
Haskell, Arnold, 190, *187*
Havas, Ferenc, 231
Hayden, Melissa, 216
Hayer, Dora, 185
Heberlé, 103
Heinel, Anne, 66, 78
Helpmann, Robert, 192, 193
Henri II, 29, 42
Henri III, 22, 31, 43, *20*
Henri IV, 42, 43, 54
Henry (Henri Bonnachon), 95
Henry, Pierre, 177
Herbert, Haill, 185
Herbert, Lilo, 185
Hightower, Rosella, 233
Hilarides, Marianna, 226
Hilferding, Franz, 71-73, 77, 79, 83, 230
Hindemith, Paul, 226
Hinton, Paula, 191
Hirosi, Sakiko, 235
Hirsch, Georges, 167
Hirstich, 231
Hogarth, William, 192
Hoguet, François-Michel, 77
Höhermann, Rainier, 185
Honegger, Arthur, 153, 163, 185
Horn, Harald, 185
Howard, Andrée, 190, 191, 194
Hugo, Victor, 98, 202
Humphrey, Doris, 212

Ibert, Jacques, 154, 161, 173
Idzikowsky, 149, 190
Indy, Vincent d', 163
Isabella, Duchess of Milan, 20
Ivanov, 200
Ivanovna, Anna, 74

Jeanmaire, Renée (Zizi), 170, 174, *172*, *173*
Jemmiz, Sandor, 231
Jensen, Svend Erik, 228
Jillana, 217
Joffrey, Robert, 219
Jooss, Kurt, 155, 182-84, 229, *182*
Jovanovich, Milica, 232
Joyeuse, Duc de, 31
Juan, Don, of Austria, 22
Judson, 192
Julien, M.-A., 179

Kaesen, 226
Kalioujny, Alexandre, 166
Kalomiris, 231
Karalli, Vera, 200
Karelskaya, Rimma, 206
Karsavina, Tamara, 135, 136, 138, 146, 149, 189, *133*, *134*, *136*
Karsten, 79
Katchourovsky, 226
Kaye, Nora, 215, 235, *214*
Kelly, Gene, 168
Kent, Allegra, 217

Kergrist, Geneviève, 162
Khatchaturian, Aram, 202,
Khokhlov, Boris, 206
Kirstein, Lincoln, 214, *212*
Klebanov, D. 202
Kochno, Boris, 148, 149
Koesun, Ruth Ann, 215, *213*
Korovine, Constantin, 135
Koppers, Maria, *227*
Kostich, Vera, 232
Kouznetsov, 206
Kramer, Leonie, 226
Krassovska, Nathalie, 218, *191*
Kreutzberg, Harald, 182, 184
Krieger, Victorina, 200, 206
Kroller, Heinrich, 230
Kronslam, Henning, 228, *226*
Kschessinska, Mathilde, 128, 135, 136
Kun, Zsuzsa, 231
Kurtz, Catherine, 85

Laban, Rudolf von, 181, 182, 184, 185, 225, *179*
Labis, Attilio, 169, *168*
Lafon, Madeleine, 165, 169, *162*
La Fontaine, Mlle., 56, 57
Laga, 226
Lagan, 226
Lagut, Irène, *147*
Lakatos, Gabrielle, 231
Lalo, Edouard, 164
Lambert, Constant, 161
Lambranzi, Gregorio, 53
Landa, Anita, 194, 196
Lander, Harald, 79, 165, 166, 168, 215, 226, 228
Lander, Margot, 228
Lander, Toni, 196, 228
Landet (Landé), Jean-Baptiste, 75
Lang, Pearl, 212
Lany, Jean-Baptiste, 68, 81
Lany, Louise-Madeleine, 68, 69
Larionov, Mikhail, 149, *144*
Larrain, Raymundo, 233
Larsen, Niels Njórn, 228
Larthe, 162
Lashchilin, 202
Lasserre, Louis, 56
Lassus, Roland de, 29
Laurencin, Marie, 148, *145*
Laurent, Jean, 177
Lavagnolo, 20
Laval, 64
Lavrovsky, L., 202
Le Camus, 48
Lecomte, Michel, 54
Le Doux, 232
Lee, Mary Ann, 107
Leeder, Sigurd, 182
Leef, Tola, 233
Leeuwen, Hannie van, 226
Lefèvre, Dominique, 86
Legat, Nicolas, 136, 189, 200
Léger, Fernand, 163
Legnani, Pierina, 127, 189, *120*
Legrain, Victorine, 122
Legrand, Claude, 86
Legrand, Lucien, 169
Lehmann, Maurice, 165, 166
Le Menestrier, Father Claude, 40

Lepri, Giovanni, 113, 121
Lesage, 64
Lestang, 56
Lichine, David, 155, 156, 214
Liediatk, Guennadi, 206
Lifar, Serge, 138, 148, 149, 162-68, 234, 235, *157*, *158*, *160*
Limido, Giovanna, 127
Limón, José, 212
Littlefield, Catherine, 214
Livry, Emma, 107
Lobiankova, Caterina Azarevich, 75
Locatelli, 75
Lolle, Jens, 165
Lommi, Enrique, 234
Longhi, Pietro, *72*
Lopokova, Lydia, 138, 191,
Lorcia, Suzanne, 162, 165
Loring, Eugene, 214
Lorraine, Christine of, 35
Lotka, 231
Louis, XII, 29
Louis XIII, 43, 46, 50, 54
Louis XIV, 51, 53ff., 60, *52*
Louis XV, 56, 59, 68
Lovenskyold, 108
Ludovico, Palvello, 24
Lully, Jean-Baptiste, 29, 51, 54, *44*
Lumley, 100
Luynes, Duke of, 48

Mabarak, 233
Macleary, Donald, 194
Magallanes, Nicholas, 216, *214*
Magri, 123
Mail, Léone, 169
Malherbe, 43
Mallarmé, Stéphane, 140
Malter, Henri, 78
Malvezzi, 35
Manen, Hans van, 226
Manet, Édouard, 107, 190
Manfredini, 73
Mantovanina, La, 85
Manzotti, Luigi, 121, 122, 124, *112*, *113*
Marais, 48, 50
Marchand, Colette, 174, 194, *175*
Maré, Rolf, de, 153, 229
Marenzio, 35
Maria Theresa of Austria, 40, 72, 230
Mariette, 56
Markova, Alicia, 149, 157, 159, 189-91, 194, 234, *154*, *193*
Martin, Frank, 169
Martinoli, Lida, 234
Maslow, Sophie, 212
Massine, Léonide, 138, 144-46, 148, 149, 154-56, 158, 159, 191, 194, 214, 217, *139*, *140*
Masson, André, 156
Matisse, Henri, 159
Matteini, Marisa, 225
Mauri, Rosita, 125
Maywood, Augusta, 113
Mazarin, 51, 53
Mazzantini, 231
Medici, Bianca Cappello de', 25
Medici, Catherine de', 25, 28, 29, 31, 35, *17*
Medici, Ferdinando de', 35
Medici, Francesco de', 42
Medici, Lorenzo de', 15, 20, *7*
Medici, Marie de', 43
Medina (Mayer), Maria, 88, 89, *75*, *77*, *79*, *80*
Mendelssohn, Felix, 216
Mérante, Louis, 124, 125, *115*
Mérimée, Prosper, 174
Messager, 124
Metastasio, 74, 83, 85
Meursius, Van, 61
Meyerbeer, Giacomo, 97
Milhaud, Darius, 148, 149, 153, 154
Mille, Agnès de, 211, 215
Miller, 96
Milloss, Aurel, 225, 230
Milon, 95
Miró, Joan, 149, 155
Miskovich, Milorad, 177, 232
Mitchell, Arthur, 217
Moiseyev, Igor, 206
Molière, 57, 96, *51*
Molinari, Nicola, 92
Mollerup, Mette, 228, *226*
Monplaisir, Hippolyte, 112
Montefeltro, Guidobaldo, di, 20
Monteverdi, Claudio, 35, 42
Mordkin, Michel, 136, 199, 212, 214
Morel, Horace, 48, 50
Moreton, 192
Moriana, Harrild y, 234
Moro, Ludovico il, 20
Morriss, Norman, 191
Motte, Claire, 169, *178*
Moulène, 166
Mozart, Wolfgang Amadeus, 62, 156, 216
Muller, Liane, 185
Mulys, Gérard, 169
Murat, King of Naples, 81, 103
Muravieva, Martha, 117, 130
Musil, Karl, 230
Mussorgsky, Modest, 135, 163
Muzzarelli, Antonio, 81, 85, 87

Navarre, Henri de, 28
Negri, Cesare, 22-24, *9*, *10*
Nemchinova, Vera, 155
Nemours, Duke of, 48, 50
Nerina, Nadia, 194
Newton, 192
Nietzsche, Friederich, 223
Nijinska, Bronislava, 135, 146, 148, 155, 161, 217-19, 230, 233
Nijinsky, Vaslav, 135, 136, 138, 140, 142-44, 161, 162, 194, 212, *136*, *138*
Nikitina, Alice, 148
Nikolais, Alwin, 218
Noriega, 233
Nouvel, Walter, 135
Novak, 212
Novaro, Luciana, 225
Noverre, Jean-Georges, 59-69, 71, 73, 77-9, 83, 86, 87, 93, 95, 224, 230, *53*
Nureyev, Rudolph, 194, *195*, *222*

Oblakov, 128
Oboukhov, 136
Offenbach, Jacques, 154
Oliva, Pepita de, 107
Orleans, Duke of, 27
Orlov, Nicolas, 184
Orosz, Adele, 231
Ossipienko, Alla, 206

Paganini, Niccoló, 218
Pagava, Ethery, 172, 177
Page, Ruth, 184, 214
Pallerini, Antonia, 92
Palucca, 182
Parlich, Dimitri, 230-32
Parnell, Felix, 233
Parnel, Ruth, 232
Patin, Jacques, 31
Pavlova, Anna, 135, 136, 138, 139, 161, 189, 213, 235, *130*
Pavlova, Éliane, 235
Paysanne, 48
Pecourt, Louis-Guillaume, 55, 56, *45*
Pélin, 69
Peracini, *see* Coralli
Peretti, Serge, 162, 165, 169
Peri, Jacopo, 42, 226
Perugini, Giovanni, 225
Perugini, Giulio, 225, *224*
Perraud, Adelaide, 103
Perrault, Charles de, 132
Perrault, Serge, *175*
Perrot, Jules, 98, 100, 118, 122, 129, 131, *92*, *100*, *106*
Pesaro, Ambrosio da, 14, 15
Pescht, Rudolph, 234
Petipa, Jean-Antoine, 128-32, 193, 226
Petipa, Lucien, 98, 114, 226, *98*
Petipa, Marie, 130, *125*
Petipa, Marius, 108, 118, 127, 128, 226, *124*
Petit, Roland, 164, 165, 170, 172-74, 225, 228, *173*
Petrovna, Elisabeth, 74
Philibois, Alexandre, 77
Philippart, Nathalie, 172, 173
Philippe II, 23
Philippe IV, 40
Piacenza, Domenico, da, 10-16, 22
Picabia, Francis, 153
Picasso, Pablo, 145, *142*, *143*
Pichler, Carolina, 88
Pichler, Gusti, 230
Picot, 48
Picq, Le, 78, 83
Pierné, Gabriel, 161
Pisan, Christine de, 27
Pistoni, Mario, 225
Pitrot, Antoine, 77
Pleasant, Richard, 214
Plestcheev, 126
Plissetskaya, Maia, 206
Pochini, Carolina, 122, *111*
Poe, Edgar Allan, 121
Poiret, 139
Poli, 225
Poliziano, 21, *7*
Pontelibero, 86
Poulenc, Francis, 148, 153
Preisser, Suse, 185
Preobrajenska, Olga, 128, 194, 200, *121*
Prete, 35
Prevost, Mlle. 48, 56, 60, 64, 66

Priora, Olimpia, 113, 114
Prokofiev, Serge, 149, 194, 202, 204, 228, 231
Prokofieva, 202
Pulcinella, 146
Pushkin, 161, 202

Quinault, 57

Racine, 71, 165
Radice, 225
Ralov, Borge, 228
Ralov, Kirsten, 228
Ramaccini, Caterina, 85
Rambert, Marie, 190, 191, *188*
Rameau, Jean-Philippe, 68, 166
Ramirez, Eduardo, 233
Ravel, Maurice, 140, 154, 156, 161
Rayet, Jacqueline, 169, *167*, *169*
Reinhardt, Max, 184
Reinholm, Gert, 185
Renault, Michel, 165-67
Rennart, Günther, 185
Respighi, Ottorino, 146
Revueldas, 233
Rhijn, Alexandra von, 226
Riabouchinska, Tatiana, 155
Ricasoli, Lisa, 9, *4*
Ricaux, 161
Ricci, Angelo, 38
Richard, Zina, 125
Richardson, P.J.S., 189, 190, *185*
Rich, John, 64
Richelieu, 38, 50, 51
Rieti, V., 149, 163
Rimsky-Korsakov, 135, 144, 203
Rinaldi, Antonio, 74, 75, 77
Rinuccini, Ottavio, 35, 43
Ritz, 164, 165
Robbins, Jerome, 185, 211, 215-17, 228
Robichon, 57
Robin, J., 179
Roerich, Nicholas, 135
Rona, Victor, 231
Ronsard, 50
Rosati, Carolina, 114-16, 130, *105*
Ross, 226
Rossi, Giuseppe de, 87
Rossini, Gioacchino, 146
Rota, Giuseppe, 121
Rota, Vittorio, 113, 117
Rouault, Georges, 149
Rouché, Jacques, 161, 162
Roussel, Albert, 161
Ruanova, Maria, 234
Rubinstein, Ida, 135, 136, 154, 167
Rues, Marga, 185

Sacco, Andreina, 75
Sacco, Antonio, 75, 79
Sacco, Libera, 75
Sacrati, 53
Saint-Aignan, Count de, 57
St Denis, Ruth, 210
Saint-Léon, Arthur, 100, 103, 107, 111, 117, 118, 131, *108*
Saint-Mard, Rémond de, 61
Saint-Saëns, Camille, 135
Saintot, 48
Sales, Anna Conti de, 75
Salfi, 86
Salin, Klaus, *228*
Sallé, Marie, 56, 60, 64, 66, 69, *57*
Salomoni, Giuseppe, 75, 85
Salvioni, Guglielmina, 117
Samengo, *82*
Samsova, Galina, 233
Samuel-Rousseau, Marcel, 164
Sand, George, 202
Sand, Inge, 228
Sandbrook, June, 191
Sanders, Job, 226
Sanfina, Vera, 232
Sanftleben, Nika, 185
Sangalli, Rita, 124
Sapagov, Anatole, *205*
Saracco, 122
Satie, Erik, 145, 149, 153, 154
Sauguet, Henri, 149, 154, 165, 168, 172-74
Sauveterre, François, 78
Savina, Vera, 189
Sawicka, Olga, 233
Schaeffer, Pierre, 177
Schaufuss, Frank, 228
Schollar, Ludmilla, 155, *136*
Schroer, Fred, 185
Schubert, Franz, 135
Schuh, Oscar, Fritz, 185
Schwartz, Solange, 164, 165, *156*
Schweikart, Hans, 185
Scio, Anna, 77
Sedaine, 88
Seigneuret, Michèle, 177, *225*
Seki, Naoto, 235
Selinder, Anders, 79, 229
Semenova, Marina, 201
Semenovich, Boublikof Timofay, 73
Sergeyev, Constantin, 201, 202, *201*
Serrano, Lupe, 215
Severo, Raoul, 233
Sforza, Gian Galeazzo, Duke of Milan, 15, 20
Shanne, Margrethe, 228
Shawn, Ted, 210
Shearer, Moria, 193
Shostakovich, Dimitri, 158
Sibelius, Jean, 191
Sifnios, Douska, 232
Siimola, Aino, 182
Sijablom, Robert, 229
Silvain, 107
Simon, 226
Simone, Kirsten, *226*
Skibine, George, 158, 168, 220, 234, *165*, *218*
Skorik, Irène, 172
Skouratoff, Vladimir, 172
Slavenska, Mia (Corak), 162, 194
Slavinsky, Thadeo, 155
Slingsby, Simon, 79
Smeraldi, 231
Smirnova, Elena, 136
Smith, George Washington, 107
Sokolova, 149
Sokolow, Anna, 212
Sourovchikova, 129
Souza, 216
Spessivtzeva, Olga, 144, 149, 161, 162, 234, *157*
Staats, Léo, 161
Starzer, 71, 72
Stanislavsky, 199
Steel, Barbara, 235
Stefano, Martinello, 23
Stendhal, 90, 92, 93
Stepanoff, Vladimir, 199
Strauss, Richard, 132, 144, 194, 210, 230
Stravinsky, Igor, 136, 138, 140, 143, 144, 148, 149, 154, 161, 194, 210, 216, 224, 226, 231
Strindberg, August, 230
Strozzi, 35
Subligny, Marie-Thérèse de, 56, *47*
Sue, Eugène, 107, 122
Szyfer, 162
Szyfman, Arnold, 233
Szymanky, Stanislas, 233

Tabor, Gyorgy, 231
Taglioni, Carlo, 81, 85
Taglioni, Filippo, 79, 85, 97, 100, 228, 232
Taglioni, Giuseppe, 85
Taglioni Luigia, 78, 85
Taglioni, Marie, 97, 98, 100, 103, 105, 107, 112, 114, 127, 149, 157, 189, 229, 230, *86*, *91*, *95*, *97*, *100*
Taglioni, Marie (daughter of Paolo), 101
Taglioni, Paolo, 101, 103
Taglioni, Salvatore, 81, 100, 103, 173
Tailleferre, Germaine, 153
Tallchief, Maria, 217, *217*
Tallchief, Marjorie, 220, 234, *165*, *218*
Tani, Moniko, 235
Taras, John, 228, 234
Tasso, 41
Taylor, Paul, 212
Tchaikovsky, 127, 132, 156,
Tchérina, Ludmilla, 167
Telloli, Bruno, 225
Terpis, Max, 184
Tesi, Cosimo Damiano, 74
Thalia, Rita, 169
Thierry, 115
Tikanova, Nina, 155
Tikhomirov, Vassili, 189, 200, 202
Tillet, Mlle. de, 79
Timofeieva, Nina, 206
Tomin, Jorge, 234
Tommasini, Maria Pia, 225
Torelli, 53
Toscani, Luisa, 78
Toumanova, Tamara, 155, 157, 165, 194, 234, *140*
Traffieri, 87
Trefilova, Vera, 189, 194, *140*
Trissino, 28
Trujol, Antonio, 234
Tudor, Antony, 190, 214, 235
Turchi, Domenico, 85
Turczynowicz, Roman, 232

Ulanova, Galina, 201-3, *199*
Uskova, Tatiana, 155
Uthoff, Ernst, 234

Vaganova, Agrippina, 200-4

Vainonen, 231
Valence, Lola de, 107
Valéry, Paul, 154, 235
Valois, Ninette de, 190-4, 228, *194*
Valville, 76
Varkovizky, 202
Vaudemont, Mlle. de, 31
Vazem, 130
Vega, Lopez de, 202
Venditti, Walter, 225
Verdi, Giuseppe, 191
Verdy, Violette, 172, 217, *190*
Véron, Doctor, 103
Verstegen, Aart, 226
Vertès, Marcel, 167
Vestris, Auguste, 66, 68, 79, 96, 100, 128, 132, *60*
Vestris, Gaetano, 62, 66, 68, 78, 79, 81, 83, 87, 95
Veyré, 48
Viazemsky, Prince, 73
Vigano, Maria Medina, *see* Medina
Vigano, Salvatore, 69, 87-90, 92, 93, 103, 162, 225, *75-79*, *81*
Vigarani, 57
Vigée-Lebrun, *55*
Villella, Edward, 217
Vilzak, Anatole, 155, 233
Vinci, Leonardo da, 21
Vinogradova, Sofia, 206
Visconti, Valentina, 27
Vlassova, Eleonora, 206
Vlassy, Christiane, 169
Volinine, Alexander, 199, 213
Volkova, Vera, 234
Voltaire, 66, 71, 73
Vondrak, Paul, 230
Vulcani, Andrea, 81
Vulcani, Antonia, 81
Vyroubova, Nina, 167, 172, 173, *215*, 218, *164*

Wagner, Richard, 121, 185, 199, 209
Wagner, Wieland, 185
Wakhevich, 166, 167, 173
Waldeen, 233
Wallmann, Marguerite, 230
Weaver, John, 78
Weber, Carl Maria von, 174
Webern, Anton, 216
Weidman, Charles, 212, 213
Wells, Doreen, 194
Wigman, Mary, 182, 184, 185, 189, *180*, *181*, *183*
Wilde, Patricia, 217
Williams, E. Virginia, 219
Wilson, Billy, 226, *227*
Woizikowsky, Léon, 149, 233
Wright, Belinda, 191, 196
Württemburg, Duke of, 62

Youskevich, Igor, 158, 159, *154*
Yuriko, 212

Zhdanov, Yuri, *200*
Zalicha, Piotr, 233
Zambelli, Carlotta, 125, 161
Zappolini, Walter, 225
Zimmerl, Christi, 230
Zoubkovskaia, Inna, *202*
Zucchi, Virginia, 125, 127, *118*
Zverev, Nicolas, 226